BICAMERALISM

POLITICAL ECONOMY OF INSTITUTIONS AND DECISIONS

Editors
James E. Alt, *Harvard University*
Douglass C. North, *Washington University of St. Louis*

Other books in the series

Alberto Alesina and Howard Rosenthal, *Partisan Politics, Divided Government, and the Economy*

Lee J. Alston, Thrainn Eggertsson, and Douglass C. North, *Empirical Studies in Institutional Change*

James E. Alt and Kenneth Shepsle, eds., *Perspectives on Positive Political Economy*

Jeffrey S. Banks and Eric A. Hanushek, *Modern Political Economy: Old Topics, New Directions*

Yoram Barzel, *Economic Analysis of Property Rights*

Robert Bates, *Beyond the Miracle of the Market: The Political Economy of Agrarian Development in Kenya*

Peter Cowhey and Mathew McCubbins, *Structure and Policy in Japan and the United States*

Gary W. Cox, *The Efficient Secret: The Cabinet and the Development of Political Parties in Victorian England*

Jean Ensminger, *Making a Market: The Institutional Transformation of an African Society*

Murray Horn, *The Political Economy of Public Administration: Institutional Choice in the Public Sector*

Jack Knight, *Institutions and Social Conflict*

Michael Laver and Kenneth Shepsle, *Making and Breaking Governments*

Michael Laver and Kenneth Shepsle, *Cabinet Ministers and Parliamentary Government*

Brian Levy and Pablo T. Spiller, *Regulations, Institutions, and Commitment*

Leif Lewin, *Ideology and Strategy: A Century of Swedish Politics* (English Edition)

Gary Libecap, *Contracting for Property Rights*

Mathew D. McCubbins and Terry Sullivan, eds., *Congress: Structure and Policy*

Gary J. Miller, *Managerial Dilemmas: The Political Economy of Hierarchy*

Douglass C. North, *Institutions, Institutional Change, and Economic Performance*

Elinor Ostrom, *Governing the Commons: The Evolution of Institutions for Collective Action*

J. Mark Ramseyer, *Odd Markets in Japanese History*

J. Mark Ramseyer and Frances Rosenbluth, *The Politics of Oligarchy: Institutional Choice in Imperial Japan*

Jean-Laurent Rosenthal, *The Fruits of Revolution: Property Rights, Litigation, and French Agriculture*

Charles Stewart III, *Budget Reform Politics: The Design of the Appropriations Process in the House of Representatives, 1865–1921*

John Waterbury, *Exposed to Innumerable Delusions: Public Enterprise and State Power in Egypt, India, Mexico, and Turkey*

David L. Weimer, *The Political Economy of Property Rights*

This book argues that the interaction between the two chambers in bi-cameral legislatures is central to comprehending behavior within each chamber, a point thus far neglected in the study of bicameral legislatures. The authors examine how the bicameral legislatures of some fifty countries produce legislation. They use both cooperative and noncooperative game-theoretic models to understand the interactions between the chambers observed in these fifty countries. Cooperative models are used to establish that bicameral legislatures, when compared with unicameral ones, increase the stability of the status quo and reduce intercameral differences to one privileged dimension of conflict. Noncooperative game-theoretic models are used to investigate the significance of a series of institutional devices governing intercameral relations: where a bill is introduced, which chamber has the final word, how many times a bill can shuttle between chambers, whether conference committees are called. The models are corroborated with data from the French Fifth Republic, supplemented with case studies from Germany, Japan, Switzerland, the United States, and the European Union.

BICAMERALISM

GEORGE TSEBELIS
*University of California,
Los Angeles*

JEANNETTE MONEY
*University of California,
Davis*

CAMBRIDGE
UNIVERSITY PRESS

PUBLISHED BY THE PRESS SYNDICATE OF THE UNIVERSITY OF CAMBRIDGE
The Pitt Building, Trumpington Street, Cambridge CB2 1RP, United Kingdom

CAMBRIDGE UNIVERSITY PRESS
The Edinburgh Building, Cambridge CB2 2RU, United Kingdom
40 West 20th Street, New York, NY 10011-4211, USA
10 Stamford Road, Oakleigh, Melbourne 3166, Australia

First published 1997

Printed in the United States of America

Typeset in Sabon

Library of Congress Cataloging-in-Publication Data
Tsebelis, George.
Bicameralism / George Tsebelis, Jeannette Money.
p.   cm. – (Political economy of institutions and decisions)
Includes index.
ISBN 0-521-58037-4 (hc.). – ISBN 0-521-58972-X (pbk.)
Legislative bodies.   I. Money, Jeannette.   II. Title.
III. Series.
JF541.T76   1997
328.3 – dc20   96-43839
                                                      CIP

*A catalog record for this book is available from
the British Library*

ISBN 0-521-58037-4 hardback
ISBN 0-521-58972-X paperback

To Miriam and Alexander, who brighten my life
GT

To my mother, who bestowed optimism, and
to my father, who bestowed intellectual curiosity
JM

Contents

Contents

Tables and figures

List of tables and figures

Series editors' preface

The Cambridge series on the Political Economy of Institutions and Decisions is built around attempts to answer two central questions: How do institutions evolve in response to individual incentives, strategies, and choices, and how do institutions affect the performance of political and economic systems? The scope of the series is comparative and historical rather than international or specifically American, and the focus is positive rather than normative.

Tsebelis and Money make a pathbreaking contribution to the "transactions benefits" theory of political institutions, which holds that a role of institutions is to prevent some collective choices from arising, or otherwise limit the number of enforceable policy outcomes. By doing so, institutions can provide outcomes or opportunities for transacting that improve on the status quo, and that would not happen in their absence. The intuition of Tsebelis and Money's work is that outcomes in a bicameral legislature are both political and efficient. By the latter they describe a form of stability; namely, the bicameral outcome has to be overturned by two majorities, whereas outcomes in either unicameral legislature of which the bicameral one is composed are more prone to being overturned, more prone to cycling, and thus less likely to produce an outcome and to remain at the status quo. Politics is also always likely to be involved no matter what the second chamber does, whether it contributes information or expertise or represents the preferences of more and different people. When different preferences are involved, bicameralism can frustrate several tyrannies: of the majority (by supplying some minority a veto), of the minority (by involving more nearly 50 percent in outcomes), of colluders, or of agenda setters. In every case, both the location and the feasibility of outcomes can differ in a bicameral setting from what a unidimensional legislature would have produced.

Tsebelis and Money's high-quality, careful analysis of the origins and working of an important political institution features a combination of theory and empirical work, within which different methodologies (quantitative and case study) are skillfully blended. Their book points out an exciting direction for future research.

Acknowledgments

This project on bicameral institutions originated in the late nineteen eighties when we were both at UCLA. It was then a conference paper so long that it was difficult to publish so we ended up dividing it into two articles. Since then, the project expanded beyond its original scope. Over the course of the years, we presented parts of the project, in the form of papers, to different audiences, and we profited from their comments. In particular we would like to thank the participants of a conference on parliaments in Western Europe, organized by Herbert Doering.

Some of the arguments presented in this book were published for the first time in the form of articles. While we have reworked all the material in order to present it in book form, we would like to thank Butterworth-Heinemann Ltd, Cambridge University Press, and Frank Cass and Company Ltd, for granting us permission to use parts of the argument in its initial form. We would also like to thank the editors and anonymous referees of the following journals: *British Journal of Political Science, International Political Science Review, Journal of Legislative Studies,* and *Legislative Studies Quarterly.*

Over the years, George Tsebelis has collaborated on related projects with other colleagues and discussions with them have influenced this work. In this respect, the acknowledgment of Kathleen Bawn and Bjorn Erik Rasch is necessary.

We would also like to thank Nicos Alivizatos, Jeffry Frieden, William Heller, Jih-wen Lin, Gary Schwartz, Steven Smith, Michael Wallerstein, Robyn Wornall, and two anonymous reviewers for providing us with comments on the entire book manuscript.

Another series of colleagues provided us with information, advice, and comments on different parts of this book. In this capacity we would like to thank Geoffrey Brennan, Gary Cox, Herbert Doering, John Ferejohn, Miriam Golden, Jean Grangé, Bernard Grofman, Alan Hamlin, Sada Kawato, Bill Keech, Gerhart Loewenberg, Jean Mastias, Stephen New-

Acknowledgments

house, Philip Norton, Larry Peterman, William Riker, Frances Rosenbluth, Andreas Ryll, Norman Schofield, Thomas Schwartz, Ken Shepsle, Kaare Strom, Albert Weale, and Barry Weingast.

For information provided from sources inaccessible to us, we also extend our gratitude to Mark Hallerberg, Simon Hug, and Jih-wen Lin; and for research assistance that helped to speed the completion of the project, thanks go to Neal Jesse, Amie Kreppel, Elizabeth Schneider-Huffman, Lisa Sharlack, and Tressa Tabares.

Financial support for the project was provided by several institutions. We would like to thank the Hoover Institution, the Academic Senate of UCLA, and the Academic Senate of the University of California, Davis.

Finally, we would like to thank Jim Alt, series editor, whose comments and encouragement facilitated the revision and ultimate completion of the manuscript. All of our colleagues and friends helped us to improve this project; for the remaining errors, the responsibility lies with us.

Introduction

Here then is the fundamental constitution of the government we are treating of. The legislative body being composed of two parts, one checks the other, by the mutual privilege of refusing. . . . Sufficient it is for my purpose to observe that [liberty] is established by their laws.

Montesquieu[1]

If the second chamber agrees with the first, it is useless, and if not, it is bad.

Abbé Sièyes[2]

Approximately one-third of the world's countries have bicameral legislatures, that is, legislatures that involve two distinct chambers in their deliberations.[3] These bicameral legislatures are not merely relics of long-forgotten constitutional compromises. Although many of them have long constitutional histories, a number of newly forged constitutions, in Central Europe and Latin America in particular, also provide for dual legislative bodies. But there is surprisingly little agreement on the actual impact of bicameral institutions. As the quotations cited above suggest, bicameralism has both advocates and opponents. In this book, we address the debate and examine the effect of bicameral institutions on political outcomes.

The existence of a second chamber appears to have little effect on the relationship between the legislature and the executive.[4] In presidential systems, the executive is elected directly and does not need the political support of the legislature to survive. In parliamentary systems, where the government needs the political support of the parliament to survive, this

[1]Montesquieu (1977: 210–11).
[2]Quoted in Walsh (1915: 331).
[3]See Trivelli (1975) for a more extensive list of features defining bicameral legislatures. His list includes separate sessions of the two legislative chambers, separate determination of voting outcomes, different composition of members, no overlapping membership, etc. Although these features help determine whether two distinct assemblies exist, the defining characteristic of bicameral legislatures is the requirement that legislation be deliberated in two distinct assemblies.
[4]This is probably the reason not only why Norton's (1990) collection of the most influential articles written about legislatures fails to include a single article on bicameralism, but also why the articles themselves do not address the distinction between unicameral and bicameral legislatures.

1

support is measured almost exclusively in the popularly elected lower chamber. Consequently, the relationship between legislative and executive is rarely altered directly by the existence of a second chamber.[5]

However, in terms of lawmaking, the existence of a second chamber may alter outcomes significantly, as the following examples indicate. Consider first a bicameral legislature that requires the agreement of both chambers for the passage of legislation, like the U.S. Congress. One house may vote for a politically popular version of a bill, counting on the other chamber to reject it. The House of Representatives' zeal for tax cuts in 1995 may be interpreted in a different light given the knowledge that the Senate would refuse such cuts. Alternatively, both chambers may vote different versions of a bill, which then is referred to conference committee never to surface again, or to surface only to be rejected by one of the houses. Bawn (1996) reports that, in the United States, the 1979 conference committee version of the bill promoting domestic energy sources (by reducing the costs of complying with environmental regulations) included provisions never voted by either chamber. As a result, it was killed on the floor of the House.

Consider now a different pattern of bicameralism where the lower chamber can override the disagreement of the upper, such as the British Parliament. The United Kingdom's House of Lords underwent two reforms (1911 and 1949) that ultimately placed the power of decision in the lower house. The maximum leverage the House of Lords may apply is to delay the passage of nonfinancial legislation for a year. However, the political significance of delaying a bill may become paramount in the year before an election, when delaying may mean killing a bill. This weak House of Lords was able to affirm its political position and to abort legislation under both Conservative and Labour governments (Mastias and Grangé 1987: 275–76). For example, the Lords returned the 1974 Trade Union and Labour Relations bill to the Labour-controlled House of Commons on three separate occasions, ultimately resulting in the failure of the legislation. In yet another case, Mrs. Thatcher was forced to postpone her project to dissolve the Greater London Council when the Lords rejected her legislation in 1984. Such maneuvers, which actually reverse floor votes, are impossible in a unicameral legislature.

If outcomes in a bicameral legislature can differ from those in a unicameral parliament, the strategies of legislators may be affected as well. Our examples illustrate behavior that, in a unicameral legislature, would

[5]The most notable exception is Article 81 of the German constitution, according to which the government can retain power for six months and legislate with the support of the upper house (Bundesrat), despite the loss of support in the lower house (Bundestag). Also, in Italy a government headed by Andreotti resigned after losing a vote of confidence in the Senate in 1979 (Ginsborg 1990: 402).

be considered as legislating, while in a bicameral legislature, the same behavior could be considered as position taking or credit claiming.

If strategies and outcomes are affected by the existence of a second chamber, it is obvious that the study of legislation in bicameral legislatures must focus not only on each of the chambers separately, but on the interaction between these chambers as well. Put in a stronger and more accurate way, the study of strategies or outcomes of bicameral legislatures that focus on one chamber alone, usually the popularly elected lower house, introduces a bias in the results. In the example noted above, tax cuts introduced in the U.S. House with opposition in the Senate, observing floor or even committee member behavior in the House may lead to the mistaken inference that House members are actually legislating, when, in fact, they are position taking. One-chamber studies of bicameral legislatures are biased because of the very assumption that legislators are rational, an assumption that is obviously central in rational choice analyses, but also extremely common in legislative studies more generally. Rationality of legislators specifies that they make their calculations backward, from the anticipated results, that is, from the compromise between the two chambers – a process labeled backwards induction. On the basis of these calculations, legislators determine what strategies to adopt inside committees or on the floor of each chamber. Consequently, the student of legislatures should follow these calculations and start the analysis from the compromise between the two chambers.

To argue that analysis of bicameral legislatures must begin with their interaction assumes that both houses affect legislative outcomes. This assumption, however, is not universally accepted. For example, in his influential study of the political systems of democratic countries, Lijphart (1984) classifies countries with bicameral legislatures on the basis of two criteria: congruence, or the similarity of the two houses' political composition, and symmetry, or the equality of the two houses' power over legislative outcomes. On the basis of these criteria he classifies bicameral legislatures as strong (incongruent and symmetric), weak (congruent and symmetric, or incongruent and asymmetric), and insignificant (congruent and asymmetric). In addition, journalistic accounts of upper houses sometimes describe them as "useless" (Grangé 1981: 39).

Our example of the British House of Lords provides one case where a "weak" upper chamber aborted legislation. In Chapter 2, we discuss another example from Italy, where chambers with identical political composition (congruence) disagree, leading to the abortion of legislation. These are visible cases of upper house influence on legislation when, according to some perspectives, there should be none. However, the examples suggest that bicameral influence may not be readily visible to the untrained eye. The legislation may shuttle from one house to the other

3

and be modified en route without an outward sign of disagreement. Or one house may anticipate and incorporate the preferences of the other and make a legislative proposal that is immediately accepted.

This book demonstrates that second chambers do exercise legislative influence. We provide theoretical arguments as well as empirical evidence substantiating the legislative influence of second chambers in various countries. Is it worth writing an entire book to demonstrate that "second chambers matter" in terms of legislation? Our answer would be affirmative even if this were the only contribution of the book, because the immediate consequence of an affirmative answer is that bicameral legislatures must be studied mainly as the interaction between two chambers. This conclusion calls for a significant change to our research agenda on legislatures.

However, demonstrating that second chambers matter is not the only goal of the book. In the chapters that follow we examine critically different theories of bicameralism, as well as different institutional structures that are associated with this form of legislatures. We demonstrate that the theoretical arguments on bicameralism, expressed in similar terms some 200 years ago on both sides of the Atlantic by Madison and Montesquieu, have diverged in more recent debates, and their common origin has been lost in most analyses.[6] Both Madison and Montesquieu were interested in the improvement of legislation that a second legislature can produce, as well as in the balance of power between the two chambers. In contrast, the contemporary constitutional debates focus on improvement alone, as in France, or balance of power almost exclusively, as in the United States.

We also examine a series of institutional devices employed around the world to resolve intercameral differences. The two most important such devices are the navette system and the conference committee. The former requires a bill to shuttle from one house to the other until there is an agreement or until some other stopping rule applies; the latter brings together representatives from both chambers for the elaboration of a compromise that will be voted up or down by each of the two chambers. In the course of the analysis we will see that a series of institutional "details" has systematic effects on the legislative process and outcomes.

We make several arguments in the book. First, bicameralism makes changes to the status quo more difficult than unicameralism. Second, bicameralism reduces all possible disagreements of legislators, or of parties in the chambers, to one privileged dimension. Third, the existence of second chambers alters legislative outcomes even if these chambers have no veto power, and even if they are politically similar to the first cham-

---

[6]But see Riker (1992a, 1992b) and Buchanan and Tullock (1962) for exceptions.

bers. Finally, the institutions regulating conflict resolution between the two chambers affect legislative outcomes. It matters in a systematic way where a bill is introduced first, which house (if any) takes the final decision, how many times a bill can shuttle from one chamber to the other, who comprises the conference committee, and how the conference committee decides – by majority rule, by qualified majority, by concurrent majorities of the two delegations, or by concurrent qualified majorities of the two delegations.[7] The details for most countries with bicameral legislatures are provided in Chapter 2.

These arguments are presented here in terms of bicameralism. However, the astute reader will see that the models presented and the arguments made are also applicable in the interaction between legislatures and executives in presidential systems (if the president has veto power over legislation). For example, the legislative procedure in Holland requires the lower house to make a take-it-or-leave-it proposal to the upper house; if the upper house rejects the proposal, the status quo prevails. This procedure is very similar to the adoption of a bill in the U.S., where the legislature as a whole makes a take-it-or-leave-it proposal to the president, and if this proposal is turned down (veto override aside) the status quo prevails. Similarly, the legislative procedure in Italy specifies that a bill will shuttle from one house to the other until agreement is reached. Similarities to the budget process in the U.S. are not coincidental. Therefore, although we concentrate on the interaction between legislative houses in bicameral systems, the presentation has wider applicability to other political processes.

1. OVERVIEW OF THE BOOK

The book consists of a series of arguments and empirical tests woven together. It includes a discussion of the historical evolution and the geographic distribution of bicameralism, models of bicameral institutions, and empirical tests of these theories with data from France and other advanced industrialized countries. We also evaluate the different accounts and theories of bicameralism in light of the theories and the data presented in the book. None of the discussion is intended to be the final word. In fact, we believe that we are very far from such a goal. Our goal in this book is to demonstrate that despite the diversity in terms of histories, representation of interests, and institutional devices for the resolution of intercameral differences, bicameral institutions present sufficient similari-

---

[7]Majority rule is employed in France, Germany, and Switzerland, qualified majority rule in Japan, concurrent majorities of the two delegations in the United States, and concurrent qualified majorities of the two delegations in the European Union. See Chapter 8 for details.

Introduction

ties to be examined as a whole. Such an examination, whether it focuses on several legislatures or on only one, must begin with the fact that bicameral institutions, by definition, consist of the interaction between two chambers. Any abstraction from this fact biases the results of the analysis. In addition we present a conceptually coherent way of looking at bicameral institutions and examine some empirical evidence that corroborates our approach. In our eyes, the major achievement of the book is that we weave these different threads together into a coherent whole.

The book is organized in three parts. The first part (Chapters 1 and 2) focuses on the diversity of bicameral institutions, both historical and geographic. The second part (Chapters 3, 4, and 5) presents a series of models investigating different aspects of bicameralism. The third part (Chapters 6, 7, 8, and 9) presents empirical evidence corroborating the different predictions of the models, compares our arguments with other theories of bicameralism, and evaluates the implications of our findings for various research agendas. The conclusions summarize the argument.

Chapter 1 presents the historical evolution of bicameral institutions in conjunction with the different theories or justifications of such institutions at the time they emerged. Although strictly speaking bicameral legislatures are a relatively new phenomenon, originating with the British practice of meeting in two separate chambers beginning in the fourteenth century, bicameral-like institutions have existed since ancient Greece. Chapter 1 demonstrates that bicameralism developed first in unitary states as a method of representing different social classes. Confederal states did not have bicameral legislatures, but employed qualified majority or unanimity rules in a single assembly to make political decisions. To our knowledge, the first place where bicameral institutions were used for the political representation of different territorial units (federalism) was the United States. The model of bicameral federalism spread so widely that today all federal countries have bicameral legislatures.[8] On the other hand, in unitary states, second chambers became less important as the power of the nobility declined. Either disagreement between the two chambers was reduced by modifying the composition of the upper chamber to resemble the lower chamber (Holland, Italy), or they were institutionally constrained (the House of Lords in Britain), or they disappeared altogether (Sweden, New Zealand) (Longley and Olson 1991).

The intellectual history of bicameralism paralleled these developments. From the origins of dual legislative institutions until the eighteenth century, the discourse on bicameralism was very similar. The founding fathers of the American Constitution discussed bicameralism in terms similar to

[8]See Chapter 2 for an overview; two minor exceptions to bicameral federalism are the Federated States of Micronesia and the United Arab Emirates, which are federal unicameral systems (*Europa Yearbook* 1994).

those of Montesquieu. Both advocated two important dimensions of bi-cameralism. The first was efficiency: improvement of the legislative prod-uct, finding the common grounds between the two chambers. The second was political and redistributive: representation of societal preferences, seeking a compromise between the two chambers, reflecting the relative balance of power. However, the arguments in favor of bicameralism sub-sequently diverge. In federal states the political arguments remain strong, while in unitary states the representational element is diminished and the discourse in favor of bicameralism refers to efficiency gains.

Chapter 2 presents the geographic distribution of bicameral institu-tional diversity. Using data from dozens of countries, we focus on two empirical questions. Whom do second chambers represent? What are the methods of resolving bicameral differences? We discover that, in addition to federalism, there are many other principles of representation. More significantly for a book focusing on institutional structures, we demon-strate that the diversity of bicameral institutions is enormous. For exam-ple, in the Netherlands, legislation is always initiated in the lower house; upon approval, it is submitted to the upper house, which votes it up or down without the possibility of amendments. On the other hand, in Switzerland, the chamber that introduces a bill sends it to the other, and the bill shuttles back and forth until one chamber decides to turn the current bill into an up or down vote for the other. The process may last for years or for as many as ten readings.[9] In fact, in the period between 1973 and 1989, 62 laws required more than five readings or more than two years to receive the approval of both legislative houses (Huber-Hotz 1991). The countries and institutions that exhibit the greatest complexity of bicameral procedures are France, the United States, and the European Union.

In view of such diversified histories, principles of interest representa-tion, and procedures for resolving intercameral disagreements, one may wonder whether any common grounds can be laid to analyze bicameral legislatures. The second part of the book (Chapters 3, 4, and 5) provides the basis for analysis. Chapter 3 gives a macro picture of the outcomes of bicameralism. It demonstrates that if agreement of two chambers is re-quired for legislation (a frequent requirement in bicameral legislatures), the outcome will reflect a compromise between the positions of the most moderate elements of both chambers.[10] Chapter 4 focuses on the institu-tional features of the most frequently employed method of intercameral bargaining, the navette system. Chapter 5 examines the proposals that

---

[9]In 1992, an amendment to the Law on the Relations between the Councils short-ened the shuttle to a maximum of three readings.

[10]As in the small print of all advertisements, several restrictions apply; see Part II for details.

a conference committee makes as a function of its composition and decision-making rule.

Chapter 6 focuses on the process of interaction in the navette system. We assess systematically some of the hypotheses derived in Chapter 4 using empirical evidence from legislation passed by the parliament of the French Fifth Republic. In particular, we test whether incomplete information, that is, uncertainty of one chamber about the preferences of the other, leads to a higher number of iterations in the navette system. We begin Chapter 6 with a description of French bicameral institutions. We then provide one way of operationalizing the concepts of impatience and uncertainty and test whether the predictions of Chapter 4 are supported. Finally we provide an interpretation of the recent French legislative history on the basis of the relevant model in Chapter 4.

Having provided quantitative evidence to substantiate some of the model's hypotheses, we turn in Chapter 7 to a qualitative analysis of the outcomes of bicameral bargaining. Using a series of case studies from the French legislature, we examine some predictions deduced from the models presented in Part II. In particular, we examine whether impatience for reaching a legislative agreement is a driving force for achieving a compromise, and whether the chamber that is more impatient makes more concessions to the other. We begin Chapter 7 with a comparison of our predictions with other accounts of bicameral interactions in France. We find that the delay of legislation is the fundamental mechanism by which second chambers exercise influence on legislation even if they do not have the power to veto the proposals of the lower chamber. Chapter 7 provides empirical evidence that the behavior and outcomes in the selected case studies, as well as the motives of legislators, are consistent with the accounts of Chapters 3 and 4.

Chapter 8 focuses exclusively on conference committees. We argue that conference committees are very important for the resolution of intercameral differences, because they submit their agreement to the parent chambers under closed rule. The importance, however, varies according to the composition and decision-making rule of the committee itself. Standing committees like the German conference committee will be more important, ceteris paribus, than ad hoc conference committees. Committees that decide by the unit rule (concurrent majorities of the two delegations), as in the United States, are more important than committees that decide by majority rule because the former have more leeway to strike a compromise. Finally, committees that decide by a qualified majority of their members, as in Japan, have a less important role than committees that decide by simple majority. A series of case studies from France, Germany, Japan, Switzerland, the United States, and the European Union corroborates these predictions.

Introduction

In Chapter 9 we take up the theoretical arguments on bicameralism proposed in Parts I and II in light of the evidence provided in the empirical chapters. We hope that by that time the reader will have a navigational map covering different bicameral legislatures and an understanding of several institutional methods for resolving bicameral differences and will be eager to come back to the big picture.

PART I

*The history and geography
of bicameral diversity*

Introduction to Part I

The goal of Part I is to present the diversity of bicameral institutions over time and among countries, as well as the diversity of theoretical justifications employed to promote them. Bicameral institutions have been adopted by class societies and by federal states, by republican polities and by unitary political systems. They have been used to maintain the status quo, to amalgamate the preferences of different constituencies, and to improve legislation, and have been justified in all of these terms. The diversity of bicameral legislatures extends to the institutional devices employed to resolve differences between the two legislative chambers, the navette (shuttle) system, conference committees, joint sessions of two chambers, one-chamber decisions; these are rules that may be applied individually or in combination. In a word, bicameral institutions are protean. They change forms and functions, and the arguments that justify or explain them follow these transformations.

This part of the book is divided into two chapters. Chapter 1 focuses on the history of bicameral diversity and presents the different theoretical justifications for bicameralism, while Chapter 2 provides information about the geographic dimension, the institutions regulating bicameral interactions in different countries today.

Chapter 1 begins with the earliest known political institutions that divided legislative deliberations between two or more chambers and follows the institutional evolution up to the modern period. At the same time, we trace the intellectual debate about the merits of this institutional structure. We describe the reasons proffered by various politicians and political theorists to justify the existence of two legislative bodies. The historical presentation emphasizes the dual evolution of institutional structures and intellectual debates. There is considerable continuity from ancient Greece to the eighteenth century – the membership of the two legislative bodies represented different classes or groups of citizens, who served to check each other and to improve the quality of the legislation.

The republican revolution disrupted this continuity and undermined the legitimacy of separate institutional structures to represent specific classes or groups of citizens. At the same time, the U.S. federal model of territorial representation provided an alternative justification for dual legislative bodies. Thereafter, two distinctive paths were followed. The first emphasized the territorial basis of bicameralism and usually retained upper houses, whose power is equal to the lower houses. The second tended toward upper house reform, either through institutional constraints reducing its power or through broadening its membership to resemble that of the lower house. Subsequently, theorists in federal systems focused their analyses predominantly on relative house power, while theorists in unitary systems evaluated upper house contributions to efficient legislative outcomes. Hence, we see a divergent intellectual debate over the role of bicameral institutions that accompanies their divergent institutional evolution.

Chapter 2 surveys contemporary bicameral institutions, focusing on the distinctiveness of upper house membership and on the institutional distribution of power between the two legislative bodies. We discover that bicameral legislatures are usually characterized by different selection methods in the upper and lower houses, giving rise to potential disagreements. The most common method of achieving agreement between the two houses is through the navette system, where the bill shuttles between the two houses. Finally, we find that most bicameral systems provide one or more methods of overcoming disagreements that are not resolved through the navette: a conference committee is organized, a joint session is called, or one house is granted the ultimate decision. Nonetheless, the variations on these institutional themes are numerous.

We have chosen to organize this wealth of information in a minimal way, so that we impress upon the reader the protean nature of bicameralism, as well as the inability of most prior theorists to provide a common framework for analysis. In fact, to this point, most analyses of bicameral institutions have argued that there are different types of bicameralism with different effects on legislative outcomes. Only once this diversity of forms and institutions and histories is understood will we move to Part II and provide a common framework for understanding bicameral institutions.

1

Bicameralism in historical perspective

Bicameral legislatures are those whose deliberations involve two distinct assemblies. As such, they are relatively modern political institutions that only gained popularity in the eighteenth and nineteenth centuries, despite much earlier origins in the fourteenth-century English parliament.[1] Nonetheless, earlier political institutions share some of the features of more modern bicameral legislatures, and the intellectual debate over the merits of multiple deliberative assemblies is centuries old. In this chapter, we trace the evolution of bicameral institutions and the intellectual justifications that underpin those structures. We do so by following two threads of analysis, what we call the *political* and *efficient* dimensions of bicameralism.

We begin with a definition of the political and efficient dimensions of bicameralism, as these two themes surface repeatedly in the text. We proceed via a chronological overview of the institutional evolution of dual deliberative structures in various eras, accompanied by an intellectual history. In Sections 1 through 3, we review the pre-bicameral institutions of ancient Greece and Rome, the development of the first, class-based bicameral legislature in Britain, and the creation of an alternative federal model in the United States. In Sections 4 and 5, we trace the divergent paths of institutional development in Europe that privilege the distinctions between federal and unitary political systems. Finally, we summarize the contemporary debate on bicameralism, which tends to emphasize *either* the political *or* the efficient dimension of bicameral legislatures.

1. THE TWO DIMENSIONS OF BICAMERALISM

Legislation changes the previously established way of doing things. Whether it regulates behavior in a new way or deregulates behavior and

---

[1]Trivelli (1975) notes the existence of bicameral legislatures prior to the eighteenth century. However, the number is nominal.

permits individual choice, legislation changes the status quo. In bicameral legislatures, the status quo may be modified in two ways.

The *efficient* dimension of bicameralism recognizes that the two legislative houses have common interests. We label this the "efficiency" dimension of bicameralism because it produces an outcome that makes both houses better off.[2] As a result, the analysis focuses on the quality of the legislation, as well as on the stability of legislative outcomes. The term "quality" has both substantive and procedural meanings. The substantive meaning of "improved quality of legislation" in a democracy is one that suggests a movement from the status quo closer to the preferred outcome of the citizens, as indicated by their representatives. The procedural meaning suggests that there are various methods of achieving the desired outcome, the most efficient outcome being the one that achieves it at least cost. Both indicate a common interest of the two legislative houses, a decision that will make both better off.[3]

In contrast, the *political* dimension of bicameralism recognizes that different interests or preferences may be expressed in the two legislative bodies. Where preferences differ, conflict between the two houses arises over the legislative outcome. We label this dimension *political* because of its redistributive nature: an outcome closer to the preferences of one house leaves the other house worse off. As a result, the analysis focuses on the relative balance of power between the two legislative houses, that is, the ability of each house to veto unsatisfactory outcomes and/or to prevail in imposing its preferences.

Briefly put, we argue that both these dimensions of bicameralism were recognized by political philosophers throughout the period from ancient Greece and Rome to eighteenth-century Europe. Since then, various factors have intervened to bifurcate the institutional development and the intellectual analysis of bicameralism. In the contemporary literature, some upper houses are classified as "weak" or "insignificant," promoting improved legislation only through expert advice; others are classified as "strong," where the preferences of upper houses, reflected in their political composition, affect the final legislative outcome (Lijphart 1984: 99).[4]

---

[2]In Tsebelis (1990) two different kind of institutions are defined, "efficient" institutions, which improve the outcomes for all interests involved, and "redistributive" institutions, which promote the interests of some actors at the expense of others. We will expand on this discussion in Chapter 3.

[3]As noted below, the substantive meaning of "quality" differs between early Greek and Roman philosophers and modern democratic analysts. See note 5.

[4]More recent, formal models of bicameral legislatures do acknowledge the connection between the efficient and political dimensions. See, e.g., Riker (1992a, 1992b) and Buchanan and Tullock (1962).

In the intellectual history of bicameralism that follows, we focus our analysis on these two dimensions.

2. PRE-BICAMERAL INSTITUTIONS IN ANCIENT GREECE AND ROME

Although bicameral legislatures in the contemporary sense are absent from ancient Greece and other contemporaneous Mediterranean cultures, some political entities of that era created representative institutions to govern the polity. Because the executive, legislative, and judicial functions of these assemblies were not clearly separated, and the powers of the citizens' assembly often limited, it is inappropriate to speak of a bicameral legislature in the modern sense. Nonetheless, the dual deliberations that characterize modern bicameral legislatures were present in these early political institutions.

Greek philosophers evaluated the quality of these institutions according to a theory of "mixed government." Good government was attributed to the wisdom or virtue of the participants, but even wise governors – legislators, administrators, adjudicators – could falter without a countervailing force achieved through the representation of the society's constituent parts: the monarchy, the aristocracy, and the people.[5] The Romans adopted the Greek principles of mixed government but emphasized the superiority of the aristocracy in producing stable and good government rather than the countervailing force to plebeian representation.

Institutional evolution. Governments in both ancient Greece and early Rome relied on dual or multiple councils whose advisory functions overlapped, providing an early parallel to more modern institutions. Some of these bicameral-like institutions are described by Aristotle, who drew on his knowledge of 158 constitutions from the Mediterranean world (Brunschwig 1983). Dual advisory–legislative councils were visible in Athens, Sparta, Crete, and Carthage. In the latter three polities, separate assemblies represented various classes of citizens. The executive,[6] consisting of a

---

[5]For our purposes, it is important to note that early philosophers were interested in achieving "good government" rather than representing the interests of various groups or classes. In other words, preferences were defined by reference to some exogenously defined system of societal organization rather than being endogenously defined by some summing of individual preferences. We thank Larry Peterman for helping us to clarify this distinction.

[6]The magistrates or administrators of government were called *ephors* in Sparta, *cosmes* in Crete, and the Council of 104 in Carthage. The magistrates clearly had the power of proposition and often had extensive legislative power as well (Aristotle 1959, Book 2).

collective leadership, gathered a small council for advice, drawing on "wise" men who were usually representatives of the wealthy and powerful classes. Athens had a more democratic basis of political organization, so the counterpart to the council of wise men was a council chosen by lot, 50 from each of the 10 tribes (Aristotle 1959: 247–307).[7] All four societies also created broad-based assemblies wherein the "citizens" of the society were represented (Aristotle 1959, 51–61).[8] The council and the assembly deliberated the same issues, providing a parallel to the dual deliberations found in modern bicameral legislatures.

Bicameral-like institutions evolved in early Rome as well.[9] There, the earliest kings appointed a council of elders to advise them, providing the name that would later identify many of the upper houses of modern bicameral legislatures – the Senate. A second consultative body was the *comitia curiate,* an assembly that organized the three tribes of Rome into 10 *curiae* each. The *comitia curiate* was called upon to endorse the new king, selected by the Senate after the death of the preceding king, and to approve the king's imperium, or rule over the army. As the Roman institutions evolved, multiple representational structures developed, often with different deliberative responsibilities, so that the parallel to modern-day bicameral legislatures diminished over time.[10]

Intellectual evolution. Greek philosophers propounded the virtues of "mixed government" over those of "simple government."[11] Simple government encompassed the interests of only one societal class – the one (monarchy), the few (aristocracy), or the many (republic) – while the mixed government included representatives of two or three of these con-

---

[7]Political life in Athens was initially based on four tribes. This number was enlarged through the constitutional reforms of Cleisthenes as a mechanism to enhance popular support for his rule. Emancipated slaves and resident aliens became citizens with rights of political participation (Aristotle 1959: 247–307).

[8]In both Greece and Rome, citizen participation excluded large portions of the population, such as women and slaves. As a result, representative government in that era was much different from representative government today.

[9]See von Fritz (1954) for the evolution of Roman institutions.

[10]The seventh king of Rome, Servus Tullius, divided the population into 193 *centuriae,* organized by class. These 193 *centuriae* were brought together in a *comitia centuriata,* a body consulted for elections of officials and in the legislative process. The *comitia curiata* retained responsibility for the *lex de imperio.* Finally, under the republic, the office of *tribuni plebis* was created; its role was to protect the plebeians from arbitrary acts of the patrician magistrates. The *tribuni* were gathered into a *comitia tributa,* which was also consulted on specific pieces of legislation. All three *comitia* coexisted with the Senate.

[11]See, in particular, the writings of Plato (1966) and Aristotle (1959), as elaborated below. Also see von Fritz (1954) for an analysis of the theory of mixed governments in ancient Greece and Rome.

stituent interests.[12] According to this line of reasoning, the various interests served to balance each other, to prevent the degeneration of the political system into either tyranny or anarchy. Aristotle describes the degenerate forms of the three simple governments:

> The deviation forms of government are as follows: of kingship, tyranny; of aristocracy, oligarchy; of polity, democracy. For tyranny is the rule of a monarch who has only his own interest at heart, oligarchy has in view the interest of the well-to-do; democracy, of the have-nots. None of them looks to the common good of all. (Aristotle 1959: 78)

Avoidance of these degenerate forms of government required a balance of power achieved through representation of different social classes. Thus, Aristotle cites Plato's ideal republic, which is "neither a democracy nor an oligarchy, but an average of the two, that which is called a constitutional government" (Aristotle 1959: 116). He himself argues that the downfall of oligarchies and democracies comes because they fail to combine the popular component and the oligarchic component.

The benefits of mixed government derive from the power balance achieved through multiple interest representation. No single element in society is able to employ the instruments of government to exploit the remainder of society, thereby avoiding the explosion of discontent and the ultimate overthrow of the political order. The Athenian constitution, despite the presence of dual deliberative institutions, was flawed because it called for a simple government. Stable constitutional government must contain a mixture of democratic, oligarchic, and monarchic elements to ensure that the common good of society is not sacrificed to the interests of one particular class.

This established, Greek philosophers were less interested in demarcating the actual institutional structures through which mixed representation could be achieved. The contours of government included an executive, a legislature, and a judiciary; each represented a potential avenue for interest representation. The senate-like institutions noted above were criticized by Aristotle because of the potential for corruption that arose from lifetime appointments and the oligarchic nature of their membership. Aristotle's prescriptions (1959, Book 4) seem to point away from a bi-

---

[12]It is difficult to select a vocabulary that adequately describes the segments of society to be represented in political decision making spanning more than two millennia. Wood (1969), for example, argues that "interest representation" is a distinctly modern term inappropriately applied to earlier eras; "class," according to the same text, fails to capture the essence of medieval "estates" or the Greek societal distinctions. Without rejecting the notion that societies understand internal divisions in different ways, we use the term *interest* to encompass these societal distinctions in the various historical eras as a method of facilitating the comparison of institutional structures over time.

cameral legislature. The appropriate mix of interests in government institutions includes an aristocratic magistrature and a democratic deliberative body, rather than a bicameral legislative body (Aristotle 1959: 103–87).

In Greek philosophy, there is a subtle distinction between the efficient and political (redistributive) dimensions of constituent representation. An aristocratic government was admired for the presence of a virtuous elite who conducted affairs properly (Aristotle 1959: 112–13). However, the aristocracy was always in danger of degenerating into an oligarchy, and it was only through the balance of democratic and monarchic elements that the tyranny of the oligarchy was prevented. So, although the potential for greater efficiency through an educated and wise elite was acknowledged, it was the balance of power established through multiple interest representation that ensured the stability of government (von Fritz 1954).

Roman philosophers placed greater emphasis on the alleged contributions of the senators to the efficiency of government. Although mixed government is touted for its stability,[13] each type of simple government was valued for a particular strength. Cicero recounts, "Thus I prefer monarchy for the love which the king bears to his subjects; aristocracy for its wisdom in counsel; and democracy for its freedom" (Cicero 1929: 140).

And the senate, in particular, provided the core of Cicero's ideal state. The council of elders applied the wisdom acquired by age as a moderating influence over the people (Wood 1969). Because of their wisdom and virtue, the senators were reserved a dominant place in government. In Cicero's words, "When the good are worth more than the many, the citizens should be weighed, not counted" (quoted in Wood 1969). And unlike Aristotle, Cicero was less concerned with the senators' potential corruption; they would naturally refrain from immoral and illicit conduct. Thus, Cicero concludes:

The safety of the state has been founded upon the wisdom of its ablest members. This is particularly true since nature has contrived to make the men who are superior in courage and ability rule over the weak and the weak willing to submit themselves to the best. Thus, between the weakness inherent in a single ruler and the recklessness inherent in the many, aristocracy has come to hold a middle place. Nothing, in fact, can be more perfectly balanced; and as long as an aristocracy guards the state, the people are necessarily in the happiest condition. (Cicero 1929: 138–39)

[13]"There is, accordingly, a fourth kind of commonwealth which, in my opinion, should receive the highest approval, since it is formed by the combination, in due measure, of the three forms of state which I described as original" (Cicero 1929: 134).

Cicero begins to depart from the Greek ideal of mixed government, where the contributions of the aristocracy are inextricably bound to the presence of countervailing forces. It is the specific characteristics of the aristocracy, their "courage and ability," that represent a contribution to the polity. The emphasis on the benefits of senatorial wisdom is reflected in more contemporary debates on bicameral legislatures and becomes a distinct and separate justification for a two-chambered house irrespective of the interests represented in the second chamber.

As the examples given above indicate, there are many historical instances of dual deliberation; most are based on multiple interest representation in political decision making, often in the form of bicameral-like institutions. The idea of an advisory council, a senate, that could improve the efficiency of government is never entirely absent from the dialogue. Nonetheless, until the eighteenth century, the emphasis is on representation of multiple societal interests as a mechanism of balancing power and rendering the political system more stable. The two dimensions that characterize dual deliberative structures, political and efficient, are inextricably intertwined: one is not available without the presence of the other.

3. BICAMERALISM PROPER

The earliest appearance of a bicameral legislature in the modern sense is in fourteenth-century England.[14] By the eighteenth century, the British parliament was widely regarded among Western philosophers as a model political institution (Wood 1969). England's legislative practice of meeting in two distinct decision-making assemblies – the House of Commons and the House of Lords – was then recast in terms of the ancient Greek theory of mixed government (Wood 1969). The legislature was defined as the locus of decision making, and the principles of mixed government were then applied to the legislature. The lower house represented the democratic element of society; the upper house, the aristocratic element; and the king's veto power, the monarchic element. The two dimensions of bicameralism – political representation and legislative efficiency – were still inextricably intertwined. The balance of power between the various societal interests represented in government ensured that the political system would not deteriorate into tyranny of one group over the others.

Institutional evolution. The bicameral legislature evolved out of the king's Great Council, an assembly of advisors to the king. The evolution involved three separate stages spanning two centuries. The process began

---

[14]See Freeman (1863), Trivelli (1975: 51), and additional citations in Trivelli.

with the Great Council's retention of power over taxation; this was followed by the expansion of representation in the Great Council; the final stage was the division of these various estates into two distinctive chambers.[15]

Initially, English political institutions were similar to those evolving on the continent. The king drew upon two advisory councils (*curia regis*) for advice, the Small Council (*concilium*), composed of "professional administrators" and close personal advisors, and the Great Council (*concilium magnum*), composed of feudal lords, both religious and secular. The former was a permanent council in constant session, while the latter was summoned periodically to discuss extraordinary issues, especially taxation. The English aristocracy was able to extract a written guarantee of power over taxation, creating the basis of continually enlarged control over legislation. The Magna Carta signed by King John in 1215 required consent of the Great Council for all royal requests for taxation other than customary feudal aids; it also shifted the basis of membership in the Great Council from feudal tenure to special summons. Thus, the basis of a legislative, rather than a purely consultative, council was laid.

Membership in the Great Council was enlarged for a variety of reasons, the most common being the need for additional taxes to support the king's personal and public expenses. The call for broader representation took the form of a general summons to select local representatives, disseminated through the county sheriffs. The first record of representation from counties by knights dates from 1227; the lower clergy was first called in 1254; and the burgesses were originally summoned to the King's Council in 1283. The so-called model parliament of 1295 reflects this broadened base of representation; it included the great prelates, lay barons, representatives of the lower clergy, two knights from each of 37 counties, and two burgesses from each of 110 cities and boroughs. The label *model parliament* is somewhat of a misnomer, since many parliaments in this era had more restricted membership. Nonetheless, by the early fourteenth century, a pattern had been established of holding frequent parliaments including representatives of all three estates – the clergy, the lords, and "other privileged groups in society."

The final stage of institutional evolution involved the division of the Great Council into two separate bodies. The original division was one based on estates. In the model parliament, for example, the three estates met together to hear the king's address. Then all repaired separately to consider the king's request for taxation and each estate approved different amounts, the burgesses granting a seventh, the landed classes (barons and

---

[15]This discussion is based on Lyon (1980), who provides a detailed history of the evolution of medieval political institutions, including the parliament.

knights) an eleventh, and the clergy a tenth. But the ultimate division into the House of Lords and the House of Commons was based on the distinction between individual and general summons, between those who represented themselves and those who represented their communities.

Initially, the clergy withdrew from the parliament: they held their own annual synods during which they considered the king's request for taxation.[16] Only the prelates continued to attend the Great Councils, based on their position as feudal tenants and as church leaders. The departure of the lower clergy left the lords, summoned to parliament as individuals, and the knights and the burgesses, summoned as representatives of their communities. The distinction between collective and individual representation was reinforced by the growing perception of common interest between the knights and the burgesses. They first presented joint petitions to the king during the Great Council under the reign of Edward II (1307–27); this collaboration had become common under Edward III (1327–77). In the parliament of 1339, the knights and burgesses met together for the first time to deliberate over the royal request for a grant. Thereafter the knights and burgesses met in their separate house. Thus, by 1339, England could be said to have the basic dimensions of a bicameral legislature.[17]

This institutional structure was interrupted only once, when Cromwell abolished the House of Lords in 1655. With the restoration of the monarchy the following year, the House of Lords was quickly reestablished. Power gradually shifted from the king to Parliament and from the upper house to the lower house. It was in this environment of stable institutions that the electoral reforms of the nineteenth century took place, expanding suffrage to working-class men and women, whose votes were incorporated into the House of Commons.[18]

Intellectual evolution. The history of bicameralism in England suggests that the institutional evolution was driven by societal forces rather than a theoretical understanding of political institutions. Nonetheless, in part because of the stability and power of the British state, its political institutions became a model of efficient and stable government.[19] Unsurpris-

---

[16]Representation of the lower clergy in the Great Council ends in the 1330s.

[17]Initially, the Peers in the House of Lords had substantial control over the selection of members of the Commons, although this never meant total control over the advice that emanated from the lower house. Gradually, this control was lost and the two chambers came to represent distinct interests (Williams and Ramsden 1990).

[18]See below for institutional reforms to the House of Lords in the twentieth century.

[19]Wood (1969) argues that the British constitution was the most important model for American colonists when they drafted state and federal constitutions; we extend that argument to the European continent and attribute it to British power rather than the power of British ideas.

ingly, politicians and philosophers alike drew on ancient Greek and Roman ideals of mixed government to justify the twofold division of legislative responsibility. Montesquieu is representative of the debate on the eastern board of the Atlantic, while John Adams represents a similar understanding in the North American colonies, in the process of becoming an independent nation.

Montesquieu's philosophy of government is summarized in *The Spirit of Laws,* published in 1748.[20] There he adopts the traditional position that political liberty is forfeited when a single class holds the reins over executive, legislative, and judicial power. "Miserable indeed would be the case, were the same man, or the same body whether of the nobles or of the people, to exercise those three powers, that of enacting laws, that of executing the public resolutions, and that of judging the crimes or differences of individuals" (Montesquieu 1977: 202). From this perspective, Montesquieu judged the majority of European kingdoms as moderate because they were constrained by the presence of two or three classes in the institutions of government.

However, in distinction from the Greeks and the Romans, Montesquieu focused on the special characteristics of the monarchy, the aristocracy, and the people as indicative of the roles they should assume in government. Executive power is best located in the hands of the monarch, who can act quickly when action is needed, while legislative power is "better ordered" by many individuals rather than a single individual. Furthermore, the aristocracy would be overwhelmed if represented as individuals in a single legislative body and would fail to support such an institutional structure. Therefore, Montesquieu recommended separate and equal legislative bodies for the aristocracy and the people:

In a state there are always persons distinguished by their birth, riches, or honors: but were they to be confounded with the common people, and to have only the weight of a single vote like the rest, the common liberty would be their slavery, and they would have no interest in supporting it, as most of the popular resolutions would be against them. The share they have therefore in the legislature ought to be proportioned to the other advantages they have in the state; which happens only when they form a body that has a right to put a stop to the enterprises of the people, as the people have a right to oppose any encroachment of theirs.

The legislative power is therefore committed to the body of the nobles, and to the body chosen to represent the people, which have each their assemblies and deliberations apart, each their separate view and interests. (Montesquieu 1977: 205)

[20]This discussion draws on Montesquieu's writings, on Trivelli (1975), and on Wood (1969).

England is singled out by Montesquieu as the contemporaneous political order that retained the political liberty of its citizens through the division of political powers among the three classes. The perfect balance thus far had been achieved only in the English system of govenment.

Montesquieu also noted the distinctive qualities of a senate, whose members shared the characteristics of age, virtue, wisdom, and service to the community. Such a council would reinforce the stability of the polity through its sound advice. In other words, a senate was a wise body that could remind the society of its first principles and ensure that new legislation improved rather than corrupted the old. The potential corruption of the hereditary nobility that concerned Aristotle could be avoided, according to Montesquieu, by diminishing their legislative power to that of veto (*faculté d'empêcher*) rather than extending to this legislative chamber the power of initiative (*faculté de statuer*).

John Adams drew on the same Greek principles of mixed government but found a different method of justifying a bicameral legislature. He argued that legislative power was sovereign and therefore required the balance of constituent interests *within* its institutional structure.[21] According to Adams, "Legislative power is naturally and necessarily sovereign and supreme over the executive, and therefore the latter must be made an essential branch of the former" (quoted in Walsh 1915: 80). The perfect constitution, said Adams, was "the tripartite balance, the political trinity in unity, trinity of the legislative, and unity of executive power" (quoted in Wood 1969: 577).

For Adams, every society, including the American society, reflects the same divisions that the Greeks enumerated – the one, the few, and the many. To ensure a stable society, these divisions must be reflected in the government. His constitutional trinity was therefore a tripartite legislature, two houses representing the aristocracy and the people, and the executive – endowed with a legislative veto – representing the monarchic element. In the English government, he too discovered the perfect balance. But because the circumstances in the American colonies were distinctive from those on the continent, some adaptation of definitions was required. For Adams, there was no basic difference between hereditary monarchy and an elective executive. Either was suited to perform executive functions and represented the interests of the nation as a whole. And the aristocracy was not a hereditary one but a "natural" aristocracy, those who *achieved* superiority rather than those who were born to it. Nonetheless, the natural aristocracy was marked by wealth and wisdom lacking in the common people.

[21]This discussion draws on Walsh (1915) and Wood (1969).

The balance Adams sought in the legislature is identical to the broader government balance recommended by the Greeks:

The three natural orders in society, the monarchical, the aristocratical and the democratical are . . . constitutionally placed to watch and control each other. . . . Thereby, also, each will balance the other two. The executive will balance the upper and lower chambers, that is, the upper and lower classes, the aristocracy and the democracy, especially preserving the people from the arrogance of the nobles; the senate will balance the king and the people or their representatives, especially preserving the people from the usurpations of the king and his favorites (or from the people's own tendency to set up a tyrant); and the commons, or the people's representatives, will balance the king and the senate, especially preserving the king from the jealousy of the aristocracy. (Quoted in Walsh 1915: 80–81)

Both Montesquieu and Adams, as representative of eighteenth-century political thought, adapted the Greek philosophy of mixed government to a distinctive institutional form – a bicameral legislature. Their understanding of the political and efficient dimensions of dual deliberative assemblies was likewise similar. The aristocracy was admired for its knowledge, training, wisdom, age, and service; but it could not be relied upon to provide these skills to improve the government unless aristocratic power was checked by the power of the monarchy (either hereditary or elected ruler) and the people.

4. THE RISE OF REPUBLICANISM AND AMERICAN INSTITUTIONAL INNOVATION

Despite political philosophies that championed the representation of "the people" in the institutions of government, many, if not most, members of society in the eighteenth century were excluded from political participation. Alternatively, as in the American colonies, broader participation in local governments did not guarantee participation in colonial policies established by the mother country. As the power of various societal groups shifted, they sought and ultimately won expanded political participation.[22] Thus, the rise of republicanism challenged national political institutions by proposing to represent the people as a whole regardless of whether previous systems of representation were based on class (unitary political systems) or on territory (confederal political systems). The newly formed United States discovered an alternative political solution that combined both republicanism and federalism. Thus, the stage was set for the divergent evolution in both the principles and the practice of bicameralism.

[22]So that most Western nations achieved universal manhood suffrage after World War I and universal adult suffrage by the end of World War II.

Institutional evolution. Given the origin of most North American colonists, it is perhaps surprising that most of the colonial governments began with unicameral legislatures. Nonetheless, most of these governments evolved into bicameral systems so that at the founding of the United States, all but Pennsylvania and Georgia had bicameral legislatures. The evolutionary process varied but most involved the transformation of the executive council into a second legislative house.[23] Connecticut provides one example. The "Fundamental Orders" establishing the colony in 1639 provided for a single legislative body consisting of the governor, magistrates, and four deputies from each of the towns. The magistrates were elected by the freemen of the entire colony, while the deputies were selected by the townspeople. Because of the press of business, in May 1678, the governor, deputy governor, and assistants (magistrates) were constituted as a standing council, thereby creating a second, distinct legislative body. Dual deliberations were ensured in 1689, when the acts of the Council required the approval of the general assembly. Ultimately, the Executive Council evolved into the upper house. A bicameral legislature was adopted in October 1698; the governor and magistrates were designated as representatives to the upper house and the deputies to the lower house. Laws required the sanction of both houses.

By 1776, the American colonies had a well-established tradition of bicameralism. The Articles of Confederation failed to draw on this tradition but also failed to provide a stable national government. The Constitutional Convention of 1787 therefore debated and adopted a bicameral federal legislature. The story of the "great compromise" is well known and will not be repeated here. The agreement provided that the House of Representatives would be elected on the basis of the population, whereas the Senate would grant equal representation for each state. The compromise protected the interests of the small states against the domination of the large and obtained the consent of the small states to the new constitution (U.S. Senate 1987). The institutional innovation, foreshadowed in the evolution of bicameral state legislatures, was the shift in representation of societal classes to representation of "the people." "The people" selected representatives for both legislative houses, but these houses represented different manifestations of "the people's" will. The lower house reflected a popular dimension, while the upper house reflected a territorial dimension. This system of national representation was combined with the reservation of certain powers to the constituent political units, the thirteen original colonies.

Intellectual evolution. The most thorough justification of bicameralism in the new constitution comes from James Madison in *The Federalist*

[23]The discussion draws on Barnett (1915), Moran (1895), and Morey (1893).

27

Papers, first published in 1788 (in particular, No. 62). To promote the ratification he drew on both dimensions of the intellectual debate: representation of interests and efficiency of a second legislative body.

The representational dimension was, of course, prominent in the debate. States, it was argued, had specific and distinct interests from the population as a whole. This being the case, an "advantage accruing from the Senate is the additional impediment it must provide against improper acts of legislation. No law or resolution can now be passed without the concurrence first, of a majority of the people, and then of a majority of the states" (Hamilton et al. 1961: 402). In other words, institutional representation provided the groups represented therein with a veto over legislative outcomes.

Having noted the political dimension of U.S. bicameralism, Madison moved to the efficient dimension. The discussion can be separated into two categories, aspects that improve political stability and aspects that improve the quality of legislative decisions.

Political stability can be affected by the changing preferences of the assembly or by the changing composition of the assembly. Madison first noted the "propensity of all single and numerous assemblies to yield to the impulse of sudden and violent passions" (Hamilton et al. 1961: 379). A senate (or second chamber) provided the ballast needed to control the lower house's tendency to produce a new majority that overturned the previous majority. Madison also describes the "mutability in the public councils arising from a rapid succession of new members, however qualified they may be" (Hamilton et al. 1961: 380). This leads to the "necessity of some stable institution in the government." The Senate became the anchor for legislation subject to the changing preferences of the lower house that arise from either the "rapid succession of new members" or the advent of "sudden and violent passions" (Hamilton et al. 1961: 405).

Legislative quality is affected by the expertise and training of legislators, as well as by their potential for corruption. A senate offered a solution to both these problems. The longer electoral terms of the senators permitted them to become "professional legislators who were better supplied with a knowledge of the means by which [the object of good government] can best be obtained" (Hamilton et al. 1961: 404). And the Senate reduced corruption because it "double[d] the security to the people by requiring the concurrence of two distinct bodies in schemes of usurpation or perfidy, where the ambition or corruption of one would otherwise be sufficient" (Hamilton et al. 1961: 378–79).

Finally, Madison also noted "the propensity of all single and numerous assemblies to be seduced by factious leaders into intemperate and pernicious resolutions" (Hamilton et al. 1961: 378–79). The presence of a senate (or second chamber) reduces the likelihood that one individual will be able to sway both groups of legislators and decreases the potential for "pernicious resolutions."

In the republican debates at the end of the eighteenth century, the justifications for a dual legislative system still acknowledged both a political dimension and an efficiency dimension, but that connection begins to be severed. In addition, in its promise to represent "the people" as a whole, republicanism undermined political institutions based on distinctive representation by class (unitary political systems), as well as political institutions based on territory (federal political systems). Therefore, as republican waves shook the political establishment during the nineteenth century, institutions evolved differently.

5. THE SPREAD OF REPUBLICANISM AND THE DISSEMINATION OF BICAMERAL INSTITUTIONS

Republicanism affected the development of political institutions in two contexts, unitary (class-based) political systems and federal (territorially based) political systems. Bicameralism was a common response but the forms of bicameralism differed. In the former case, British institutions served as the primary point of departure; in the latter, the U.S. institutions provided a model.

The unitary pattern. Although patterns varied, the institutional continuity that characterized Britain was the exception rather than the rule in continental Europe. Early monarchs of nascent European states generally created a three-estate system of consultation, but the balance of power that favored the nobility in England favored the monarchs on the continent. During the period of absolutism, most Estates General fell into disuse. Then, in the wake of the French Revolution, as citizens fought to gain political representation, the upper houses of newly forged bicameral legislatures offered the nobility a place of refuge and the monarch a constitutional base of political support.

The evolution of Swedish institutions is probably closest to the British experience because there the Estates General was continuously maintained (Håstad 1957). The primitive form of the Riksdag was established in the fourteenth century and comprised members of the nobility and the clergy. Representation expanded to include representatives of the towns and the peasantry in the fifteenth century. These four estates met separately until the constitutional reforms of 1865–66 established a two-chambered Riksdag. The reform movement was motivated in large part by the unwieldiness of decision making with four estates rather than by demands for electoral reform.[24]

More typical of the continental European pattern of absolutism is Denmark.[25] There, the earliest reference to a consultative assembly is 811, when a treaty with the Franks was approved by an assembly of the leading men of the realm. As in Britain, the relative power of the nobles vis-à-vis the monarch rose and waned. In 1282, the nobles forced the monarch, King Erik Klipping, to sign the Great Charter, recognizing important restrictions on his power and calling for an annual assembly, the Danehof. By the end of the fourteenth century, the Danehof was eclipsed by a small inner circle of nobles and clergy. During the sixteenth century, in the wake of the Reformation, Christian II called a national assembly, drawing on nobles, burghers, and peasants, to support the elimination of the Catholic hierarchy from positions of wealth and power. But a century later, the monarchy was sufficiently powerful to forego this support. The Royal Law, issued in 1665, was an "unequivocal statement of absolutism," and representative assemblies fell into disuse.

The Danish monarchy reigned without societal consultation for almost 200 years until 1834, when Frederick VI reestablished consultative assemblies. But it wasn't until the revolutions of 1848 swept across Europe that Christian VII directed the drafting of a constitution limiting monarchical power. In this constitution, the parliament, or Riksdag, was divided into two assemblies, the Folketing and the Landsting. The former assembly reflected the demands of the working classes for universal (male) suffrage. To offset this new base of popular power, the latter assembly was an indirectly elected body of legislators serving eight-year terms. A bastion of conservatism, members of the Landsting were at least 40 years of age, with significant property holdings. In 1866, the conservative nature of this body was reinforced by restricting suffrage and designating 12 of the 66 members as appointees of the king.

Like Denmark, many other European countries experienced an institutional break between the medieval Estates General composed of three or four privileged classes and the modern, predominantly bicameral legislatures. France, Italy, Portugal, and Spain all reflect a similar institutional evolution: the rise of Estates General that subsequently fell into disuse during a period of monarchical absolutism, followed by the establishment

---

[24]Originally, each estate had veto power over decisions. During the eighteenth century, the principle of majority rule was adopted for most legislation, but agreement of three of the four estates was still necessary. Constitutional changes required consensus so that the 1865–66 constitutional reform was approved by all four estates (Håstad 1957). Expansion of the suffrage through electoral reform awaited the twentieth century.

[25]This discussion is based on Miller (1968).

of constitutional monarchies or republics. The issue of unicameral as opposed to bicameral legislatures was often hotly contested, but the power of the elite classes was sufficient in most cases to ensure the creation of two legislative bodies, one privileging the people, the other a landed or bourgeois elite. Thus, bicameralism in many states was a new institutional mechanism created in the wake of the changing societal balance of power.

The federal pattern. Another set of European polities confronted a different institutional tradition.[26] Confederations in Europe, such as the German Confederation (1815–66), the Swiss Confederation (1291–1798), and the United Provinces of the Netherlands (1579–1795), all had unicameral assemblies. In contrast to the modern day perception of the close connection between "strong" bicameralism and federalism, historically, confederal states were unicameral. Each constituent unit was represented in the assembly, where its representatives acted as "ambassadors" for the local governments and took instruction from them. There was no enforced congruence of the local governments. Autocratic princes coexisted with aristocracies, merchant and craft guilds, and direct democracies.

Switzerland and the United Provinces granted equal weight to each constituent unit, whereas a system of weighted voting applied in the case of the German Confederation. Nonetheless, even there, the voting weight of the largest states was significantly smaller than their actual size in terms of population.[27] Decision making required unanimity of the member states, providing each member, even the smallest, with veto power. Again, the German Confederation was exceptional; a two-thirds majority was required in the general assembly for most issues, although unanimous consent was necessary in certain instances.

Rising republicanism triggered institutional reform in these federated states, as well as in the centralized monarchies described above. The Swiss solution was, in fact, copied from the United States. After a period of institutional turmoil under French occupation (1798–1814) and an uneasy agreement reestablishing the confederal pattern (1815–48), the Swiss finally created a bicameral legislature with a lower house based on popular representation, and an upper house based on cantonal represen-

---

[26]The discussion draws on Koch (1984) and Passant (1977) for Germany, Freeman (1863), Moses (1889), Sauser-Hall (1946), and Trivelli (1975) for Switzerland, and Barnouw (1944), Renier (1944), and Riemens (1944) for the Netherlands.

[27]The German Diet consisted of two councils. In the inner council, each of the major states designated one representative, while the remaining states (some 30-odd principalities and city-states) divided six delegates among themselves. In the general assembly, every state had at least one vote, while the larger states were granted two, three, or four votes (Passant 1977).

tation. As in the U.S. case, the smaller cantons preferred equal representation, while the larger cantons sought popular representation. The compromise there was championed by few but remained the only viable solution, one that "was unacceptable to no one" (Trivelli 1975: 155).

Germans followed a path similar to the Swiss, with a Reichstag based on universal (male) suffrage and a Bundesrat based on weighted representation of the member states.[28] The Netherlands, on the other hand, established a unitary state with an aristocratic upper house nominated by the king. Political upheaval in 1848 forced the reform of the upper house; provincial representation was reestablished but this time within a centralized unitary system of government rather than a federal system. As a result, the upper chamber is not granted coequal power to the lower chamber.

In summary, Britain and the United States represent two distinct models of institutional development. Other European states experienced some linear combination of these two paths. Confederations tended to adopt a bicameralism in which "the people" were represented in the lower house, while the constituent states were represented in the upper house. Unitary states tended to reserve the upper house for elite classes to offset the political power of "the people" in the lower house. In both cases, however, the two houses tended to have equal legislative power. Unicameral legislatures, championed by some republicans, were the exception rather than the rule.

6. THE TRIUMPH OF REPUBLICANISM AND THE BIFURCATION OF THE BICAMERAL DIALOGUE

We have argued that bicameral legislatures evolved in two different ways. The first involved the representation of societal classes. This type of bicameralism was justified by reference both to the representation of societal interests and to the specific characteristics of the legislators – their wisdom, stability, education. The second involved representation of different dimensions of the nation, population, and territory. This second type of bicameralism was also justified in terms of representation, but because pursuit of interests may contradict the wisdom of the legislators, the "efficient" aspects of bicameralism were sought in its institutional structure. Therefore, as republicanism became firmly entrenched in the twentieth century, the acceptability of these two institutional structures differed. The legitimacy of upper houses in class-based systems was repu-

[28]The North German Confederation was created in 1866 and a constitution adopted at that time. The year 1871 marks the beginning of the German Reich, whose constitution was a modified version of the earlier North German Confederation constitution.

diated, while the legitimacy in territorially-based systems was maintained. Territory provided a "competing legitimacy," in the words of Mastias and Grangé (1987), that social class lacked.[29] It is not surprising then that both the institutional dynamic and the theoretical justification of bicameral legislatures evolved along different lines. What is surprising is that the structural bases of bicameral efficiency enumerated by Madison were forgotten rather than shared.

Three separate paths were taken: bicameralism with legitimate and politically powerful upper houses; bicameralism with weak and efficient upper houses; and congruent bicameralism. These three evolutionary paths elicited three separate streams of thought in which the perceived complementarity of interest representation and legislative efficiency were erased.[30] Each path is examined in turn.

Bicameralism in federal systems. In most federal systems the legitimacy of upper houses remains unquestioned and their power unconstrained.[31] The United States, for example, retained a Senate whose power is equal to the House of Representatives. Switzerland and Germany are continental examples of politically powerful upper houses in federal systems.[32]

In the intellectual dialogue, the role of interest representation predominates, and emphasis is given to the political rather than to the efficient role of upper houses. The United States is a prime example. A recent, comprehensive survey of bicameral politics in the United States lists the classical justifications for bicameralism. Class and territorial cleavages head the list, stability is mentioned, but quality assurance and legislative efficiency never make the list (Longley and Oleszek 1989: 14–16). [33] The

---

[29]Temperley (1910, p. 62) notes that "power seems to be enjoyed by the Upper Chamber in proportion as its composition is democratized. . . . Nominee Upper Chambers are far inferior in power to Elective ones, and the reason is to be found in the profound . . . conviction that a man or a body is only to be trusted, when it is freely and directly chosen by the people as a whole." Also see Lees-Smith (1923).

[30]Temperley (1910, p. 16) notes that federal upper houses are noncomparable to unitary upper houses: "While the Upper Chamber exists in a Unitary State only to interpret the will of the people, in the Federal State, it may exist actually to oppose it." Also see Lees-Smith (1923).

[31]There are exceptions to the rule, including Canada and Austria.

[32]The powers of the Swiss houses are equal. In the Federal Republic of Germany/Germany, the Bundesrat has equal power in legislation that requires implementation by the states, which is more than half of all legislation (Mastias and Grangé 1987; Trivelli 1975).

[33]The efficiency dimension propounded by Madison has not been completely eradicated. That tradition is carried on by Rogers (1926) and Burdette (1940) in their discussions of the Senate's ability to delay legislation through filibuster. Rather than seeing this in entirely negative terms, filibuster may provide protection for individual and minority rights.

33

legitimacy of the U.S. Senate is so little questioned that it is completely excluded from contemporary discussions.

Given the emphasis on the Senate's political role, analysts immediately ask which house has the most power. Some literature deals directly with relative house power, but since most of the important legislation is referred to conference committee, it is this "third house" of the U.S. legislature that receives the most attention (Ferejohn 1975; Shepsle and Weingast 1984, 1987a, 1987b; Steiner 1951; Strom and Rundquist 1976, 1977; Vogler 1970, 1971).

Bicameralism in unitary systems. In unitary systems the role of upper houses grew problematic as suffrage was expanded and as democratic attitudes were adopted. Initially, the problem was resolved by attributing the need for a strong upper house to the representation of "minorities" rather than of the aristocracy. But eventually, upper houses were confronted with the fact that in order to stand up to the popular house on behalf of minorities, "a Second Chamber was found to need a democratic basis which could only be secured by some form of popular election" (Campion 1953–54: 20). In cases where nations chose to retain their selection procedures, the second house was relegated to efficient, apolitical functions.

The United Kingdom provides an example where a hereditary upper house was retained but its powers were severely curtailed. Schemes to abolish or reform the upper house began circulating in the 1880s and culminated in the Parliament Act of 1911, which placed the ultimate power of decision in the lower house. The Lords' power was further reduced in 1949 legislation that limited their delaying power over nonfinancial legislation from three years to one. The Lords' power over financial legislation is even more restricted.

A similar picture can be drawn of the French Sénat. In contrast to the equal power of the two houses in the Third Republic, the constitutions of the Fourth and Fifth Republics drastically limited senatorial power. The constitution of the Fourth Republic permitted the upper house only the power of delay. The constitution of the Fifth Republic, upon request of the government, grants the Assemblée Nationale final power of decision after two readings in the Senate.

The intellectual debate on the role of the upper house evolved as well. Political analysts selected those dimensions of intellectual history that confirmed an efficient role of the upper house, without addressing the linkage that connected efficiency with political representation. A series of books and articles on the role of the House of Lords in the post–World War II period confirm the political impotence of the House of Lords even as they concede the Lords' usefulness (Adonis 1988; Bromhead 1958;

34

Bicameralism in historical perspective

Bromhead and Shell 1967; Burrows 1964; Campion 1953–54; Percival 1953–54; Vincent 1966; Weare 1965). French analyses of senatorial power are devoted either to describing senatorial impotence (Georgel 1968; Grangé 1981; Lassaigne 1968; Tardan 1988) or to analyzing the normative bases of influence: independence, expertise, time for thoughtful consideration (Grangé 1984; Mastias 1980). These analyses echo Cicero's emphasis on the Senate's *auctoritas* – the upper legislative chamber retains authority and influence despite its lack of power. The reason, according to this literature, is that dedication, expertise, and moderation serve to convince the lower house of the correctness of the upper house's opinions.

Congruent bicameralism. Sweden serves as a good example of the last road (Mastias and Grangé 1987). The nation gradually reformed its electoral procedures so the upper house eventually resembled the lower house in political composition. By 1933, the political composition of the two houses was almost identical despite indirect elections in the upper house. In countries with congruent bicameralism, the debate hinges on the value of a second legislative body. In the words of a seventeenth-century political philosopher, Abbé Sièyes, "If the second chamber agrees with the first, it is useless, and if not, it is bad" (quoted in Walsh 1915: 331). As a result, Sweden in 1959, as well as countries with congruent houses, like Denmark in 1953, resolved this debate in favor of unicameralism.

7. THE CONTEMPORARY DEBATE

The contemporary debate both echoes and extends the theoretical analysis of bicameral institutions. Because we will revisit these intellectual justifications of bicameralism in our concluding chapter, we summarize here both the historical and contemporary dialogue. In fact, the contemporary debate often formalizes the intuitions of earlier political philosophers. For ease of presentation, we organize the material into the two categories we have developed throughout the chapter, the political and efficiency aspects of bicameralism.

Political. Whether bicameral legislatures represent distinct classes, occupational groups, or manifestations of the sovereign people, bicameral legislatures provide an institutionalized veto power that prevents a "tyranny of the majority" (Hamilton et al. 1961). To quote Montesquieu (1977: 210–11), "The legislative body [is] composed of two parts, one checks the other, by the mutual privilege of refusing." In the contemporary debate, this system of checks and balances is described by Levmore (1992: 146) as a "stopping mechanism, as a means of preventing some

35

kinds of government intervention based on the support of a simple majority of the members of a legislature."

Bicameralism is also purported to prevent a "tyranny of the minority." Buchanan and Tullock (1962) argue that bicameralism improves the representativeness of decisions under majority rule systems. According to their argument, majority rule in unicameral legislatures means that slightly more than one-quarter of the voters can prevail in having their preferences implemented – one-half of the representatives in the legislature, representing one-half of the voters in their constituencies. In bicameral systems, the presence of two legislative houses requires a broader constituency base to support any legislation.[34]

Finally, bicameralism reduces the potential for tyranny of an individual leader.[35] Madison noted the propensity of "all single and numerous assemblies to be seduced by factious leaders into intemperate and pernicious resolutions" (Hamilton et al. 1961: 379). In the contemporary debate, Levmore (1992) explores the role of bicameralism in reducing the power of the agenda setter. More formally, in the presence of voting cycles, the power of the agenda setter lies in the ability to structure the order in which alternatives are evaluated. Consider a three member parliament with the set of preferences presented in Table 1.1. In this scenario, A is the agenda setter, who prefers x to y, and y to z. By introducing first a choice between y and z, y is the majority-supported outcome. The agenda setter A can then pose the choice between x and y, in which x is successful. In a unicameral setting, the agenda setter, by structuring the order in which alternatives are voted upon, can control the outcome and achieve his or her preferred solution.

Under bicameralism, the agenda setter's choice must survive the competition from *all* alternatives in the second house. Control over outcomes necessitates the collusion of an agenda setter in the second house. Therefore, bicameralism reduces the power of the agenda setter.[36]

Both historical and contemporary analyses base these political and redistributive justifications on an egalitarian bicameralism, in which both chambers have equal powers of decision, where the consent of both houses is required for the passage of legislation. In those cases where the upper house is merely consultative and the lower house has ultimate

---

[34]This holds only where the two houses are noncongruent.

[35]Bicameralism also reduces agenda control without opening the legislature to cycles, an efficient aspect of bicameralism. See below.

[36]Levmore (1992) recognizes that if reconciliation of intercameral differences is by conference committee and the agenda setter has power of appointment of the conference committee delegation, bicameralism may not undermine the power of the agenda setter. An alternative way of stating this is that although bicameralism decreases the power of the agenda setter, it increases the power of those who control the appointment of conference committee members.

Table 1.1. *Power of agenda setter in unicameral legislatures*

Member of parliament	Preference ordering
A (Agenda setter)	$x > y > z$
B	$y > z > x$
C	$z > x > y$

Note: By selecting an agenda where y is compared to z and the winner to x, A assures that x will be the outcome of collective choice.

power of decision, bicameralism does not create a system of checks and balances.

Efficiency. Efficient legislatures produce both better legislation and more stable outcomes. The distinction between quality and stability is illustrated by Madison when he argues that "continual change of even good measures is inconsistent with every rule of prudence and every prospect of success" (Hamilton et al. 1961: 380). Bicameral legislatures are purported to produce both types of efficiency gains.

There are three sources of legislative instability: changes in personnel, changes in preferences (Hamilton et al. 1961), and changes in outcomes attributable to the voting cycle (Condorcet 1968; Hammond and Miller 1987; Miller and Hammond 1989). Bicameralism improves all three types of instability. However, the first two types of instability are resolved through differences in tenure, whereas the third depends on different types of membership. Stability for Madison was created by a longer term in office and partial renewal of membership.[37] Many legislative chambers are designed with differences in tenure to avoid the instability associated with "sudden and violent passions" and "rapid succession of new members."

The third type of instability is the potential instability of outcomes associated with what is today called the voting cycle.[38] Bicameral institu-

---

[37]Miller and Hammond (1989) imply that Madison was also aware of the instability created by the voting cycle, discussed below, as well as the effects of bicameral institutions in resolving this instability.

[38]The marquis de Condorcet first noted the potential instability of outcomes that today is labeled "Condorcet's paradox," or the voting cycle (Condorcet 1968). In his essay on probability and decision making published in 1785 and summarized in his discourse on provincial assemblies, Condorcet noted the inability of majority voting to

37

tions reduce "cycling" problems associated with unicameral legislatures. (Frickey 1992; Hammond and Miller 1987; Miller and Hammond 1989; Riker 1992a, 1992b).[39]

To illustrate the problem that can arise in a unicameral legislature under majority voting, take a six-member parliament whose members have preferences as noted in Table 1.2. Each alternative is considered in a pairwise comparison with the other alternatives. Suppose first that x is compared with y; x would win because a majority (A, D, E, and F) prefers x to y. Then x is compared with z; z wins this comparison because a different majority (B, C, E, and F) prefers z to x. Finally, z is compared with y; y wins this comparison because yet a different majority (A, B, C, and D) prefers y to z. But if the winner of this last round is arrayed against x, the cycle begins anew. There is always a majority-preferred alternative that can defeat the status quo, leading to cycling and unstable outcomes. Thus, even where preferences and membership are stable, outcomes may be unstable.

Dividing the legislature into two distinct groups and requiring concur-

capture the true preferences of individuals in cases where choices were greater than two, because majority voting failed to make use of knowledge of preferences over the entire spectrum of choices. However, a system that employs this knowledge, by systematically comparing all possible pairs of alternatives, may produce the "absurd" result of no stable choice. His example is reproduced in the tabulation to illustrate the instability of outcomes. Sixty voters attempt to select a representative from the field of three candidates, Paul, Pierre, and Jacques. Given the preferences outlined, Condorcet noted that in a pairwise comparison of the three candidates, Pierre was preferred to Paul (33 vs. 27 votes); Paul was preferred to Jacques (42 vs. 18 votes), and Jacques was preferred to Pierre (35 vs. 25 votes). In his words, "The election gives an absurd result, or rather it gives no result at all" (Condorcet 1968: p. 570). This cycling problem is equally applicable to legislative outcomes.

Preferences of sixty voters

Voters 1–23	Voters 24–25	Voters 26–42	Voters 43–52	Voters 53–60
Pierre	Paul	Paul	Jacques	Jacques
Paul	Pierre	Jacques	Pierre	Paul
Jacques	Jacques	Pierre	Paul	Pierre

As noted below, one solution to this problem of instability of outcomes was a second chamber. It is not clear from his writings that Condorcet himself recognized the benefits of a second legislative chamber in overcoming the voting cycle. In any case, Condorcet believed the advantages of a single legislative assembly outweighed the disadvantages associated with two legislative chambers. His preferred solution to many of the flaws associated with a single legislative assembly was the requirement of super-majorities.

[39]Bicameralism is one method of reducing cycles without delegating power to agenda setters. See above.

Table 1.2. *Voting cycles in unicameral and bicameral legislatures*

Members of unicameral parliament	Preference ordering
A	$x > y > z$
B	$y > z > x$
C	$y > z > x$
D	$x > y > z$
E	$z > x > y$
F	$z > x > y$

Members of bicameral parliament	Preference ordering
Chamber 1	
A	$x > y > z$
B	$y > z > x$
C	$y > z > x$
Chamber 2	
D	$x > y > z$
E	$z > x > y$
F	$z > x > y$

Note: The cycle $x > y > z > x$ that exists in the unicameral legislature is eliminated in the bicameral legislature.

rent majorities of both groups may reduce the number of alternatives that a majority prefers. If A, B, and C are defined as members of one legislative house, D, E, and F are defined as members of a second legislative assembly, and passage requires concurrent majorities, then some majority-supported alternatives are no longer available. Riker provides an example that illustrates this principle. In Chamber 1, y is preferred to z and z is preferred to x, but x is not preferred to y. In Chamber 2, z is preferred to x, x is preferred to y, but y is not preferred to z. The only legislation that is supported by concurrent majorities is z. However, this result is achieved only when the two assemblies reflect different preference structures. If the two houses have identical preferences, then cycling continues despite the presence of two deliberative bodies.

If stability is a desirable feature and bicameralism promotes stability, Levmore (1992) and others believe that it must be evaluated in light of other legislative systems that also encourage stability. Both bicameralism and unicameral super-majority systems promote stability, but Levmore argues, bicameralism compares favorably with unicameral super-majority systems because it fosters the selection of a strong Condorcet winner, that is, "an alternative that [is] preferred to all others in head-to-head competition" (1992: 156). In other words, when one alternative is majority supported over all other alternatives, the cycling problem disappears and legislatures should endorse such alternatives. However, unicameral super-majority voting systems permit a minority to block the will of the majority, whereas bicameral legislatures approve "strong Condorcet winners" by majority vote.[40] Thus, whereas both systems reduce instability, only bicameral legislatures promote strong Condorcet winners.

Bicameral legislatures also promote "better" legislative outcomes in a number of ways. From the time of the ancient Greeks onward, the idea of a council of elders, who could bring their experience and wisdom to the government, has been advocated (Aristotle 1959). Cicero's (1929) promotion of the aristocracy was not completely self-serving, given that this was the educated class in a society where educational opportunities were limited. Mastias and Grangé (1987) provide an example of contemporary analysts who emphasize the wisdom of the senate in ensuring better political outcomes. The institutional provisions that promote an efficient role for the senate include higher age minimums for the upper chamber than for the lower chamber and selection criteria that involve some evaluation of expertise. The longer term in office also permits the development of legislative expertise. And the disinterested nature of senatorial involvement promotes an objective look at legislation. Therefore, the senate represents the bastion of *auctoritas,* capable of improving legislation (Mastias and Grangé 1987).

However, the mere presence of a second legislative chamber creates the possibility of quality control in the more modern sense. Quality control rests on two ideas. The first is preventive: knowing that someone else will examine the product makes the producer more careful initially. Second, there is a system to discover mistakes after they have been committed. A second chamber, regardless of its level of expertise and wisdom, constitutes such a quality-control mechanism.

Bicameralism has also been touted as reducing corruption and slowing the legislative process. Following Madison, Levmore (1992) cites the ability of a second chamber to reduce corruption because bicameralism requires the collusion of more individuals than would be required in a

---

[40]A Condorcet winner is an alternative that beats every other alternative in pairwise comparisons. Levmore defines as "strong Condorcet winner" an alternative that is the Condorcet winner in both chambers. We discuss the likelihood that a Condorcet winner exists in Chapter 3 and then again in Chapter 9.

unicameral system. As for delay, according to Madison, the senate is there "to check the misguided career and to suspend the blow mediated by the people against themselves, until reason, justice, and truth can regain their authority over the public mind" (Hamilton et al. 1961: 384). In other words, bicameralism, by requiring two distinct assemblies to make decisions, delays the passage of legislation and provides "the safety which lies in sober second thoughts, to appeal from Philip drunk to Philip sober" (quoted in Walsh 1915: 334).

Riker (1992a, 1992b) presents a more formal analysis of the delaying power of the senate that also incorporates the promotion of the status quo. The essence of his argument is that the requirement of concurrent majorities is more stringent than that of a single majority. Riker uses these results to support the contention that bicameralism promotes equilibrium decisions in one dimension and avoids out-of-equilibrium decisions in two or more dimensions. The essence of the argument is based on the existence of an equilibrium outcome in one dimension – the median voter – and the lack of an equilibrium outcome in two or more dimensions, except under extremely restrictive conditions (Plott 1967). Riker (1992a: 113) notes that "when there is a one-dimensional issue configuration, then multicameralism encourages prompt adoption of the one-dimensional equilibrium" – the "global median voter."[41] At the same time, multicameralism discourages decision making in multiple dimensions by limiting the number of alternatives that defeat the status quo, rendering them more difficult to find.

Hammond and Miller (1987) also study the stability properties of bicameral institutions. For a bicameral legislature considering legislation with two policy dimensions, Hammond and Miller formally produce conditions for the existence of a *core, a set of points that cannot be defeated by concurrent majorities in both chambers*. Such a core exists only when the ideal points of the members of the two chambers are sufficiently distant from each other (1987:1160).[42]

Bicameralism is also believed to reduce decision costs. Levmore (1992)

[41]To arrive at this result, Riker assumes that tastes are distributed uniformly across the two houses: "Assuming representation works fairly well, tastes harmonize in all houses roughly simultaneously. So for each house, the single dimension is the same, and the distribution of voters similar. Then each house can arrive at its median which is about the same median as in the other houses, and the whole body and the whole society thus arrive at the equilibrium" (Riker 1992b: 168). This assumption, of course, contradicts the assumption of diversity needed to achieve stability in the face of cycling.

[42]See their 1987 article for the conditions necessary for the existence of a core when there are an even number of legislators in one or both houses and when more than one bicameral bisector exists.

argues that bicameralism promotes the creation of conference committees. Because conference committees are smaller than the full legislative bodies, it is easier for representatives to bargain and trade votes, and thereby to reach a decision. In his words (1992: 150),

interchamber conferences can be seen as a means towards more efficient logrolling, either because the participants are bargaining agents (and smaller numbers of people can bargain better than larger numbers) or because . . . a conference committee is a thinned down form of unicameralism, and interest groups may in the long run trade votes most efficiently in a single arena with relatively few players. Bicameralism might therefore be seen . . . as a preliminary step to conference committees which lower [decision] costs.[43]

Thus, we have a list of justifications of bicameralism. Although some analysts (especially Buchanan and Tullock 1962; Riker 1992a, 1992b) recognize that these features are not mutually exclusive, most analysts concentrate on either the efficiency dimension or the political dimension of bicameralism, depending on the relative power of the two chambers. Where power is equal, the political dimension is paramount; where power is unequal, the focus is on bicameral efficiency.

8. CONCLUSIONS

In this chapter we have traced the evolution of dual political deliberations from the ancient Greek and Mediterranean societies to the present. There are two aspects of this description that we want to signal. The variety of effects attributed to bicameral legislatures, as summarized in the contemporary debate, presents the first puzzle: Does bicameralism produce all the enumerated effects? Are all of these explanations correct and mutually consistent?

Second, the effects of bicameralism are attributed to different institutional features. The political effects – checking the majority in one house and reducing power of leaders (agenda setters) – depend on the presence of equal legislative power (Hamilton et al. 1961; Levmore 1992; Montesquieu 1977). On the other hand, some of the efficient dimensions of bicameralism rely on the rules governing the terms of office. Stability is achieved because the upper house is subject to partial rather than total renewal – senators are older and more experienced and have longer terms of office (Cicero 1927; Hamilton et al. 1961; Mastias and Grangé 1987). Should these features be absent, presumably, these aspects of stability would disappear. On the other hand, the mere presence of two legislative

---

[43]Although Levmore advances this argument, he himself finds it only "mildly convincing," and seeks the real value of bicameralism elsewhere.

houses, regardless of membership, theoretically reduces corruption and promotes the status quo (Hammond and Miller 1987; Levmore 1992; Riker 1992a, 1992b). Finally, some effects can occur only when preferences of members of the two houses differ: reduction of instability associated with the voting cycle (Riker 1992a, 1992b) and increased representativeness (Buchanan and Tullock 1962). The attribution of effects to institutional features presents the second puzzle: Do the specific institutional features affect legislative outcomes and, if so, which ones?

Before attempting to answer these questions, we turn in Chapter 2 to the institutional features of contemporary bicameral legislatures. This survey will provide the empirical base upon which to evaluate many of the claims made about the effects of bicameralism.

2

The institutions of bicameralism

Given the diverse national paths in the development of bicameral legislatures, it is not surprising to find substantial institutional variation. In this chapter, we explore these institutional differences. The characteristics of lower and upper legislative houses differ on a number of dimensions, and analysts have relied on these differences to explain cross-national variations in upper house power. Although there are variations in size, legislative term of office, turnover, membership, representativeness, and institutional power,[1] two particular characteristics have been emphasized. The first is the membership of the two houses, based on selection methods and categories of citizens represented. The second is the relative power of the two houses as reflected in their mechanisms for resolving intercameral differences. Here we focus on these two critical dimensions of variation.

Political analysts who examine the variation in bicameral institutions argue that bicameralism produces disparate results across countries. Lijphart (1984) attributes variation to the degree of congruence between the two legislative houses and power asymmetries, whereas Mastias and Grangé (1987) focus on upper house legitimacy as the important independent variable.

Lijphart (1984: 99) defines "congruence" as similarity of political composition. Regardless of the variations in selection methods, if the two houses have similar political representation, they are deemed congruent. Disparities in power range from full symmetry, where agreement of the two houses is necessary to enact a law, to total asymmetry, where one house is granted decision-making power. Using these two categories, Lijphart constructs three types of bicameralism. He argues that "strong" bicameral legislatures are characterized by significant differences in composition and by relatively symmetric power. "Weak" bicameral legislatures are characterized *either* by asymmetric power *or* by congruent

---

[1]Lijphart (1984) enumerates these institutional variations.

chambers. And "insignificant" bicameralism is characterized by both asymmetric power and congruence.

Alternatively, the methods of selection are hypothesized to affect the legitimacy and therefore the perceived usefulness of upper houses (Lijphart 1984; Mastias and Grangé 1987; Trivelli 1975). Mastias and Grangé (1987) emphasize the legitimacy of the upper house as determinative of its institutional structure and therefore of its influence over legislative outcomes. Legitimacy is defined in terms of direct citizen input; the less direct the method of selection, the less legitimate the chamber. Mastias and Grangé (1987, Chapter 4) find a systematic correspondence between the level of legitimacy and the institutional power (*moyens d'actions*) accorded to upper houses. Those houses that link the citizen most directly to the selection of upper house representatives tend to have powers coequal to the lower house, whereas appointed or hereditary houses tend to have limited legislative powers. For them, it is not surprising that Switzerland and the United States, with directly elected senators, have powerful upper houses, whereas the appointed and hereditary British House of Lords has only a power of delay.

It is interesting that these analyses tend to replicate the bifurcation of the intellectual debate referred to in Chapter 1. Lijphart, for example, does not discuss an efficient dimension of bicameral legislatures; Mastias and Grangé attribute political effects to legitimate upper chambers and efficient effects to "illegitimate" chambers.

In order to evaluate these claims, we explore institutional variations in bicameralism associated with methods of membership selection and modes of intercameral reconciliation. This chapter serves as an empirical basis for a theoretical exploration of institutional effects on legislative outcomes in Part II. The chapter is divided into two parts, the first focusing on upper house membership and the second focusing on methods of intercameral reconciliation. We survey 53 of the 56 nations whose constitutions provide for bicameral legislatures as of 1994 even though some constitutions are not in force (*Europa Yearbook* 1994).[2] Some readers may think the inclusion of nondemocratic countries odd, as institutional structures currently play little role in political outcomes. However,

---

[2]Because copies of constitutions were unavailable for Bosnia-Herzegovina, Lesotho, and Uruguay, the tables include only 53 of the 56 countries with bicameral legislatures. Of the 192 countries listed in the 1994 *Europa Yearbook,* 126 are unicameral, 56 are bicameral, and 10 are designated as "other" (usually monarchies without legislatures). We classify Indonesia as unicameral because, although there are constitutional provisions for a People's Congress, called into session every five years, legislative power is clearly vested in the House of Representatives, a unique legislative body. Sierra Leone has a 1994 draft constitution with a bicameral legislature, but this has not been ratified yet.

in the event of a democratic transition, the conflict may be played out in these institutions, and their relative power, as determined by the constitution, may affect the political outcome. The survey is based on a close reading of the constitutional provisions affecting the legislative process. In many cases, our knowledge of country practices allows us to supplement the constitutional survey. Where constitutional provisions were unclear we consulted country experts whenever possible to reduce the possibility of error. However, because of the number of countries we include and the newness of many of the constitutions, there may be additional bicameral procedures detailed in laws or internal regulations that are not included in the tables.

1. VARIATIONS IN REPRESENTATION

In most cases, lower houses in representative systems are elected directly by a nation's citizens, with equal weight given to each eligible voter. Electoral systems may vary from single-member districts to various types of proportional representation, passing by way of two-round elections. Regardless of electoral system, the lower house normally serves as a repository of legitimacy because it is elected by the citizens of the country, each accorded an equal weight: one citizen, one vote.

In contrast, upper house selection varies on two dimensions. The first involves the method of selection, the second, the type of representation. These data are summarized in Table 2.1. On the first dimension, there are four basic methods of selecting upper house representatives: heredity, appointment, indirect elections, and direct elections. Many houses combine two or more methods and are therefore listed more than once.

Systems of hereditary nobility are historically common, as described in Chapter 1, but rare in the contemporary era. The aristocracy's membership in the upper house was granted by (or extracted from) the monarchy and passed down from generation to generation. Membership was enlarged or renewed through new grants of nobility by the crown. However, only one contemporary legislative house can be described as partially hereditary: the British House of Lords.

There are a number of reasons that hereditary systems declined in popularity in representative democracies. In some cases, they simply became unwieldy as the number of members increased.[3] Moreover, whether "wise" or "unwise," upper house members may disagree with the government. Where the issue is politically salient, the government may opt to override the upper house by appointing new members to change the

---

[3]Per Lijphart (1984: 95), the House of Lords exceeds 1,000 members, approximately three-quarters of whom are hereditary peers.

prevailing opinion. Hence, a second system evolved – appointment for life or for shorter tenures.

Thus, hereditary membership in the House of Lords is now supplemented by lifetime appointments. And many other systems retain fully or partially appointed houses: Antigua, the Bahamas, Barbados, Belgium, Belize, Canada, Germany, Grenada, Ireland, Jamaica, Jordan, Madagascar, Malaysia, the Russian Federation, Swaziland, Thailand, and Trinidad and Tobago. Upper houses in Chile, Croatia, India, and Italy also include a nominal number of presidential appointees. Appointments may be designated by the monarchy (Jordan, Malaysia, and Thailand), but more commonly, members are designated by an elected government. In Germany and the Russian Federation (the 1993 constitution), regional governments appoint members to the upper house to represent regional interests. In Belgium, one-seventh of the members are selected by the senators themselves. More frequently, national governments appoint individuals to serve in the upper house. Selection may be based on outstanding performance or service to the government or to a particular profession, recalling the Roman model of wise legislators seasoned by experience and age.

Nonetheless, in democratic systems, even this method may be viewed as illegitimate because the people, as citizens, are perceived as the repository of wisdom. Hence, the selection of upper house members is often delegated to the citizenry either indirectly or directly. Indirect elections are fairly common and include such countries as Austria, Belgium, Comoros, the Congo, France, Haiti, India, Ireland, Madagascar, Mauritania, the Netherlands, Pakistan, South Africa, Spain, and Swaziland. In most cases, local or provincial governments, elected directly by the citizens, elect upper house members. In other cases, such as France, an electoral college, formed by local and provincial councils, selects senators.

But the most frequently employed method of selecting upper house membership is direct election by the citizens. Nations whose upper house is directly elected, in whole or in part, include Argentina, Australia, Bolivia, Brazil, Chile, Colombia, Croatia, the Czech Republic, the Dominican Republic, Haiti, Iceland, Ireland, Italy, Japan, Liberia, Malaysia, Mexico, Nigeria, Norway, Paraguay, the Philippines, Poland, Romania, Spain, Switzerland, the United States, Venezuela, and (the new) Yugoslavia.

In contrast to lower houses, in upper houses, there is also a question of *who* is represented. One common answer is to replicate the lower house and represent the citizens on an equal basis. This is the case in Italy and Japan for the past few decades and in the bicameral legislatures in 49 of the 50 U.S. states, for example.[4] Often subnational geographic units are

---

[4]Nebraska is the only state with a unicameral legislature.

Table 2.1. *Overcoming disagreements between houses on bills*

Country[a]	Most recent revision of constitution[b]	Mode of selection of upper house	Congruence	Decision system
Antigua and Barbuda	March 1982	Appointed by governor-general	No	Navette (lower house decisive)
Argentina	May 1995	Direct election (3 per province), by partial proportional representation	No	Navette (originating house decisive)
Australia	November 1991	Direct election (6 per state)	No	Navette (new elections, then joint session)
Austria	December 1985	Indirect election by provincial legislatures, by proportional representation (3 to 12 per province, based on population)	Yes[c]	Navette (lower house decisive)
Bahamas	April 1989	Appointed by governor-general	No	Navette (lower house decisive)
Barbados	September 1989	Appointed by governor-general	No	Navette (lower house decisive)
Belgium	November 1994	Indirect election by linguistic communities; cooptation by Senate; children of the king	No	Navette (lower house decisive)
Belize	June 1995	Appointed by governor-general	No	Navette (lower house decisive)
Bolivia	December 1995	Direct election (3 per department, 2 for the majority and 1 for the minority)	No	Navette (joint session)
Brazil	September 1995	Direct election, by simple majority (3 per state and federal district)	No	Navette (reviewing house decisive) or joint session (for budget)
Canada	March 1991	Appointed by governor-general	No	Navette (conference committee)
Chile	September 1994	Direct election (2 or 4 per region); former top officials appointed	No	Navette (conference committee, then reviewing house decisive)

48

Table 2.1. *(cont.)*

Country[a]	Most recent revision of constitution[b]	Mode of selection of upper house	Congruence	Decision system
Colombia	August 1995	Direct election in one national district, by proportional representation plus representatives of indigenous communities	No	Navette (conference committee, both houses retain veto power)
Comoros	February 1994	Indirect election by electoral college (5 per island)	No	Navette (government decisive)
Congo	December 1993	Indirect election by councils, districts, regions, arrondissements, and communes	No	Navette (conference committee, then lower house decisive)
Croatia	May 1992	Direct election (3 per county); president may nominate up to 5 members; former presidents are lifelong members	No	Navette (lower house decisive)
Czech Republic	June 1993	Direct election, by majority	No	Navette (lower house decisive)
Dominican Republic	May 1973	Direct election (1 per province and national district)	No	Navette (reviewing house decisive)
European Union	1996	Council of Ministers: 1 representative per country, weighted vote	No	Navette (upper house, the Council, decisive; lower house, the European Parliament, has veto power in some procedures)
Fiji	November 1990	Appointed by president	No	Navette (lower house decisive)
France	December 1995	Indirect election by electoral colleges	No	Navette (conference committee, then lower house decisive)
Germany	June 1995	Appointed by state governments (3 to 6 per state)	No	Navette (conference committee or lower house decisive; upper house retains veto power in certain cases)
Grenada	June 1990	Appointed by governor-general	No	Navette (lower house decisive)

Table 2.1. *(cont.)*

Country[a]	Most recent revision of constitution[b]	Mode of selection of upper house	Congruence	Decision system
Haiti	September 1987	Indirect election by local assemblies (3 per department)	No	Navette (conference committee on financial legislation, otherwise both houses retain veto)
India	September 1994	Indirect election by state legislatures by proportional representation; 12 appointed by president	No	Navette (joint session)
Ireland	March 1994	Indirect election of individuals nominated by panels (49/60), by proportional representation; appointed by prime minister (11/60)	Yes[c]	Navette (conference committee or lower house decisive)
Italy	November 1994	Direct election, by proportional representation (by region, based on population); 5 appointed by president; past presidents	Yes[c]	Navette (conference committee or lower house decisive)
Jamaica	April 1983	Appointed by governor-general	No	Navette (lower house decisive)
Japan	December 1993	Direct election	Yes[c]	Navette (conference committee or lower house decisive)
Jordan	November 1984	Appointed	No	Navette (joint session)
Liberia	September 1985	Direct election (2 per county)	No	Navette
Madagascar	February 1994	Indirect election (2/3); appointed by president (1/3)	No	Navette (conference committee, then lower house decisive)
Malaysia	November 1995	Partly elected (2 per state); partly appointed by the Yang di-Pertuan Agong	No	Navette (lower house decisive)
Mauritania	August 1993	Indirect election by territorial districts	No	Navette (lower house decisive)
Mexico	April 1988	Direct election, by majority (2 per state and federal district)	No	Navette (reviewing house decisive)

Table 2.1. *(cont.)*

Country[a]	Most recent revision of constitution[b]	Mode of selection of upper house	Congruence	Decision system
Netherlands	November 1990	Indirect election by provincial councils, by proportional representation	Yes[c]	Navette (upper house decisive)
Nigeria	October 1990	Election (3 per state)	No	Navette (joint session for financial bills only)
Norway	October 1993	Direct election; nominated by unified chamber from among its own members (1/4 total membership)	Yes[c]	Navette (joint session)
Pakistan	June 1993	Indirect election, by provincial assemblies or federally administered tribal areas (14 per province, 3 for tribal areas)	No	Navette (joint session)
Paraguay	April 1993	Direct election, one national district	No	Navette (lower house decisive for financial legislation; reviewing house decisive for other legislation)
Philippines	December 1986	Direct election, one national district (at large)	Yes[c]	Navette
Poland	October 1993	Direct election, by voivodeship (territorial unit)	No	Navette (lower house decisive)
Romania	March 1992	Direct election (with special provisions for national minorities)	Yes	Navette (conference committee, then joint session)
Russian Federation	May 1994	Appointed by state governments (2 per territory, 1 from the representative and 1 from the executive bodies of state authority)	No	Navette (conference committee, then lower house decisive)
South Africa	June 1995	Indirect election by provincial legislature (10 per province), by proportional representation	No	Navette (conference committee, then joint session for ordinary bills; lower house decisive for financial bills)

Table 2.1. *(cont.)*

Country[a]	Most recent revision of constitution[b]	Mode of selection of upper house	Congruence	Decision system
Spain	March 1991	Direct election (4 per province); indirect election by "autonomous communities"	No	Navette (lower house decisive in some cases; conference committee, then lower house decisive in other cases)
Swaziland	May 1991	Indirect election by lower house (1/2); appointed by the King (1/2)	No	Navette (joint session or lower house decisive)
Switzerland	August 1994	Direct election (2 per canton)	No	Navette (conference committee)
Thailand	November 1993	Appointed by king	No	Navette (conference committee; lower house decisive after 180 days)
Trinidad and Tobago	September 1988	Appointed by president	No	Navette (lower house decisive)
United Kingdom	July 1992	Hereditary and appointed	No	Navette (lower house decisive)
United States	November 1992	Direct election (2 per state)	No	Navette or conference committee; also possibility of concurrent examination of legislation
Venezuela	November 1994	Direct election (2 per state and federal district); additional senators for minority representation; former presidents	No	Navette (followed by joint session)
Yugoslavia	March 1994	Elected (20 per republic)	No	Concurrent examination of legislation; conference committee then dissolution of both houses

[a]Constitutions unavailable for Bosnia-Herzegovina, Lesotho, and Uruguay.
[b]Date of latest release of constitutions or supplementary updates, as of December 1995.
[c]These bicameral legislatures are designated congruent by Lijphart (1984: 99) along with Belgium, which underwent a constitutional revision in 1994.
Sources: Flanz (1995), Maddex (1995), Department of Justice, Canada (1989), Hogg (1977), Morgan (1990), Casy (1992), Inter-parliamentary Union (1986).

represented in the upper house. This is characteristic of all federal systems, such as Austria, Germany, India, Mexico, Switzerland, and the United States. But this system also functions in unitary nations such as Argentina, Bolivia, the Netherlands, and Spain. Because populations are not evenly distributed across territory, frequently citizens are not represented equally. In upper houses where local political units (states, cantons, regions, departments, or counties) are granted equal representation, such as the United States and Switzerland, some citizens' votes are weighted much more heavily than others. This pattern is visible in approximately one-third of all bicameral legislatures. In Germany and Austria, where the allocation of representatives is partially proportional to the population, the degree of over- or underrepresentation diminishes and, in the Austrian case, disappears altogether.

Other types of representation are infrequently employed. Ireland's upper house is selected in part by professional occupation; Venezuela ensures some degree of minority ethnic representation. And Belgium has modified its constitution so that linguistic communities are represented in the Belgian Senate.

Taken together, the methods of selection and the constituent groups determine the degree of congruence between the upper and lower houses in bicameral parliaments. We have found no instances where the methods of selecting legislators in upper and lower houses are completely identical. However, where proportional or semiproportional representation is employed, the two houses tend to resemble each other politically, even though election methods may differ, as in the Netherlands and in Italy (Lijphart 1984: 98). For these or any other reasons, where party composition of one chamber mimics the composition of the other, it is often assumed that preferences of the houses are also similar or identical. As noted above, these systems are labeled by Lijphart (1984) as systems of congruent bicameralism and, when combined with asymmetric power, are designated as "insignificant" due to the identity of preferences.

However, congruence should not be equated with identity of positions. Opinions may vary within the same party, and individual legislators in the two chambers may have differences of opinion despite membership in the same party. In Italy, for example, where the two houses are politically congruent, some disagreements between the two chambers have lasted for years. Allum (1973: 131–32) describes a "kind of shuttle between the Houses [that] can continue for years and lead to a bill being 'killed' by a dissolution, which has the effect of annulling all uncompleted legislation. Thus, for example, the legislation setting up the Constitutional Court was shuttled between both Houses for eighteen months." And Sassoon (1986: 193) refers to a communist political scientist, Giuseppe Cotturri, [who] has pointed out that there are other reasons for the abolition of one of the two chambers: the incessant negotiations which occur between the Chamber and the Senate over every piece of legislation works to the advantage of the DC [Christian Democrats]. The time it takes for a bill to go from one chamber to the other enables the DC to make deals between its various factions and lobbies.[5]

Another reason that congruence may not be equivalent to identity of preferences is the difference in constituency representation. Upper houses tend to be smaller than lower houses and thus to represent larger constituencies. As a result, legislator preferences may vary. A case in point is the 1995–96 U.S. Congress, where both houses had Republican majorities yet disagreed over many issues.

Yet another reason that congruent chambers may have differences in opinions is the presence of different decision-making rules in each chamber. The United States again serves as an example. There, a three-fifths majority is required to end a filibuster in the Senate, but there is no possibility of filibustering in the House. As a consequence, there is a blocking minority of two-fifths in the U.S. Senate, but not in the House. This implies that the pivotal voter in the Senate is likely to be different from the pivotal voter in the House, even assuming similar distributions of overall preferences.[6] These examples suggest that congruence does not invariably reduce disagreements between the two houses to zero.

However, as we see in Table 2.1, the vast majority of bicameral legislatures are not congruent. When the two chambers exhibit different preferences, procedures to resolve the differences are necessary. Consequently, the institutionalized rules for the resolution of differences become relevant. We turn now to a description of these institutional mechanisms.

2. VARIATIONS IN INTERCAMERAL CONFLICT RESOLUTION

One observer of bicameral legislatures has suggested that "American legislatures stand alone among modern bicameral legislative bodies in providing a formal method for adjusting differences between them" (George Galloway quoted in Longley and Oleszek 1989: 27). As Tables 2.2A and 2.2B indicate, nothing could be further from the truth. There are a variety of methods for resolving disagreements between houses: the navette, the conference committee, the joint session, the ultimate decision by one house, and new elections. We discuss the mechanics of each procedure below; the data are summarized in the last column in Table 2.1 and

[5]The reference is to a 1982 article by Cotturri that appeared in *Rinancita*.
[6]For a very interesting argument along these lines, see David Jones (1993).

54

described in more detail in Tables 2.2A and 2.2B, which are divided into nonfinancial and financial legislation because these types of legislation are often handled differently. We begin by describing the procedures governing nonfinancial legislation, summarized in Table 2.2A.

The most common method of resolving disagreements is the *navette*, or shuttle system. In this system, the house that first passes a bill sends that legislation to the second house. If the second house ratifies the legislation, the process ends and the legislation proceeds through the remainder of the promulgation procedure. When the second house disagrees in whole or in part with the first house, it amends the legislation and returns it to the originating house. Hence, the legislation "shuttles" between houses. This procedure is employed in 52 of the 53 bicameral legislatures in our population. The one exception is Yugoslavia, the only state that systematically provides for concurrent examination of legislation; the United States represents a partial exception because legislation there can be examined either sequentially or simultaneously.

However, the navette may not ultimately resolve the disagreement, so numerous rules were developed to achieve an outcome should the navette fail. In fact, many nations employ a series of stopping rules in a specified sequence. In some cases, where no alternative procedure exists and disagreements persist, the legislation is aborted. This is the case in Belgium (for some legislation), Italy, Liberia, Nigeria, the Philippines, and the United States (for some legislation). In France, Madagascar, and Mauritania, the shuttle will persist unless the government intervenes.

In most cases, though, the navette is limited either voluntarily (such as in the United States in the case of important legislation) or by the application of institutional rules. One dimension of variation is captured by the number of rounds the bill can shuttle between the two houses before another method of resolving disagreements is applied. In rare cases, a solution rule is applied immediately upon disagreement. In Pakistan and in South Africa, for example, if the second house to review the legislation disagrees with the first, a joint session is called immediately (preceded in the case of South Africa by a conference committee). More frequently, the two houses can communicate about their disagreements and attempt to reach a voluntary compromise. In Belgium, for example, for specific types of legislation, the bill shuttles between the houses for at least two readings before another resolution method is implemented.

The other dimension of variation is the type of resolution rule implemented. One method of breaking a deadlock between the two houses is a conference committee. This is the case for Chile, Colombia, the Congo, France, Germany, Haiti, Ireland, Japan, Madagascar, Romania, the Russian Federation, South Africa, Switzerland, Thailand, the United States, Yugoslavia, and in one procedure (codecision) the European Union. In

Table 2.2A. *Institutional features of the navette (nonfinancial)*

Country[a]	Introduction of nonfinancial legislation	Number of rounds[b]	Final decision	Comments
Antigua and Barbuda	Either house	3/2 or 2	Two successive approvals by lower house	3 months must elapse between 1st and 2nd approval by lower house; legislation is not returned to lower house after 2nd upper house rejection; 2 positive lower house votes are sufficient for passage
Argentina	Either house	1	Originating house	Originating house must meet absolute or 2/3 majority depending on vote in reviewing house; "law-conventions" must originate in upper house
Australia	Either house	5/2 or 3	Dissolution/ new election; if continued disagreement, joint session	Absolute majority of total membership of the legislature required for passage; 3 months must elapse between 1st and 2nd approval of lower house
Austria	Lower house	1	Lower house	Upper house has 8 weeks to raise objections
Bahamas	Either house	3/2 or 2	Two successive approvals by lower house	9 months must elapse between 1st and 2nd approval by lower house; legislation is not returned to lower house after 2nd upper house rejection; 2 positive lower house votes are sufficient for passage
Barbados	Either house	3/2 or 2	Two successive approvals by lower house	7 months must elapse between 1st and 2nd approval by lower house; legislation is not returned to lower house after 2nd upper house rejection; 2 positive lower house votes are sufficient for passage
Belgium, Article 77 legislation	Upper house	Indefinite	No stopping rules	Lower house retains right of legislative initiative, in which case legislation is introduced in lower house
Belgium, Article 78 legislation	Lower house	2	Lower house	Upper house retains right of legislative initiative, in which case legislation is introduced in upper house, adding 1/2 round

Table 2.2A. *(cont.)*

Country[a]	Introduction of nonfinancial legislation	Number of rounds[b]	Final decision	Comments
Belize	Either house	3/2 or 2	Two successive approvals by lower house	6 months must elapse between 1st and 2nd approval by lower house; legislation is not returned to lower house after 2nd upper house rejection; 2 positive lower house votes are sufficient for passage
Bolivia	Either house	1	Joint session	Each house retains veto power; in the case of disagreement regarding amendments, joint session called at the discretion of either house's president, within 20 days
Brazil	Government bills in lower house; otherwise either house	1/2, 1, or 3/2	Reviewing house	If reviewing house rejects bill, it is aborted; amended bills are returned to originating house; governmental legislation designated urgent limits review to 45 days in lower house, 10 days in upper house
Canada	Either house	3/2	Conference committee	Formally, upper house has the same powers as lower house; in practice, upper house rarely rejects or even amends legislation and thus plays mainly an advisory role
Chile	Either house	2 or 3	Conference committee, then reviewing house	If conference committee unsuccessful, president may request initiating house to insist, then reviewing house may reject only with 2/3 majority
Colombia	Either house; international relations in upper house	3/2	Conference committee, both houses retain veto power	Draft from committee submitted for final decision in each house
Comoros	Lower house	3/2	The government	After 2 upper house rejections, the government decides whether legislation is defeated or if lower house version is enacted; a law passed by the lower house but contested by all upper house members of an island is defeated if, after a 2nd reading by the lower house, the law is equally contested by a majority of lower house members from the same island

Table 2.2A. *(cont.)*

Country[a]	Introduction of nonfinancial legislation	Number of rounds[b]	Final decision	Comments
Congo	Either house	3	Conference committee, then lower house	Conference committee and final decision by lower house at the discretion of the government
Croatia	Lower house	1	Lower house	Upper house has 15 days to review; lower house accepts or rejects recommendations by simple majority or 2/3 majority when passed by upper house with 2/3 majority
Czech Republic	Lower house	1	Lower house	Upper house has 30 days to review legislation
Dominican Republic	Either house	3/2	Reviewing house	
European Union, consultation procedure	Lower house (European Parliament)	1/2	Upper house (Council of Ministers)	Legislation is introduced by a third body, the European Commission
European Union, cooperation procedure	Lower house (European Parliament)	3/2	Upper house (Council of Ministers)	European Commission introduces legislation and can modify it at any time before the second reading by the European Parliament
European Union, codecision	Lower house (European Parliament)	2 or 5/2	Conference committe, then upper house (Council of Ministers) *unless* lower house overrules by absolute majority	European Commission introduces legislation and can modify it at any time before the second reading by the European Parliament; conference committee report is approved by qualified majority in the Council and by simple majority in the Parliament *or* Council makes proposal to Parliament
Fiji	Either house	3/2 or 2	Two successive approvals by lower house	6 months must elapse between 1st and 2nd approval by lower house; legislation is not returned to lower house after 2nd upper house rejection; 2 positive lower house votes are sufficient for passage

Table 2.2A. *(cont.)*

Country[a]	Introduction of nonfinancial legislation	Number of rounds[b]	Final decision	Comments
France	Either house	Indefinite; 3 (2 if urgent)	Conference committee, then lower house	Government decides where bills are introduced, the number of rounds, and whether lower house decides
Germany	Government bills in upper house; otherwise either house	2 or 5/2	Conference committee; lower house decides by majority or 2/3 majority in specific cases; otherwise, upper house retains veto power	
Grenada	Either house	3/2 or 2	Two successive approvals by lower house	6 months must elapse between 1st and 2nd approval by lower house; legislation is not returned to lower house after 2nd upper house rejection; 2 positive lower house votes are sufficient for passage
Haiti	Either house	5/2	Conference committee; both houses retain veto power	Legislation must be introduced in 2nd legislative session
India	Either house	1/2 or indefinite	Joint session	Joint session called by president if reviewing house fails to act on legislation within 6 months or if it rejects the legislation or if disagreement on amendments persists
Ireland	Either house	2 or 5/2	Conference committee, or lower house after 90 days	Upper house has 90 days to review legislation; lower house must pass decisive resolution within 180 days thereafter
Italy	Either house	Indefinite	No stopping rules	
Jamaica	Either house	3/2 or 2	Two successive approvals by lower house	7 months must elapse between 1st and 2nd approval by lower house; legislation is not returned to lower house after 2nd upper house rejection; 2 positive lower house votes are sufficient for passage

59

Table 2.2A. *(cont.)*

Country[a]	Introduction of nonfinancial legislation	Number of rounds[b]	Final decision	Comments
Japan	Either house	1	Conference committee or lower house by 2/3 majority	Upper house may have a maximum of 60 days to review legislation
Jordan	Lower house	1 or 3/2	Joint session with 2/3 majority of members present	
Liberia	Either house	Indefinite	No stopping rules	
Madagascar	Either house	Indefinite; 3 (2 if urgent)	Conference committee, then lower house	Conference committee and final decision by lower house at the discretion of the government
Malaysia	Either house	3/2 or 2	Two successive approvals by lower house	1 year must elapse between 1st and 2nd approval by lower house; legislation is not returned to lower house after 2nd upper house rejection; 2 positive lower house votes are sufficient for passage
Mauritania	Either house	Indefinite; (3/2 or 2 if urgent)	Conference committee, then lower house	Conference committee and final decision by lower house at the discretion of the government
Mexico	Either house	3/2	Reviewing house, by majority	Partially approved bills may be forwarded to executive for promulgation
Netherlands	Lower house or joint session	1/2	Upper house	Upper house has no amendment powers
Nigeria	Either house	Indefinite	No stopping rules	
Norway	Lower house	3/2	Plenary session of united chamber (2/3 majority)	
Pakistan	Either house	1/2 or 1	Joint session, by majority	Joint session called at request of initiating house; upper house can send amended bill to lower house only once

Table 2.2A. *(cont.)*

Country[a]	Introduction of nonfinancial legislation	Number of rounds[b]	Final decision	Comments
Paraguay	Dept. and municipal in lower house; treaties and international agreements in upper house; otherwise, either house	3/2	Reviewing chamber (absolute majority vote for amendments; 2/3 majority for rejection)	Maximum review period is 90 days after which legislation is considered approved; urgent status reduces review to 30 days in either house
Philippines	Either house	Indefinite	No stopping rules	President may certify necessity of immediate enactment
Poland	Lower house	1	Lower house, by absolute majority	Upper house has a maximum of 30 days to review legislation
Romania	Either house	3/2	Conference committee, then joint session (for amendments)	For rejected rather than amended legislation, reviewing house can veto by 2 successive rejections
Russian Federation	Lower house	1	Conference committee, then lower house by 2/3 majority	Upper house has 14 days to review legislation
South Africa	Either house	1/2	Conference committee, then joint session	
Spain, Article 74 legislation	Upper or lower house, depending on content	5/2	Conference committee, then lower house	Article 74 deals with treaties and autonomous communities
Spain, Article 87 legislation	Lower house	1	Lower house	Upper house has 2 months to review legislation (20 days in case of urgency)
Swaziland	Either house	1/2	Joint session	Upper house has 90 days to review legislation, then lower house decisive
Switzerland	Either house	7/2	Conference committee	Each house retains veto power

61

Table 2.2A. *(cont.)*

Country[a]	Introduction of nonfinancial legislation	Number of rounds[b]	Final decision	Comments
Thailand	Lower house	3/2	Conference committee, then lower house after 180 days	Upper house has 60 days to review general legislation (30 days for financial bills)
Trinidad and Tobago	Either house	3/2 or 2	Two successive approvals by lower house	6 months must elapse between 1st and 2nd approval by lower house; legislation is not returned to lower house after 2nd upper house rejection; 2 positive lower house votes are sufficient for passage
United Kingdom	Either house	3/2 or 2	Two successive approvals by lower house	1 year must elapse between 1st and 2nd approval by lower house; legislation is not returned to lower house after 2nd upper house rejection; 2 positive lower house votes are sufficient for passage
United States	Either house	Indefinite	Conference committee (at any time)	
Venezuela	Either house, unless specified	1	Joint session	
Yugoslavia	Either house	Concurrent examination of text	Conference committee	If no agreement after conference committee (time limit of 1 month), either lower or upper house version temporarily adopted (according to subject of statute); after 1 year, lack of passage leads to dissolution of houses

[a]Constitutions unavailable for Bosnia-Herzegovina, Lesotho, and Uruguay.
[b]Each round indicates the reintroduction of a bill in the originating chamber. The count comprises the movement of the legislation from the introduction of the bill until the ratification of the law, including the various stopping rules.
Sources: Flanz (1995), Maddex (1995), Department of Justice, Canada (1989), Hogg (1977), Morgan (1990), Casy (1992), Inter-parliamentary Union (1986).

Canada and Ireland, conference committees are available but rarely called. When a conference committee is called, the two houses each appoint an equal number of delegates, who meet jointly and attempt to craft a compromise. The United States is an exception to the general rule because House delegations need not be equal in size. However, because the U.S. system requires concurrent majorities of the two delegations in conference committee, the number of delegates is not critical. In most cases, the conference committee acts as a unicameral mini-parliament under majority rule, which then proposes a compromise to the parent bodies under closed rule (without accepting amendments).

Alternatively, both legislatures meet in a common session to vote on the legislation. This is true for Australia, Bolivia, Brazil, Iceland, India, Jordan, Nigeria (for financial legislation), Norway, Pakistan, Romania, South Africa (for nonfinancial legislation), Swaziland, and Venezuela. This procedure ultimately favors the lower house in most/all cases because the lower house is generally larger than the upper house. The combined vote of the two legislative houses therefore pulls the outcome toward the lower house position.

In some cases, one house, usually the lower house, is decisive. In France, for example, if the navette and conference committee fail to produce a compromise, ultimately the government can ask the lower house to decide the outcome. In other cases, the decision automatically reverts to one house. The lower house is decisive in Antigua, Austria, the Bahamas, Barbados, Belgium (for certain legislation), Belize, the Congo, Croatia, the Czech Republic, Fiji, Germany (for some bills), Grenada, Ireland, Jamaica, Japan, Madagascar, Malaysia, Mauritania, Poland, the Russian Federation, South Africa (for financial legislation), Spain, Swaziland, and the United Kingdom, among others. In other cases, either the initiating house or the reviewing house is decisive, so the distribution of power depends on where the bill is introduced. This is true in Argentina, Brazil, Chile, the Dominican Republic, and Mexico. In the sole example of systematic upper house decisive power, the Dutch "first house" has ultimate veto power over legislation, although it has no powers of amendment.

Finally, some countries resort to new elections to poll the citizens on the divisive issue. Australia is a country that, failing to reach agreement, calls for legislative elections as a method of resolving the contentious issue. The new Yugoslavian constitution also makes provisions for dissolution of both legislative houses if they fail to reach agreement after a year's time.

In almost all cases, the importance of financial legislation has caused countries to modify the negotiation process between the two houses. We outline in Table 2.2B the rules for financial legislation. Usually, the navette is reduced and the review process limited in time. The British pat-

Table 2.2B. *Institutional features of the navette (financial)*

Country[a]	Introduction of financial legislation	Number of rounds[b]	Final decision	Comments
Antigua and Barbuda	Lower house	1/2	Lower house	Upper house can delay a maximum of 1 month
Argentina	Either house; tax legislation in lower house	1	Originating house	By absolute or 2/3 majority depending on vote in reviewing house
Australia	Lower house	1	Lower house	Upper house has no power of amendment but may communicate suggestions to lower house
Austria	Lower house	0	Lower house	Upper house cannot raise objections to federal budget, among other restrictions
Bahamas	Lower house	1/2	Lower house	Upper house can delay a maximum of 1 month
Barbados	Lower house	1/2	Lower house	Upper house can delay a maximum of 1 month
Belgium	Lower house	0	Lower house	Article 74 defines budgetary legislation as the responsibility of the king and the lower house only
Belize	Lower house	1/2	Lower house	Upper house can delay a maximum of 1 month
Bolivia	Lower house	1	Joint session	
Brazil	Joint session	0	Joint session	
Canada	Lower house	3/2	Conference committee	Formally, upper house has the same powers as lower house; in practice, upper house rarely rejects or even amends legislation and thus plays mainly an advisory role
Chile	Lower house	2 or 3	Conference committee, then reviewing house	Time limit of 60 days, then budget is enacted by decree

Table 2.2B. *(cont.)*

Country[a]	Introduction of financial legislation	Number of rounds[b]	Final decision	Comments
Colombia	Lower house	3/2	Each house retains veto power	Urgency limits navette to 30 days
Comoros	Lower house	3/2	The government	After 2 upper house rejections, the government decides whether legislation is defeated or if lower house version is enacted; a law passed by the lower house but contested by all upper house members of an island is defeated if, after a 2nd reading by the lower house, the law is equally contested by a majority of lower house members from the same island
Congo	Lower house	1/2 or 1	Joint session	Budget must be submitted by October 15 and passed by December 31 every year
Croatia	Lower house	1	Lower house	
Czech Republic	Lower house	1	Lower house	
Dominican Republic	Either house	3/2	Reviewing house	
European Union	Upper house (Council of Ministers)	3/2	Lower house (European Parliament)	Council decides by qualified majority; parliament can reject by absolute majority, with 2/3 of members present
Fiji	Lower house	1/2	Lower house	Upper house cannot amend and is constrained by a 1-day maximum delay for appropriations bills and a 21-day maximum delay for other financial legislation
France	Lower house	3 (2 if urgent)	Conference committee, then lower house	Government decides number of rounds; budget must be enacted within 70 days or the government can enact by decree

65

Table 2.2B. *(cont.)*

Country[a]	Introduction of financial legislation	Number of rounds[b]	Final decision	Comments
Germany	Upper house	2 or 5/2	Conference committee; lower house decides by majority or 2/3 majority in specific cases; otherwise, upper house retains veto power	
Grenada	Lower house	1/2	Lower house	Upper house can delay a maximum of 1 month
Haiti	Lower house	1/2	Conference committee	
India	Simultaneous for budget; otherwise, lower house	1	Lower house	Upper house has 14 days to review legislation
Ireland	Lower house	1	Lower house	Upper house may recommend changes to lower house within a maximum of 21 days
Italy	Alternately in lower and upper houses	Indefinite	No stopping rules	
Jamaica	Lower house	1/2	Lower house	Upper house can delay a maximum of 1 month
Japan	Lower house	1	Conference committee, then lower house	Upper house has 30 days to review
Jordan	Lower house	1 or 3/2	Joint session with 2/3 majority of members present	
Liberia	Lower house	Indefinite	No stopping rules	
Madagascar	Lower house	3 (2 if urgent)	Conference committee, then lower house within 60 days	Time limit of 60 days, then budget is enacted by decree

Table 2.2B. *(cont.)*

Country[a]	Introduction of financial legislation	Number of rounds[b]	Final decision	Comments
Malaysia	Lower house	1/2	Lower house	Upper house can delay a maximum of one month and has no power of amendment
Mauritania	Lower house	3/2 or 2	Conference committee, then lower house	Ultimately, government can enact by ordinance
Mexico	Lower house	1/2 or 3/2	Lower house for budget of expenditures; upper house for taxes or loans	
Netherlands	Lower house or joint session	1/2	Upper house	Upper house has no power of amendment
Nigeria	Either house	Indefinite	Joint finance committee, then joint session	Time limit of 2 months before joint committee is called
Norway	United chamber	0	United chamber	
Pakistan	Lower house	0	Lower house	
Paraguay	Lower house	1	Lower house	Initial review in both houses limited to 15 days; second reading in lower house limited to 10 days
Philippines	Lower house	Indefinite	No stopping rules	
Poland	Lower house	1	Lower house, by absolute majority	Upper house has a maximum of 20 days to review legislation; government may dissolve lower house if it fails to enact the budget within 3 months
Romania	Joint session	0	Joint session	
Russian Federation	Lower house	1	Conference committee, then lower house by 2/3 majority	Budget introduced by lower house only with corresponding resolution by the government

67

Table 2.2B. *(cont.)*

Country[a]	Introduction of financial legislation	Number of rounds[b]	Final decision	Comments
South Africa	Lower house	1	Lower house	Upper house has a maximum of 30 days to review the legislation and limited powers of amendment
Spain	Lower house	1	Lower house	
Swaziland	Lower house	1/2	Lower house	Upper house has 5 days to review appropriation legislation and 30 days for other financial legislation (7 days if urgent)
Switzerland	Alternately in lower and upper houses	7/2	Conference committee	Both houses retain veto power
Thailand	Lower house	3/2	Conference committee, then lower house	Lower house has a maximum of 30 days to review annual appropriations bill; upper house has a maximum of 15 days to review
Trinidad and Tobago	Lower house	1/2	Lower house	Upper house can delay a maximum of 1 month
United Kingdom	Lower house	1/2	Lower house	Upper house can delay a maximum of 1 month
United States	Lower house	Indefinite	Conference committee (at any time)	
Venezuela	Lower house	1	Joint session	
Yugoslavia	Either house	Concurrent examination of text	Conference committee	(Same as nonfinancial legislation)

[a]Constitutions unavailable for Bosnia-Herzegovina, Lesotho, and Uruguay.
[b]Each round indicates the reintroduction of a bill in the originating chamber. The count comprises the movement of the legislation from the introduction of the bill until the ratification of the law, including the various stopping rules.
Sources: Flanz (1995), Maddex (1995), Department of Justice, Canada (1989), Hogg (1977), Morgan (1990), Casy 1992), Inter-parliamentary Union (1986).

tern, followed by several Commonwealth member states, illustrates a more general trend. In these countries, nonfinancial legislation may shuttle one and a half to two rounds before the lower house decides, whereas financial legislation is reviewed by the upper house once, often with no powers of amendment, before being promulgated with a maximum one-month delay.

Despite the many variations on the theme, our description should make clear that there are basically three ways of resolving differences in bicameral legislatures. The navette is a consultative process where the bill shuttles back and forth until agreement is reached. The conference committee is usually a unicameral decision process, which involves a subset of the parent house membership. The other methods, joint session and decision by one house, can be understood through unicameral models. Finally, new elections may modify membership and therefore preferences but do not provide a new decision rule; therefore, the outcome can be understood with reference to the normal decision rules.

3. CONCLUSIONS

This short description of bicameral institutions provides evidence that institutional structures vary widely. Representation is most often associated with territorial units, even in unitary systems. Alternatively, membership is based on appointment, which leaves substantial discretion in the hands of the individual or institution granted powers of appointment. More rarely, economic interests and ethnic or linguistic groups may be represented. Representation is also unequal in many cases; like the United States, many countries provide equal representation for territorial units so that individual citizen votes are overweighted or underweighted. Because of the need to legislate, countries have been ingenious in creating methods of overcoming disagreement between the two legislative bodies. Bills shuttle between the two houses; conference committees or joint sessions are called into play; and in many cases, one house is given ultimate decision-making power, after alternative methods of reaching agreement have failed.

Other analysts have attempted to make sense of this diversity by classifying bicameral institutions in terms of congruence, decision rules, and legitimacy (Lijphart 1984; Mastias and Grangé 1987; Trivelli 1975). Our overview suggests that political congruence does not necessarily lead to identity of preferences, so that even congruent legislative houses experience disagreements. Moreover, as illustrated in Table 2.1, almost all bicameral legislatures are noncongruent. Thus, the preferences of upper houses, whose power is symmetrically distributed, are clearly important for legislative outcomes.

History and geography of bicameral diversity

The same political analysts also argue that political differences between the two houses do not matter if the upper house is powerless, if it lacks the institutional power to impose its preferences because the lower house is granted the last word (Lijphart 1984; Mastias and Grangé 1987; Trivelli 1975). Yet we see that, even though their power has been curtailed, many long-standing upper houses have not been dissolved; moreover, bicameral systems continue to be included in newly drafted constitutions, such as those in Central Europe and South America.

Thus, this overview of bicameral institutions presents two puzzles. First, how can we understand the diversity of bicameral institutions? How do different institutional settings affect legislative outcomes? Second, what is the role of bicameral institutions in "weak" upper houses? Do the political preferences of "weak" upper houses affect legislative outcomes? In Part II, we turn to a theoretical examination of the institutions of bicameralism in an effort to find answers to these puzzles.

PART II

Models of bicameral institutions

Introduction to Part II

What difference does it make if a country has a bicameral legislature instead of a unicameral one? Our purpose in Part II is to outline a framework to answer this question and to analyze the historical and geographic diversity of bicameral institutions. Thus, the overarching research question is supplemented by more detailed investigations of the specific mechanisms of intercameral reconciliation. What difference does it make if the navette system can last for one, or two, or an infinite number of rounds, as exemplified in the procedural rules of Austria, France, and Italy, respectively? What is the effect of a conference committee at the end of the navette instead of a final decision by the upper chamber or the lower one, as exemplified in the procedural rules of Switzerland, the Netherlands, and Spain, respectively? Does it make any difference if the government introduces legislation in the lower house first, as required by many constitutions for budgetary matters? Do conference committees affect the outcomes of bicameral bargaining and, if so, how?

Our account demonstrates that bicameral institutions share features that differentiate their outcomes from unicameral ones. In addition, we show how the institutional variations of bicameralism affect relative house power, providing a series of hypotheses that can be tested systematically. Part II constitutes the theoretical foundation on which we conduct empirical analyses in subsequent chapters, so that, in the conclusions, we will be able to assess critically the arguments on bicameralism proposed by various analysts.

Figure II.1 presents in a nutshell the problem we investigate in this part of the book. The current policy, the status quo, is indicated in the figure by the point SQ. Imagine that each chamber of a bicameral legislature has a new ideal policy. This policy choice can be represented by a single *ideal point,* that is, *a point in space at which it would prefer to locate the legislative outcome.* If this choice is impossible, the chamber would prefer to see legislation producing outcomes as close as possible to this ideal

73

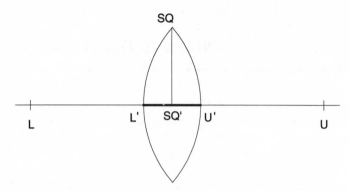

Figure II.1. Simplified decision making in a bicameral legislature

point. More precisely, each chamber is indifferent among points that are equally distant from its own ideal point.[1]

Suppose that in a multidimensional space (two-dimensional in our figure), the two houses have different ideal positions, indicated by U and L for the upper and lower chambers, respectively. For the moment, disregard how the multiplicity of legislators in each chamber is reduced to a single point. The two houses may have different ideal points for a variety of reasons. They may represent different constituencies or may have different rules of deliberation, as we saw in Chapter 2; they may be involved in different games, as when one house is playing an electoral game while the other is not (Tsebelis 1990); or the divisions generated by some issue may not be identical with the overall political alignments despite overarching political similarities.

This setting produces several conclusions. With a unicameral legislature (assume the lower chamber, L), *the winset of the status quo,* that is, *the set of points that defeat the status quo,* would be the entire area of a circle with center L and radius, the segment LSQ. With the addition of a second chamber, the winset of the status quo is reduced to the intersection of two such circles, one with center L and the other with center U. Therefore, the set of outcomes that defeat the status quo is significantly reduced by the existence of a second chamber. As we saw in Chapter 1, this is exactly the point that Riker (1992a) made concerning bicameralism; it also echoes the remarks of Montesquieu and Madison. Furthermore, it is easy to demonstrate that the larger the distance between the ideal points of the upper and lower chambers, the smaller the winset of the status quo (Tsebelis 1995a, Proposition 2). This status-quo-

[1]The technical term for the preferences we just introduced is *Euclidean.* Throughout the book we assume all actors have Euclidean preferences.

preserving capacity is the first major characteristic of bicameralism. We will single it out for subsequent discussions.

Proposition II.1: *Compared with unicameralism, bicameralism makes a change to the status quo more difficult.*

Now, compare any point in space, such as the status quo SQ, to its projection SQ' on the line that connects the ideal points of the upper and lower chambers, the UL line. Assuming that the degree of preference is defined by the distance between the ideal point and the policy alternative represented by the status quo, then both the upper and lower houses prefer SQ' over SQ since SQ' is closer to their positions than SQ. So, some point on the segment UL is preferred to any other point in space by both houses. However, along the UL segment, each player prefers a point that is closer to its own ideal point. This representation helps visualize the difference between the efficient and the political roles of the houses. A movement toward UL represents a gain in efficiency and both houses can agree on it, while a movement along UL represents a conflict of interest between the two houses, a zero-sum, or redistributive, game between the two chambers.

Is there an educated guess about which point these two chambers will select to replace the status quo? For a unicameral legislature the answer to this question is simple: a unique chamber, L for the sake of this illustration, would move the status quo from SQ to its own ideal point. For a bicameral legislature, we are able to narrow the choice to the segment of the line that connects U and L and is included inside the circles with centers U and L that pass through the status quo (segment $L'U'$ in the figure). But which one of these points will be chosen? And what characteristics of the chambers does one need to investigate in order to narrow down the possible outcomes?

The answer depends in part on two distances, the distance between the ideal points of the two chambers and the distance from the status quo to the line connecting the two chambers' ideal points. Each of these distances may be large or small. If the two chambers have ideal points close to each other, which occurs if they are congruent, and are far from the status quo, then it will be relatively easy for the two chambers to reach an agreement. This is because both houses confront the choice of accepting a new solution that is near their own ideal points or preserving a very undesirable status quo because of their disagreement. Conversely, if the status quo is close to the line $L'U'$ and the distance between the two chambers on the LU line is large, a compromise between the two chambers becomes more difficult because the joint gains from altering the status quo are insufficient to compensate for the differences of opinion (the points along the line $L'U'$). If the ideal points of the two chambers are far away from each other, then the specific institutional provisions that regulate the interaction between the two chambers are of paramount importance. If, on the other hand, the two ideal points are close to each other, then the specific mechanisms of reconciliation become less important.

These conclusions are based on the heroic simplifying assumption that collective players have unique ideal points. If we relax this assumption, can we retain these expectations? Chapter 3 provides an affirmative answer to the question. Under a wide set of assumptions, the expectation that the outcome will be "around" the segment $L'U'$ is reasonable. In fact, we argue that *a second major feature of bicameralism, in addition to preserving the status quo, is that it reduces the conflict between the two chambers to one predominant dimension.*

In Chapter 4, we narrow further the interval of the final outcome and provide a point estimate. However, we do so on the basis of more restrictive assumptions about the interaction of the chambers. Our investigation of bicameralism concludes that the institutional features of the two chambers' interaction, such as where a bill is introduced, how many times it can shuttle between chambers, and who has the final word, systematically affect the outcome. The location of the outcome also depends on political factors, such as the impatience of each chamber to reach a compromise.

Finally, in Chapter 5, we analyze the properties of one particular decision-making procedure in bicameral legislatures, the conference committee. We argue that the importance of conference committees stems from the fact that they control the agenda, that is, they can make a take-it-or-leave-it proposal to both chambers. We use spatial voting models to locate the area in which this proposal will be made.

To evaluate the effects of bicameral legislatures, we use both cooperative and noncooperative game theories. The fundamental difference between the two is that cooperative game theory assumes that agreements are enforceable, while noncooperative game theory does not. The consequences of these opposed assumptions are dramatic. When agreements are enforceable, institutional features such as agenda setting become irrelevant. Agendas merely determine the sequence in which different decisions are reached and strategic players act at every stage in a manner that promotes their (enforceable) agreement. Keeping the set of feasible alternatives constant, the only institution that matters in a cooperative game-theoretic analysis is the decision-making rule itself. In this sense, cooperative game theory is almost institution-free. In contrast, noncooperative game theory is the basis for any rational choice analysis of institutions.

Cooperative game theory provides us with two important insights. First, it equips us with a bird's-eye view of bicameralism, that is, the fundamental consequences of using a bicameral legislature rather than a unicameral one (Chapter 3). Second, it gives us a tool that sheds light on the black box of conference committee deliberations (Chapter 5). Conference committees usually operate in a secretive way; their deliberations frequently are unrecorded, or classified and declassified only after many years. Consequently the analyst does not have systematic access to data. Furthermore, we lack information on rules of procedure and whether they mean very much in small-group meetings, where rules can be obfuscated by a majority agreement on a specific outcome. This is exactly the situation where other methodologies are less helpful and where cooperative game theory can provide invaluable insights.

The use of cooperative game theory represents a departure from previous practice in two ways. First, cooperative game theory is used here in exactly the opposite way than usual. Normally, cooperative game theory provides a reduced form solution that is validated only to the extent that there is a noncooperative model that arrives at the same outcomes. Game theorists want to know *how* agreements become enforceable in order to accept a cooperative game-theoretic solution; that is, before accepting the conclusions of a cooperative game-theoretic model, they want to know the sequence of moves, the restrictions in choice, or the information available to different players that ensures the enforcement of agreement. Here we assume that agreements *are* enforceable, either because of the existence of political parties or because of the frequent interaction of participants, and use the results of cooperative game theory in Chapter 3 as the basis for the development of noncooperative models in Chapter 4. In particular, we use cooperative game theory to reduce the number of dimensions of conflict from many to one and then apply one-dimensional noncooperative models.

Readers who object to the use of cooperative game theory to *derive* one predominant dimension of conflict can *assume* such a dimension and focus on the institutional results of Chapter 4. However, there are two reasons that support our choice of methodology. First, the solution concept we employ presupposes that direct comparisons of all possible outcomes are feasible, a feature that would be present in any realistic noncooperative game equilibrium.[2] Second, recent noncooperative game-theoretic models of unicameral legislatures, the so-called sequential choice theory of institutions (Baron 1993, 1995; Baron and Ferejohn 1989), also lead to conceptually similar predictions.[3]

This leads us to a second possible surprise for some of our readers. Cooperative game theory does not lead to single point predictions but to

---

[2]The solution concept we employ is Schwartz's (1990) tournament equilibrium.
[3]The sequential choice theory of institutions leads to predictions of solution sets that are centrally located in space, solutions that are similar to ours.

a set of possible outcomes.[4] Some readers may be dissatisfied by the concept of a set prediction. How can one corroborate a theory that suggests that an entire set of results is possible? We provide two responses. First, set predictions are not uncommon where rational choice methodology is employed. For example, the concepts of mixed strategies and mixed strategy equilibria provide set predictions together with a probability distribution over the set of possible outcomes. Similarly, the spatial noncooperative models we mentioned in the previous paragraph lead also to set predictions. Second, processes of collective decision making are genuinely indeterminate most of the time. The radical form of this statement is provided by the so-called chaos theorems, according to which majority rule can lead to any possible outcome, even under very weak assumptions (McKelvey 1976; Schofield 1978). However, we do not have to examine formal models to conclude that even the most astute observers of the U.S. Congress often cannot predict the outcomes of votes. And if one looks inside committees, uncertainty about the possible outcomes, the bargains struck, and the coalitions supporting one plan or another is pervasive.

However, we do share the belief of epistemologists that simple hypotheses (in our case predictions) are easier to test (Hempel 1964; Popper 1962), and we try our best to be more precise in our predictions. In fact, in Chapter 4, we do arrive at point predictions. However, this accuracy comes at the expense of introducing a series of additional assumptions. Some of these assumptions are uncontroversial, such as the introduction of parameters corresponding to different institutional structures; others, such as the assumption that legislators are impatient to reach agreement, are more difficult to operationalize and to measure (see Chapters 6 and 7).

Part II is organized into three chapters. Chapter 3 describes some general features of bicameral legislatures, generated by the fact that, at least initially, the agreement of both chambers is sought. We examine three different solution concepts of cooperative game theory – the core, the uncovered set, and the tournament equilibrium – and we demonstrate that all three solutions point to one predominant dimension of conflict. Chapter 4 uses this finding as the point of departure and introduces a one-dimensional bargaining model of intercameral reconciliation. This model explores the political significance of the different mechanisms developed to resolve intercameral differences. Finally, the model indicates that a conference committee, where it is employed, has a decisive power,

---

[4]In our case, these are the core, which exists only rarely, and the uncovered set and tournament equilibrium, which exist always. See below for definitions.

that is, to make an offer to both chambers under closed rule. Chapter 5 examines this decision-making process, which is usually quite secretive, and tries to get a theoretical handle on the location of conference committee proposals that very frequently become bicameral legislative outcomes.

3

The core and the uncovered
set of bicameral legislatures

The basic problem with identifying the possible outcomes of a majoritarian decision-making process, such as decisions of unicameral or bicameral legislatures, is the fact that collective preferences, unlike individual ones, are not transitive. This means that although a legislature can prefer outcome *a* over *b*, and outcome *b* over *c*, by majority rule, it is still possible for the same legislature to prefer outcome *c* over *a*.[1] This set of preferences results in unstable decision making; any outcome may be defeated by a majority, and that outcome in turn may be defeated by yet another majority. And the process may be repeated endlessly.

For this reason, the concept of the *core* became a basic tool in social choice theory and cooperative game theory. The core is *the set of points that cannot be defeated by the application of the decision-making rule*. So the core of a unicameral institution is the set of points that cannot be defeated by majority or any other decision-making rule; the core of a bicameral legislature is the set of points that cannot be defeated by concurrent majorities in both chambers; and so forth.

For unicameral legislatures, Plott has shown that the necessary and sufficient conditions for the existence of a core are very restrictive (Plott 1967: 790). He demonstrated that in a legislature with an odd number of members, a core exists in an *n*-dimensional legislative space ($n > 1$) only when it is located on the ideal point of at least one member and the remaining even number of members are "divided into pairs whose interests are diametrically opposed." In the absence of these restrictive conditions, majority rule outcomes can cycle anywhere in the *n*-dimensional space (McKelvey 1976; Schofield 1978).

In the absence of a core, social choice theory has developed other, weaker concepts of stability. The most important is the *uncovered set* (Cox 1987; Miller 1980; Ordeshook and Schwartz 1987; Shepsle and

[1]For a definition of *cycling*, see Chapter 1.

80

Weingast 1984). Roughly, the uncovered set is *the set of points that cannot be defeated directly and indirectly by any other point.*[2] Consequently, the uncovered set collapses to the core, if the core exists. This literature has demonstrated that if legislators are sophisticated, under certain agendas, the legislative outcome will be located inside the uncovered set. McKelvey (1986) has proven that in an *n*-dimensional space, the uncovered set is centrally located. This means that the possible outcomes are in an area that divides the differences between the legislators rather than privileges extreme positions.

More restrictive assumptions produce outcomes in some subset of the uncovered set (Banks 1985; Schwartz 1990). One of these results, for our purposes the most significant, is Schwartz's *tournament equilibrium set.* Schwartz assumes that contracts between legislators are enforceable (cooperative decision making) but legislators are free to recontract; that is, if they find a proposal that a majority coalition prefers, they can write an enforceable contract to support it. He also assumes that any two proposals can be directly compared. He calculates the smallest set within which this cooperative recontracting process is likely to produce outcomes. He calls this set the tournament equilibrium set and he proves that it is a subset of the uncovered set.

Such formal analyses of bicameral institutions do not exist, with three exceptions. Cox and McKelvey (1984) have demonstrated, at a high level of abstraction, the conditions for the existence of a core of multicameral legislatures when the preferences of the legislative houses do not overlap. In social choice terminology, when the ideal points of one chamber's members are not located "within" the other chambers' sets of ideal points, their Pareto sets do not overlap. Hammond and Miller (1987) produce conditions for the existence of the core of a bicameral legislature in two dimensions. And Brennan and Hamlin (1992) inaccurately claim to have generalized the Hammond and Miller argument in more than two dimensions.[3]

We extend the formal analysis of bicameral institutions in an effort to clarify the theoretical foundation underlying the existing informal analyses of bicameral institutions by Montesquieu, Madison, and others reviewed in Chapter 1. In Section 1 we present the conditions under which there is a core in bicameral legislatures; we demonstrate that, if the core exists, it will be a segment of a straight line. In Section 2 we argue that the uncovered set always exists and that it is always elongated along one dimension. In Section 3 we conclude that, in bicameral legislatures –

[2]The exact definition can be found in Appendix 3B.

[3]Tsebelis (1993) has demonstrated that they mistakenly assume that once a bicameral median exists it is unique. The same paper provides counterexamples to the Brennan and Hamlin argument.

with or without a core, whether the two chambers overlap or not – there is always one privileged dimension of intercameral conflict and compromise.

1. EXISTENCE AND LOCATION OF BICAMERAL AND QUALIFIED MAJORITY CORES

In this section we present the intuition underlying the argument that a bicameral core exists in one and two dimensions and explain why this does not generalize to more than two dimensions. To enable the reader to evaluate the proposition advanced by some analysts that the properties of bicameral legislatures are similar to unicameral legislatures with qualified majority rule, we also present the qualified majority core of a unicameral legislature.[4] The proofs of the propositions concerning bicameralism in n dimensions can be found in Appendix A, this chapter.

First, let us assume that the policy space has a single dimension, such as the traditional Left–Right continuum. In this case, it is easy to locate the median voter of each chamber. From Figure 3.1 we can predict that the bicameral outcome will be located somewhere between the medians of the two chambers.

Let us now consider a simple case of two-dimensional policy space where the two chambers have distinct policy positions, as is the case in Figure 3.2. In this case, there is one *bicameral median;* that is, there is only *one line that divides the bicameral legislature in such a way that on it and on either side of it, there is a majority of members of both chambers.* This line is the line passing through points L_2 and U_2. Indeed, on it and on one side of it, one can find points L_1 and L_2, as well as points U_1 and U_2; and on it and on the other side of it, one can find points L_2 and L_3, as well as points U_2 and U_3. It is easy to demonstrate that any point in space can be defeated by its projection on the bicameral median. Indeed, for any point above or below line LU, its projection on the line is majority preferred in each chamber, so any point off the line can be defeated by its projection on the line by concurrent majorities of the two chambers (the line LU is an "attractor"). Similarly, any point to the left of L or to the right of U can be defeated by L or U by concurrent majorities in both chambers. Any point on the segment LU cannot be defeated by any other point in space by concurrent majorities of both chambers. Consequently, the segment LU is the core of the bicameral legislature.

This argument cannot be generalized to the case where the policy preferences of the two chambers overlap, as depicted in Figure 3.3. In this case, there are three different bicameral medians, and points on each one

[4]For references, see Chapter 1.

Figure 3.1. Core of a bicameral legislature in one dimension

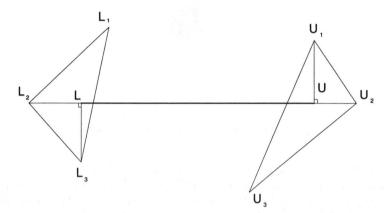

Figure 3.2. Core of a bicameral legislature in two dimensions

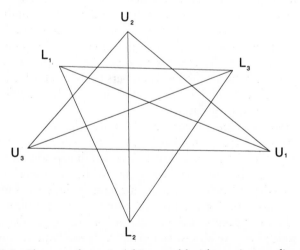

Figure 3.3. Absence of core in a bicameral legislature in two dimensions

of them can defeat points outside the line. Consequently, there is no invulnerable point, except for the (very rare) case where all three bicameral medians pass through the same point. In that case, the point of intersection of all medians is the bicameral core.

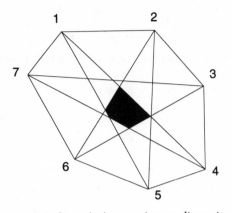

Figure 3.4. $5/7$ majority core in two dimensions

For purposes of comparison, we present the core of a unicameral legislature that decides with qualified majority of $5/7$. Figure 3.4 presents such a legislature in a two-dimensional policy space, and the core, represented by the shaded area in the figure, can be proven to exist always. In fact, Greenberg (1979) has demonstrated that a legislature that decides by qualified majority always has a core in n dimensions, as long as $q > (n/(n + 1))$, where q is the qualified majority and n is the number of issue dimensions. A simple comparison of the bicameral core with the qualified majority core (Figures 3.3 and 3.4) indicates that the points that are invulnerable in the two legislatures are very different. Only points that are on a straight line between the two chambers belong to the bicameral core, while the set of centrally located points belong to the qualified majority core of a unicameral legislature.

Let us now examine the core of a bicameral legislature in more than two dimensions. For reasons that become apparent in Appendix A, this chapter, in general, the core in more than two dimensions ceases to exist even if the two chambers are far apart. Although there are multiple bicameral medians,[5] unless all these medians include the same straight line, there is no core. For a bicameral core to exist in n dimensions, the layout of the ideal points of the legislators has to be peculiar indeed. In fact, the conditions are almost as restrictive as the Plott conditions for a unicameral legislature. However, regardless of the dimensionality of the space, the general result indicates that, if the core exists, it will be a

---

[5]Medians are lines that divide both chambers in such a way that a majority of members in each chamber is located on either side of the line *and* on the line itself. In the case of a three-dimensional space the medians are planes, and in the general case of an n-dimensional space the medians are $(n - 1)$-dimensional hyperplanes.

segment of a straight line (or a single point). Consequently, if legislators resolve the efficiency problem, that is, if they move by concurrent majorities into the core, the problem remains which one of the points of the core to select. However, the most important result of this analysis is that in more than two dimensions, the core rarely exists.

Why discuss the cases that lack a core? Why not assume that the space is "close enough" to two dimensions and leave the analysis at this point? This is the solution adopted by Hammond and Miller (1987) in their excellent article that formally analyzes the U.S. Constitution. They claim, on the basis of empirical results presented in Poole and Rosenthal (1985, 1987), that the dimensionality of the political debates in the United States has rarely exceeded two, except in periods of realignment, so that a two-dimensional analysis is adequate. Our problem with this approach, even if we accept the dimension-reducing technique of Poole and Rosenthal, is that the relevant problem is not the *actual* dimension of the policy space but the *potential* one. As Riker (1983) has convincingly argued, political entrepreneurs scan the entire political space to discover new dimensions that will disrupt existing coalitions. To determine whether a core exists (i.e., points that are invulnerable to such strategic maneuvers), we must examine all issues that political entrepreneurs consider; that is, we must scan a multidimensional space, not a two-dimensional one. Therefore, although the concept of the core has the convenient property of reducing the *n*-dimensional problem of bicameral negotiations to a single dimension, it usually lacks another essential property for it to be useful: existence. Therefore, we turn to the other solution concept, the uncovered set.

2. LOCATION OF THE BICAMERAL UNCOVERED SET AND TOURNAMENT EQUILIBRIUM

In this section we demonstrate that the uncovered set of a bicameral legislature always exists and is located centrally between the two chambers. We also demonstrate that the uncovered set is almost always contained in an area that is cylindrically symmetric, that is, an area in which all but one dimension are equal to each other, and the remaining dimension is longer than the rest.[6] As noted above, a rough definition of *covering* is *the points that cannot be defeated both directly and indirectly by any other point* (for the exact definition see Appendix B, this chapter). From this definition, it follows that points that are uncovered in *either* chamber belong to the bicameral uncovered set, although they are not the

---

[6]For the one exception, when the uncovered set is included in a hypersphere, see infra.

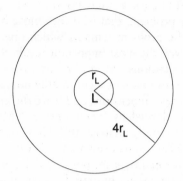

Figure 3.5. Area within which is located the uncovered set of a unicameral legislature

only points in the bicameral uncovered set. For a unicameral legislature, McKelvey (1986) calculated the size and location of the uncovered set.

The easiest way to understand McKelvey's results is to examine the uncovered set visually, as it is depicted in the two-dimensional policy space in Figure 3.5. The smaller circle in the figure is the *yolk*. The yolk is *the smallest circle intersecting with all median lines.* Intuitively, it is the closest approximation to a two-dimensional median. Where the policy space has more than two dimensions, the yolk is a sphere or hypersphere intersecting with all median planes or hyperplanes. The yolk has a center C and a radius r. The larger circle in the figure has radius $4r$ and is a circle that contains the uncovered set of the unicameral legislature. We will call it the *uncovered bound circle* (or uncovered bound sphere/hypersphere).

To calculate the radius of the uncovered bound circle, McKelvey (1986) followed Ferejohn, McKelvey, and Packell's (1984) reasoning. For any pair of points X and Y, Y defeats X by majority vote of the legislature if Y is closer to the center of the yolk than X by the distance $2r$. In other words, Y defeats X if the distance CX is greater than the distance $CY + 2r$. It follows that C (the center of the yolk) defeats any point X at a distance more than $2r$ from it. It also follows that C covers (because it can beat both directly and indirectly) any point X that is at a distance $4r$ from it. Therefore, all points more than $4r$ from the center of the yolk cannot be part of the uncovered set, and the uncovered set must be contained within the circle with a radius $4r$. For a two-dimensional policy space, *the uncovered set of a unicameral legislature is contained within the uncovered bound circle.*

To determine the area within which the uncovered set of a *bicameral* legislature must lie, we replicate McKelvey's calculations. First, we find the points that can be defeated by the line connecting the centers of the

Figure 3.6. Area within which is located the uncovered set of a bicameral legislature

yolks of the two chambers. Second, we find the boundary of this set, the points that are furthest from the line connecting the centers of the two yolks. Third, we find the points that can be defeated by these boundary points by concurrent majorities of both chambers. All these points can be defeated directly and indirectly by some point on the line connecting the two yolks and consequently cannot belong to the uncovered set. Figure 3.6 visually presents the area within which the bicameral uncovered set is located. The reader can verify that this area contains the uncovered bound spheres of each chamber, as well as the points "in between" these two spheres. The area is cylindrically symmetric; that is, it has one dimension larger than all the others, which are equal to each other.

> **Proposition 3.1:** *The uncovered set and the tournament equilibrium set of a bicameral legislature are included in the cylindrically symmetric area surrounding the yolks of the two chambers (Figure 3.6).*

The dimensions of the shaded area depend on the distance between the centers of the yolks of the two chambers and the radii of the two yolks. The size r of the radius of each yolk is usually very small, and on average, it decreases with the number of individual voters with distinct positions (Koehler 1990). Consequently, on average, as the number of legislators increases and as the distance between the centers of the yolks of the two chambers grows, the shaded area in Figure 3.6 becomes more like a straight line.

3. CONCLUSIONS

In Section 1 we demonstrated that the core of a bicameral legislature is a straight line but rarely exists. In Section 2 we demonstrated that the

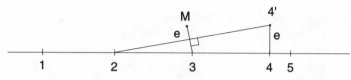

Figure 3.7. Existence of a core in a two-dimensional space (transaction costs)

uncovered set and the tournament equilibrium set always exist and are included in the cylindrically symmetric area depicted in Figure 3.6. The shaded area of the figure almost always has one dimension longer than any other, but it is multidimensional; it is *not* a straight line.

It is a recurrent and well-known theme in the theory of spatial models that any deviation from a single dimension is likely to lead to the absence of a core (Plott 1967) and to "chaos" (McKelvey 1986). Is our exercise therefore useless, or is there any way that we can claim that the area depicted in Figure 3.6 is "almost" a straight line?

We argue that one assumption common to all spatial voting models is responsible for the bifurcation of results between one dimension and more than one dimension. When this assumption is relaxed the bifurcation disappears and results become more uniform. To our knowledge, the essence of our argument can be found earliest in an article by Judith Sloss (1973) and is illustrated in Figure 3.7.

Consider a committee of five members, labeled 1 through 5, positioned on a straight line as depicted in the figure. Under majority rule, with endogenous agenda setting, the unique equilibrium outcome is the position of median voter 3, because a coalition of 3, 4, and 5 can defeat any proposal to the left of 3 and a coalition of 1, 2, and 3 can defeat any proposal to the right of 3.

Now, move one member of the committee, Member 4, by an infinitesimal distance *e* away from the line, to the point 4'. The committee is now located in a two-dimensional space and the equilibrium disappears. In fact, Member 3 can now be defeated by a coalition of 1, 2, and 4', who will vote for the point *M*. *M* itself can be defeated by many coalitions, and the infinitesimal movement of Member 4 results in "chaos." This is the standard multidimensional spatial modeling story.

There may be many implausible claims in the story, but we focus on a single claim, the implicit assumption that there are no costs of negotiation among the members of coalition 1, 2, and 4' and that there are no costs of enforcing their agreement. First, we calculate the distance the new coalition, 1, 2, and 4', is able to move the outcome from the original equilibrium at point 3. At most, the coalition can move it to point *M*, which is the symmetric of 3 with respect to the line 24′. If, to obtain an order of magnitude, we position point 3 in the middle of points 2 and 4 and if we assume that the segments 24 and 24′ are equal,[7] the distance between points 3 and M can be calculated to be e. So if one assumes some transaction costs, it does not seem reasonable to claim that movement e was worth the effort. Therefore, point 3 remains invulnerable even if we have moved from one dimension to two. The reason is that we moved very little (e) and the costs of negotiating a new coalition exceed the results achieved. In other words, in our stylized story, the actors recognize that a slight perturbation of 3 is not worth their effort if this effort is not completely costless.

This is the argument we apply to the shaded area of Figure 3.6. The larger the differences between the two chambers, the smaller their yolks, and the heavier negotiation or transaction costs, the more this area is considered by the players (and can be considered by the analyst) to be a straight line, because differences perpendicular to the line connecting the yolks are insignificant compared with differences along the line.[8]

The conclusions of the Part introduction and Sections 1 and 2 follow from this analysis. We remind the reader of their implications.

Proposition II.1: *Compared with unicameralism, bicameralism makes a change to the status quo more difficult.*

Proposition 3.1: *The uncovered set and the tournament equilibrium set of a bicameral legislature are included in the cylindrically symmetric area surrounding the yolks of the two chambers (Figure 3.6).*

Whether it is the core (which in multiple dimensions rarely exists) or the uncovered set or the tournament equilibrium set (which always exist), bicameralism produces one privileged dimension of conflict. This dimension expresses the differences of the two chambers, or the differences of the median voters of the two chambers.[9] We remind the reader that both of these statements rely on the assumptions of enforceable agreements and the Euclidian preferences of the actors. Furthermore, with respect to the uncovered set, the privileged dimension relies on the existence of some negotiation or transaction costs, which will force the participant actors to consider points close to each other as indistinguishable for practical purposes. Consequently,

[7]This second assumption is an approximation.
[8]For a similar argument introducing costs into spatial models, see Huber (forthcoming).
[9]Strictly speaking, the median in n dimensions does not exist (if it does it is the core). However, one can think of the yolk as the multidimensional equivalent of the median.

Models of bicameral institutions

Corollary 3.1: *Under the assumptions of cooperative decision making and Euclidean preferences, the line connecting the centers of the yolks of the two chambers is the privileged dimension of conflict and compromise in bicameral legislatures.*[10]

It may appear that the prediction of Corollary 3.1 is not very restrictive. However, before jumping to that conclusion, we consider two points. First, as discussed in the beginning of this section, in the absence of a core, the outcome of bicameral deliberations can wander anywhere in space. Thus, by assuming cooperative decision making, we are able to restrict the outcome to a limited space. Second, the size of the yolk generally decreases with the number of members of each chamber. For modern legislatures, whose membership numbers in the hundreds, the prediction is not only the best we can do; it is also quite good. However, in the next chapter, we take the objection seriously. Since we demonstrate that bicameralism forces conflicts to be resolved along the dimension connecting the centers of the yolks of the two chambers, we make appropriate additional assumptions and present a point prediction on that line. This analysis will introduce the institutional mechanisms of bicameral negotiations, that is, the different forms of the navette system.

[10]The assumption of Euclidean preferences is necessary for the line connecting the centers of the two yolks to be straight. If the preferences are not Euclidean, if, for example, different players weigh dimensions differently (and consequently are willing to trade), the contract curve connecting the two yolks will have a different shape. We conjecture that such a modification would significantly complicate calculations but would not alter qualitatively the results of this book.

Existence and location of the core
of bicameral legislatures

Lemma 3.AI: For any bicameral legislature with $(2n + 1)$ and $(2m + 1)$ members in each chamber in k dimensions, a bicameral median hyperplane in $(k - 1)$ dimensions exists.

Proof: Follows from Theorem 2 in Cox and McKelvey (1984). The lemma is trivially true if the number of dimensions is greater than the number of members. For $(k \leq 2n + 1, 2m + 1)$, consider a bicameral legislature in a three-dimensional space $(k = 3)$. Project the ideal points of the legislators on a two-dimensional plane, H_2. Call D_1 the direction of the projection $(D_1 \perp H_2)$. Find the bicameral median line of the projection. Hammond and Miller have proved that there is at least one such line. Call this line M and call D_2 the line perpendicular to it on H_2. Since M is median on the H_2 plane, it means that at least half the legislators of each chamber have nonpositive and half nonnegative ordinates on D_2. Consequently, the plane $D_1 D_2$ is a median (two-dimensional) plane. The proof for higher values of k is similar. Consider the projection along the direction D_{k-2} on a plane, find D_2, and construct the hyperplane generated by D_{k-2} and D_2, which is a bicameral median hyperplane in $(k - 1)$ dimensions.   QED

Consider now any point X in k dimensions and its projection X' to a $(k - 1)$-dimensional hyperplane H_{k-1}. Consider the preference relation P_X (read $AP_X B$ as A is preferred by X to B).

Lemma 3.A2: For any two points A and $B \in H_{k-1}$, $AP_X B$ iff $AP_{X'} B$.

Proof: Follows from the Pythagorean theorem applied on triangles $XX'A$ and $XX'B$.   QED

Successive applications of Lemma 3.A2 can help us reduce the dimensionality of the core. Consider a bicameral legislature in k dimensions and a bicameral hyperplane H_{k-1}. Consider now the projections of all legislators U_i and L_j on H_{k-1}; call them U_i' and L_j'.

Lemma 3.A3 (reduction of dimensions): The core of the bicameral legislature U_i and L_j in k dimensions coincides with the core of its projection U_i' and L_j' on a bicameral median hyperplane $((k - 1)$ dimensions).

Proof: Since H_{k-1} is an attractor, the bicameral core of U_i and L_j has to be on it. Now, consider the bicameral legislature U_i' and L_j' in $(k - 1)$ dimensions. For any two points A and $B \in H_{k-1}$ repeated application of Lemma 3.A2 indicates that A is majority preferred to B among U_i and L_j iff A is majority preferred to B among U_i' and L_j'.   QED

Lemma 3.A4: The core of an n-dimensional bicameral legislature is a subset of the intersection of all bicameral median hyperplanes.

Proof: By contradiction. Suppose that there is one bicameral median hyperplane that does not include the core. Then, one of the points of the core could be defeated by its projection on that bicameral median hyperplane. This is impossible by the definition of the core.   QED

Proposition 3.A1: The core of an n-dimensional bicameral legislature is at the most in one dimension.

Proof: Consider the intersection of all bicameral median hyperplanes. There are four possible cases:

1. The intersection of all median hyperplanes is empty. In this case the core of the bicameral legislature is empty.
2. All bicameral median hyperplanes pass through one point. In this case, this point is the core of the legislature.
3. All bicameral median hyperplanes pass through the same line. In this case, the core will be a subset (possibly empty) of this straight line.
4. All bicameral median hyperplanes pass through the same hyperplane (of two or more dimensions).

We show that case 4 is impossible. The core is a subset of the space (S) of the intersection of these bicameral median hyperplanes (Lemma 3.A4). By Lemma 3.A3, in order to locate the core, we find the induced ideal points of all legislators on S (projection of ideal points on S). We know from Hammond and Miller (1987) that if S is two-dimensional, the core does not always exist, but if it does exist it is one dimensional.

Suppose now that S has three dimensions. Consider the (two-dimensional) median hyperplanes and their intersection. The core will be on this intersection (which is in zero, one, or two dimensions). Again the problem has been reduced to two dimensions at most; consequently the core is at the most one dimensional. A similar reduction can be made if S has more than three dimensions.   QED

Appendix 3.A

Corollary 3.A1: If both chambers have a core, the segment connecting the two unicameral cores is the bicameral core.

Proof: For each chamber, any hyperplane through the core is a median hyperplane, and there is no median hyperplane that does not pass through the core. Consequently, all hyperplanes through both cores are bicameral median hyperplanes, and there is no other bicameral median hyperplane.   QED

Corollary 3.A2: If only one chamber has a core, the bicameral core is not empty, and the core point of this chamber belongs to the bicameral core.

Proof: The winset of the core point of one chamber is empty; consequently nothing can defeat that point by concurrent majorities in both chambers.   QED

Proposition 3.A2: Every $(n - 1)$-dimensional hyperplane that includes the bicameral core is a bicameral median hyperplane.

Proof: Consider a bicameral legislature with a core. Call H_{n-1} an $(n - 1)$-dimensional hyperplane perpendicular to the core. Project all points U_i of the upper chamber on H_{n-1} and call U'_i the projections. Consider now a bicameral median hyperplane M_{n-1}. M_{n-1} is perpendicular to H_{n-1} (since the former includes the core). Call M_{n-2} *the intersection of* M_{n-1} *and* H_{n-1}. M_{n-2} is a median hyperplane of the points U'_i. Indeed, line X perpendicular on M_{n-1} intersecting the core would divide points U_i in half (half of the points would be above or on the core, and half below or on the core); the same line would divide points U'_i in half. Similarly, the intersection of any other bicameral median hyperplane with H_{n-1} is also a median hyperplane for the projections U'_i. Consequently, all median hyperplanes of U'_i pass through the same point (the intersection of the bicameral core with H_{n-1}). This point, call it U', is the intersection of all median hyperplanes of the legislature of U'_i in $(n - 1)$ dimensions and, therefore, its core. Consequently, any $(n - 2)$-dimensional hyperplane through U' is a median hyperplane of U'_i. Consider now one of these median hyperplanes; call it M'_{n-2}. From U' draw the perpendicular X' to M'_{n-2} in the H_{n-1} space. X' divides points U'_i in half (half of the points would be above or on the core, and half below or on the core); the same line would divide points U_i in half. Consequently, hyperplane M'_{n-1} generated by M'_{n-2} and the bicameral core is a median hyperplane of U_i.

Identical arguments can be made about the lower house L_j.   QED

Corollary 3.A3: If the core of a bicameral legislature exists, it is on a line intersecting the yolks of both chambers.

Proof: Otherwise there would be hyperplanes through the core that are not median.   QED

Corollary 3.A4: A bicameral core in n dimensions exists if the Pareto sets of the two chambers do not overlap and if there are two points U_c and L_c such that every two-dimensional plane through U_c and L_c that includes one ideal point of one chamber (other than L_c or U_c) also includes another ideal point of the same chamber on the other side of $U_c L_c$.

Proof: By construction, every hyperplane passing through $U_c L_c$ is a bicameral median hyperplane. We need to show that there are no other bicameral median hyperplanes. The proof is made by contradiction:

Consider bicameral median hyperplane H_{n-1} not passing through $U_c L_c$. This hyperplane either is parallel to $U_c L_c$, or intersects with it at a point X.

1. Assume it is parallel, and from a point of $U_c L_c$ draw a line D that is perpendicular to H_{n-1}. Since H_{n-1} is median, half of the points of the upper and half of the lower chamber have nonpositive ordinates on the D axis, and half nonnegative. But the only such axis on the plane (as we showed in the first part of the proof) originates on $U_c L_c$. Contradiction.

2. Assume that H_{n-1} intersects with $U_c L_c$ *at point X*. From X draw line D that is perpendicular to H_{n-1}. Since H_{n-1} is a median hyperplane, half of the points of the upper and half of the lower chamber have nonpositive ordinates on the D axis, and half nonnegative. Axis D is not perpendicular to $U_c L_c$ because in this case $U_c L_c$ would belong to H_{n-1}. Consider the (two-dimensional) plane H_2 generated by $U_c L_c$ and D. On this plane, draw the line through X that is perpendicular to D. By assumption, this is a median line, on H_2, and it is different from $U_c L_c$. Contradiction.   QED

Location of the bicameral uncovered set

In the following discussion we will assume that there is no core (if the core exists, the uncovered set coincides with it).

The proof is based on Ferejohn et al. (1984) and McKelvey (1986). Ferejohn et al. (1984) locate the area within which the *winset* of point X is located, that is, *the set of all points that defeat X by majority rule*. They demonstrate that if the distance between point X and center of yolk L of a (unicameral) legislature is d, all points Y that belong to the winset of X are closer than the distance $(d + 2r)$ from L, where $2r$ is the diameter of the yolk. Consequently, for a bicameral legislature, the winset of point X is located inside the intersection of two circles with radii equal to the distance between X and the two centers of the yolks, increased by the diameter of the corresponding yolk. In fact, Ferejohn et al. (1984) go further and calculate that the entire winset can be included inside an area smaller than these circles, inside a "cardioid" for which they calculate the polar coordinates. Their analysis is our starting point.

For the bicameral legislature, we calculate the intersection of the two cardioids of point X (one for each chamber). The bicameral winset of X lies inside this intersection. At this point, we replicate McKelvey's calculations. McKelvey considered the center of the yolk of a unicameral legislature and found that it cannot be defeated directly by any point located at a distance of $2r$ from it; the points in the circumference of this circle with radius twice as big as the yolk cannot be defeated by points that are another $2r$ further away from the center of the yolk. Consequently, the uncovered set of a legislature is included within a sphere with radius $4r$ and center the center of the yolk.

Definition 3.B1 (median hyperplane of a chamber): An $(n - 1)$-dimensional hyperplane will be called median if a majority of members of the chamber have ideal points on it or on one side of it, and a majority of members of the chamber have ideal points on it or on the other side of it.

Definition 3.B2 (yolk): The yolk of a chamber is the smallest sphere intersecting with all median hyperplanes.

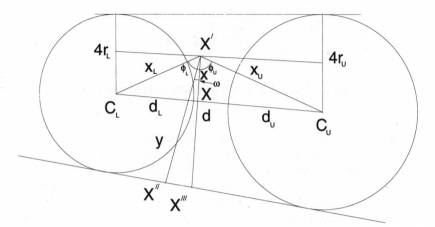

Figure 3.B1. Location of a bicameral uncovered set

Definition 3.B3 (covering relation): For a pair of points $x, y \in R^n$, yCx(read y covers x) iff (1) $y \in W(x)$ (y belongs to the winset of x) and (2) $W(y) \subset W(x)$ (the winset of y is a subset of the winset of x).

Definition 3.B4 (uncovered set): $UC = \{x/x \in R^n$ and $\forall_y \in R^n$, not $yCx\}$ (read the set of all points that are not covered by any point in space).

Consider the line connecting the centers C_U and C_L of the two yolks and a point X on it (see Figure 3.B1). Call r_U and r_L the radii of these two yolks. Call d_U and d_L the distances of X from C_U and C_L and d the distance of the centers of the yolks. Consider also the two outer cardioids and their intersection. Distance x is defined as

$$x = 2(r_U + 2d_U \cos \vartheta_U) = 2(r_L + 2d_L \cos \vartheta_L) \tag{3.B1}$$

$$\text{where } \vartheta_U + \vartheta_L = \pi \tag{3.B2}$$

From (3.B1) and (3.B2) we get

$$x = \frac{2(r_U d_L + d_U r_L)}{d_L + d_U} \tag{3.B3}$$

Consider now line XX' perpendicular to $C_U C_L$ with the point X' at distance x from X. Point X' is outside the intersection of the winsets of X with respect to the upper and lower chambers. Consider now the segments connecting X' with C_U and C_L, respectively, and the angles between XX' and these segments as indicated in Figure 3.B1.

$$x_U^2 = d_U^2 + x^2 \quad \text{and} \quad x_L^2 = d_L^2 + x^2 \tag{3.B4}$$

$$\cos \varphi_L = \frac{x}{x_L} \quad \text{and} \quad \cos \varphi_U = \frac{x}{x_U} \tag{3.B5}$$

$$\sin \varphi\, L = \frac{d_L}{x_L} \quad \text{and} \quad \sin \varphi\, U = \frac{d_U}{x_U} \tag{3.B6}$$

Consider now the set of points included in the winset of X'. These points are inscribed inside two cardioids facing toward C_U and C_L, respectively. Call X'' the intersection of these cardioids and y the segment $X'X''$. Finally, call ω the angle between x and y.

$$y = 2(r_U + x_U \cos(\varphi_U - \omega)) = 2(r_L + x_L \cos(\varphi_L + \omega)) \tag{3.B7}$$

And in combination with (3.B5) and (3.B6)

$$\sin \omega = \frac{r_L - r_U}{d_L + d_U} \tag{3.B8}$$

$$y = 2r_U + 2x \cos \omega + 2d_U \sin \omega < y' \tag{3.B9}$$

where $\quad y' = 2r_U + 2x + \dfrac{2d_U(r_L - r_U)}{d_L + d_U}$

Consequently, the point on X''', on the other side of X on the XX' segment and distance $(y' - x)$ from X, is defeated by X'. So the uncovered set of a bicameral legislature is included in the cone around the line that connects the yolks and at distance

$$y' - x = \frac{4(r_U d_L + d_U r_L)}{d_L + d_U} \tag{3.B10}$$

Note that for $d_L = 0$ the bounds of the uncovered set of the lower house are generated, and for $d_U = 0$ the bounds of the uncovered set of the upper house are produced. Proposition 3.1 follows from this analysis.

4

A model of intercameral bargaining

In the preceding chapter we argued that bicameralism stresses one dimension of conflict, the line connecting the centers of the yolks of each chamber. Here we take this finding for granted. We assume conflict along one dimension, either because there is only one policy dimension or because, on the basis of the previous argument, the two chambers are negotiating along line *UL* of Figure 3.6. This dimension represents the redistributive, or political, dimension of bicameralism described in Chapter 1.

In the following account we present complete and incomplete information models of bargaining. *Complete information* is the technical term indicating that the *two players know each other's payoffs*, while *incomplete information* indicates that *some characteristic of one player is unknown to the other player*.

Consider the lower house and the upper house as unified players and their ideal positions *L* and *U* on a particular bill. Along line segment *LU*, each house prefers a point that is closer to its own ideal point. Rubinstein (1982, 1985) developed the first bargaining model where two players divide an object between them – in this case, a dollar. One can think of the dollar as a unit segment with each player bargaining for the largest part. Our spatial representation of bargaining in legislatures is similar to the Rubinstein model;[1] one difference is that, in the dollar model, each player is interested in obtaining the biggest possible part, while in our spatial representation, each player wants the smallest part.[2] For reasons of

---

[1]More precisely our representation is isomorphic; that is, there is a correspondence between the two models, so that one can solve any problem on one model and then transpose the solution to the equivalent solution of the other in a unique way.

[2]There is, however, one major difference between the bargaining games of "divide the dollar" and "agree on a bill." Although both games assume the initial position of each player is known, the "divide the dollar" game is safe in assuming that each player's initial position is to want the whole dollar, while in our game there is room for strategic misrepresentation of (initial) preferences. For example, if the upper house

A model of intercameral bargaining

mathematical convenience we will adopt the Rubinstein representation, where each player is interested in maximizing his or her share of the dollar.

Rubinstein produced one complete and one incomplete information model of bargaining. Following his steps, a series of formal models of bargaining with incomplete information have been developed. In our complete information model we follow the Rubinstein model and calculate the effects of various procedures on legislative outcomes, such as the maximum number of readings, which house has the first or the last word, and so on; in our incomplete information account we adopt a similar model developed by Grossman and Perry (1986a, 1986b), which is closer to the problem at hand than the original Rubinstein model.

1. BARGAINING WITH COMPLETE INFORMATION

In our representation L and U negotiate to split the dollar, but instead of the infinite rounds of the Rubinstein model, we apply the institutional constraints created by the constitutions of different countries (Tables 2.2A and 2.2B). The game is driven by impatience; both players prefer an agreement today over an agreement tomorrow. Their impatience is expressed by their time discount factors, d_L for the lower house and d_U for the upper house, both in the [0,1] interval. The time discount factors d_L and d_U are the respective values of a dollar in the next time period of negotiations if agreement is not reached immediately. A *time period* refers to *each time one of the houses reads a bill;* a *round* refers to *each time the bill is reintroduced into the same house.* Consequently, each round is composed of two time periods.

Impatience for agreement can be generated by a series of factors, by the sheer passage of time or by pressures of public opinion. Citizens dislike seeing their institutional representatives, the legislators, in disagreement. Legislatures are elected for the purpose of legislating and are often perceived by the public as inefficient when unable to produce legislation on a timely basis. The idea that time is an important aspect of the discount factor is also visible in those rules governing the legislative process that define the maximum delay of legislation by the upper house. There is, however, another more important reason for impatience: each round without an agreement pushes a bill one step further toward possible abortion or may swing some votes in one or the other house, so that the compromise tomorrow may be worse, from one house's point of view, than an agreement today.[3]

wants a smaller (but positive) deficit than the lower house, it could start the bargaining process by claiming that it wants no deficit at all.

[3]See Chapter 7 for a more detailed account of the logic underlying this concept of

99

Models of bicameral institutions

In order to solve the bargaining problem, we start from the final position and work backward. Assume that the lower house has the final word, as is true for many legislatures. Also assume the legislature has reached the last round and it is the upper house's turn to make a proposal. If the proposal is not accepted, in the next time period, the lower house makes the final decision. In this case, U knows that if its proposal is rejected by L, L will keep the whole (discounted) dollar in the next time period. So L is ensured of d_L. Therefore, it will not accept any proposal that would offer less in this time period. Knowing this, U can keep $(1 - d_L)$ and leave d_L for L. Similar reasoning can be applied for L in the preceding period and would lead to a different split of the dollar. The algorithm can be applied as many times as necessary until the final outcome is reached.

This model permits us to draw several conclusions. First, agreement is always reached in the first round; public disagreement is avoided. Since U knows that L finally prevails, it concedes what L would have obtained in any case and keeps the rest. The appendix to this chapter provides the different divisions of the dollar if the process lasts one, two, three, or an infinite number of rounds. However, if one of the players is patient, if, for him, the passage of time or the existence of public disagreement is positive instead of negative, then disagreements will occur. The model can be extended to values of d_L or d_U greater than one. The player with a discount factor greater than one will always reject the opponent's offers and will make unacceptable offers. Therefore, if the number of negotiating rounds is finite, the players will always exhaust the rounds until the final decision rules come into play; if the number of rounds is infinite, there will be no legislation. Discount factors greater than one and, consequently, strong public disagreements between the upper house and the lower house may occur when the two chambers are controlled by opposing sides of the political spectrum. We will see such cases when we analyze events of the Mitterrand presidency in Chapter 7.

The second general observation is that the more impatient a player is, the less his or her share of the dollar. Impatience is an indication of impotence: you are willing to give up a lot in order to reach an agreement sooner rather than later. The third general observation is that it makes a difference whether there is an explicit stopping rule or the bargaining process continues forever. Comparing U's share under different constraints on the number of negotiating rounds leads to the following conclusion (see the appendix to this chapter):

---

legislative impatience. Certainly, most observers of legislative behavior would agree that unless the status quo is preferred to change, legislators attempt to seal the new legislative deal as quickly as possible.

A model of intercameral bargaining

Proposition 4.1: *When the lower house has the final word, the power of the upper house increases with the number of negotiating rounds.*

Consider now the case where disagreements are resolved in a conference committee. This institutional structure cannot be explicitly studied by the model in this chapter.[4] However, we can assume that the outcome of this procedure is known. For example, suppose that the conference committee will split the difference in half – since it is frequently composed of an equal number of members from each house – or any other default solution. If the default solution is different than the outcome without stopping rules, then the house that has the advantage in the default solution will lose power as the number of negotiating rounds increases.

Proposition 4.2: *If the default solution is a conference committee, the most powerful house loses power as the number of negotiating rounds increases.*[5]

The fourth general observation is that it makes a difference where a bill is introduced first. As the appendix to this chapter indicates,

Proposition 4.3: *If there is an integer number of possible negotiating rounds, the house where the bill is introduced first has an advantage. This advantage is independent of the stopping rule and increases with the number of rounds.*[6]

For example, suppose that the lower house and the upper house are going to split their differences in half after a certain number of rounds ($x_0 = 1/2$) and that they have the same time discount factor d. If the split occurs after one round, the house where the bill is introduced first will receive $(1 - d)^2$ more than the other. If the split occurs after two rounds, the house where the bill is introduced first will receive $(1 - d)^2 (1 + d^2)$ more than the other. If there is no stopping rule, the first mover will receive $(1 - d)^2/(1 - d^2)$, or $(1 - d)/(1 + d)$, more than the other. This example is an extreme simplification, because we assume that the players are identical with the exception of move sequence. Proposition 4.3 (equation 4.A14) permits many more comparisons, in particular the comparison between the share of one player if he or she moves first with the share

---

[4]For this problem see the next chapter.
[5]The most powerful house in the conference committee is defined relative to the power distribution without the conference committee.
[6]If the number of rounds is not an integer, that is, if one house introduces the bill and the other applies the stopping rule, the advantage depends on the time discount factors of both houses.

101

of the same player if he or she moves second, keeping the number of rounds and the default alternative constant.

2. BARGAINING WITH INCOMPLETE INFORMATION

The analysis here replicates the results of an incomplete information bargaining model developed by Grossman and Perry (1986a, 1986b). According to this model, two impatient players with time discount factor d are bargaining over the price of an object (one sells and the other buys). Although the buyer knows the announced price of the object, the seller does not know the buyer's willingness to buy. In fact, the buyer can be "strong" (have a low valuation price for object p_L) or "weak" (have a high valuation price for object p_H), or, with equal probability, the buyer can have any other valuation price in the $[p_L, p_H]$ interval (a uniform distribution). The two players alternate in making offers to each other until one of them accepts the offer made by the other, in which case the game stops and they exchange the object at the agreed price.

This model can be adapted easily to the political situation existing in the negotiations between two chambers because, according to the rules of the navette, the two houses take turns making proposals to each other about the content of a bill, and whenever they agree on the content, they stop the negotiation. One can consider the case where both players know the ideal point of the upper house but the lower house's ideal point is known only by the lower house itself, while the upper house has a probabilistic assessment: a uniform distribution between p_{LH} and p_{LL}. If L's ideal point is close to U, L has high valuation price p_{LH}, or L is "weak." If L's ideal point is far away from U, L has low valuation price p_{LL}, or L is "strong." In any intermediate case, it will have some p_L in the $[p_{LL}, p_{LH}]$ interval. Here we investigate only the infinite-round case.

The intuition underlying this representation is straightforward. The distance between ideal points reveals the degree of compromise required to strike a deal (controlling for the time discount factor). A lower house whose ideal point is far from the upper house's ideal point will be less willing to compromise than a lower house that is closer, because, holding discount factors constant, it will have to move further to conclude negotiations successfully.

First, Grossman and Perry demonstrate a series of properties of *any Bayesian perfect equilibrium*.[7] Here we present a short verbal account of

---

[7]A Bayesian perfect equilibrium is an equilibrium where both players play equilibrium strategies in every subgame and update their beliefs along the equilibrium path using Bayes's rule. This equilibrium concept generates an infinity of equilibria, all of which have the properties described in the text. Grossman and Perry use an additional

A model of intercameral bargaining

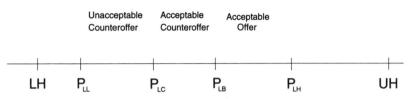

Figure 4.1. Bargaining with incomplete information between upper and lower chambers

the intuition underlying their model.[8] Instead of using their example (buyer and seller), we use the upper house and the lower house as players. As Figure 4.1 indicates, there are two points p_{LB} and p_{LC} that divide the interval in three parts. These points may be distinct or coincide with each other or with the ends of the interval $[p_{LL}, p_{LH}]$; in the latter two cases some of the three parts will be empty. (1) If L has an ideal point in the $[p_{LB}, p_{LH}]$ interval, it will make an acceptable offer to the upper house; if L's ideal point is not in this interval, it will make an unacceptable offer. (2) If U receives an unacceptable offer, it updates its beliefs about L; it understands that L's ideal point is in the $[p_{LL}, p_{LB}]$ interval. U makes an offer that would be accepted by any L with ideal point in the $[p_{LC}, p_{LB}]$ interval. (3) If the offer is rejected, U realizes that L's ideal point is in the $[p_{LL}, p_{LC}]$ interval and updates its beliefs accordingly. If the game has more than one round, then the process repeats itself with U having increasingly accurate beliefs about L. That is, if L has an ideal point in the $[p_{LL}, p_{LC}]$ interval and U has this knowledge, the negotiating process will last one round less than if U knew that p_L was in the $[p_{LL}, p_{LH}]$ interval.

Alternatively, we can employ Rubinstein's approach to incomplete information and consider the lower house's time discount factor to be unknown by the upper house. The lower house could be patient (have a high discount factor, in which case we would call it strong) or impatient (have a low discount factor, in which case we would call it weak) or have any value between the two extremes. The results of this approach and the Grossman and Perry model are comparable regardless of whether the houses have incomplete information on initial preferences (ideal points) or on levels of impatience (time discount factors).

Grossman and Perry's model does not produce closed formulas for the calculation of equilibria, so they use computer simulations to investigate the properties of the equilibria of the bargaining process. Their simula-

criterion to define a perfect sequential equilibrium. For further information the technically inclined reader should consult Proposition 3.1 in Grossman and Perry (1986b), which provides the basis for the next paragraph.

[8]See Proposition 3.1 in Grossman and Perry (1986b).

tions lead to a series of statements, two of which we will single out and label *conjectures*.[9]

Conjecture 4.1: *The level of uncertainty has a positive effect on the length of bargaining.*

Conjecture 4.2: *As the time discount factor increases, there are more periods of bargaining.*

3. CONCLUSIONS

The combination of the two models (complete and incomplete information) provides two conclusions, which differ sharply from points made in some of the existing empirical literature.

Conclusion 4.1 (combination of Propositions 4.1, 4.2, and 4.3): *The relative power of each house in bicameral legislatures is a function of institutional constraints (number of possible iterations, stopping rules, who initiates the process) and the impatience of each legislature to reach a deal.*

Conclusion 4.2 (combination of Conjectures 4.1 and 4.2): *The number of actual negotiating rounds in bicameral legislatures increases with the uncertainty of one house about the other house's willingness to compromise and with the time discount factor of each house.*

This model enables us to make point predictions about outcomes of bicameral bargaining. Its advantage is that it can incorporate institutional variations and offer comparative statics predictions for small changes in procedure, like changing the number of rounds from two to three or introducing a bill in one house as opposed to the other. It differs from the models of the preceding chapter in terms of its single dimension and its sensitivity to additional parameters, such as time discount factors. The restriction of unidimensionality is a minor problem because we have already demonstrated that bicameralism reduces conflict to one predominant dimension, so the single dimensionality assumption is quite realistic. The sensitivity to a series of parameters is common to all noncooperative game-theoretic models of legislatures, because a small change in institutional details affects the game tree and therefore the strategy spaces of the players. Therefore, we expect that the results will be different as well. From a comparative politics standpoint this sensitivity is felicitous be-

[9]This label is given because the statements are not proven formally, but are observations generated by their simulations. Both conjectures are cited from p. 146 of the article.

cause it enables us to examine institutional variations and their effects on the outcomes of bicameral negotiations.

There is one point that remains unexplored. In the bargaining model, we assumed that if the stopping rule provides for a conference committee, both players know where a conference committee will strike a compromise. After this chapter's appendix, we will turn to this privileged method of inducing intercameral compromises and study the results it produces.

Bargaining with complete information

In all the models, the players make offers to each other in each time period sequentially. The game ends either when an offer is accepted or when a specified number of rounds is reached without agreement (in this case a prespecified default division applies). In all the models that follow, the counting is done backwards: the last period will be named 0; the period before the last, 1; and so on. Two time periods constitute a round.

Assumptions: The players are "impatient"; that is, they have time discount factors d_L and d_U in the [0, 1] interval. The remaining assumptions regard the number of rounds and the default solution; these are presented at the beginning of each game.

1. Bill introduced in L; one round of bargaining; then, L decides.

Since L has the final word, it can wait for two time periods and get the whole dollar (discounted by d_L^2). However, the whole dollar at time 0 is equivalent (from L's point of view) to d_L at time 1. Therefore, if U makes an offer at time 1 it can keep $(1 - d_L)$ and offer d_L to L. Similar reasoning indicates that $(1 - d_L)$ at time 1 is equivalent (from U's point of view) to $d_U(1 - d_L)$ at time 2. Therefore, L can make an offer that gives to U the share $d_U(1 - d_L)$ and keeps $1 - d_U(1 - d_L)$ for itself. This equilibrium is the unique subgame perfect equilibrium of the game; therefore, it is perfect.[10] Table 4.A1 summarizes the argument.

The equilibrium strategies are the following:

L: First time period, make offer $1 - d_U(1 - d_L)$; second time period, accept any offer $\geq d_L$; third time period, keep the whole dollar.

U: First time period, accept any offer $\geq d_U(1 - d_L)$; second time period, make offer $1 - d_L$; third time period, accept any ≥ 0 offer.

The outcome is the division indicated in time period 2 of Table 4.A1. From now on we will present the tables without verbal statement of the arguments.

2. Periods of bargaining: $2n$; default solution x_0 (for L and $1 - x_0$ for the upper house).

a. The bill is introduced in L first. At the end of time period 0, in the absence of agreement, L receives x_0. Table 4.A2 indicates that at the end

[10]See Selten (1975).

Appendix 4.A

Table 4.A1

Time period	Player L	Player U
0 L offers	1	0
1 U offers	d_L	$1 - d_L$
2 L offers	$1 - d_U(1 - d_L)$	$d_U(1 - d_L)$

Table 4.A2

Time period	Player L	Player U
0 L offers	x_0	$1 - x_0$
1 U offers	$x_0 d_L$	$1 - x_0 d_L$
2 L offers	$1 - d_U(1 - x_0 d_L)$	$d_U(1 - x_0 d_L)$

of time period 2, it will receive $x_{2,L} = 1 - d_U(1 - x_0 d_L)$. Note that the outcome is indexed by both the number of time periods and where the bill is introduced first.

Replication of the same reasoning for one more round (two time periods) gives

$x_{4,L} = 1 - d_U(1 - x_{2,L} d_L)$; generally, $x_{2n,L} = 1 - d_U(1 - x_{2n-2,L} d_L)$.

Expressing $x_{2n,L}$ in terms of x_0 gives

$$x_{2n,L} = \frac{(1 - d_U)(1 - (d_U d_L)^n)}{1 - d_U d_L} + x_0(d_U d_L)^n \tag{4.A1}$$

b. The bill is introduced in U first. Similar calculations produce

$$x_{2n,U} = \frac{d_L(1 - d_U)(1 - (d_U d_L)^n)}{1 - d_U d_L} + x_0(d_U d_L)^n \tag{4.A2}$$

3. Infinite number of rounds.

a. Bill introduced in L. Taking the limit of Equation (4.A1) when $n \to \infty$ produces

$$x_{\infty,L} = \frac{1 - d_U}{1 - d_L d_U} \tag{4.A3}$$

b. Bill introduced in U. Taking the limit of Equation (4.A2) when $n \to \infty$ produces

$$x_{\infty,U} = \frac{d_L(1 - d_U)}{1 - d_L d_U} \tag{4.A4}$$

107

Models of bicameral institutions

Comparison of (4.A3) and (4.A4) indicates that L gets less if it moves second.

4. Proof of monotonicity of the share of L with the number of rounds (Propositions 4.1 and 4.2). Proposition 4.1 is a special case of Proposition 4.2 when the default solution is $x_0 = 1$ (for the lower house). Therefore, it is sufficient to prove Proposition 4.2.

   a. Decreasing sequence; bill introduced in L. Suppose that L's share if there is no agreement is

$$x_0 > \frac{1 - d_U}{1 - d_L d_U} \tag{4.A5}$$

We will show that

$$x_{n,L} > x_{n+2,L} > \frac{1 - d_U}{1 - d_L d_U} \tag{4.A6}$$

The proof is by induction; the proposition holds for $n = 0$. From Section 2 of this appendix, we have

$$x_{2,L} = 1 - d_U(1 - x_0 d_L) \tag{4.A7}$$

If $x_0 \leq x_{2,L}$ then, from Equation (4.A7) we conclude that (4.A5) is false; therefore,

$$x_{2,L} < x_0 \tag{4.A8}$$

If

$$x_{2,L} \leq \frac{1 - d_U}{1 - d_L d_U}$$

substitution in (4.A7) and simplification lead to the conclusion that Equation (4.A5) is false; therefore,

$$x_{2,L} > \frac{1 - d_U}{1 - d_L d_U} \tag{4.A9}$$

Combining (4.A8) and (4.A9) we get

$$x_0 > x_{2,L} > \frac{1 - d_U}{1 - d_L d_U}$$

We need to show that if (4.A6) is true for $2n$, it is also true for $2n + 2$. Assume that

$$x_{2n-2,L} > x_{2n,L} > \frac{1 - d_U}{1 - d_L d_U} \tag{4.A10}$$

From Section 2 of this appendix, we have

108

$$x_{2n+2,L} = 1 - d_U(1 - x_{2n,L}d_L) \tag{4.A11}$$

If $x_{2n,L} \leq x_{2n+2,L}$, then (4.A10) is false; therefore,

$$x_{2n,L} > x_{2n+2,L} \tag{4.A12}$$

If

$$x_{2n+2,L} \leq \frac{1 - d_U}{1 - d_L d_U}$$

substitution in (4.A11) and simplification lead to the conclusion that (4.A10) is false; therefore,

$$x_{2n+2,L} > \frac{1 - d_U}{1 - d_L d_U} \tag{4.A13}$$

Equation (4.A6) is the combination of (4.A12) and (4.A13).

Reversing inequalities we can prove the proposition for the increasing sequence: if U has the first reading, the proof can be replicated after multiplying all inequalities by the positive d_L.

b. Increasing sequence; bill introduced in L.

If

$$x_0 \leq \frac{1 - d_U}{1 - d_L d_U}$$

then

$$x_{2n,L} \leq x_{2n+2,L} \leq \frac{1 - d_U}{1 - d_L d_U}$$

The proof replicates the steps of the preceding part (a) (replacing $>$ by $\leq$).

c and d. Bill introduced in U. The proof can be replicated after multiplying all inequalities by the positive d_L.

5. Proof of first-house advantage (Proposition 4.3). Taking differences between Equations (4.A1) and (4.A2) we get

$$x_{2n,L} - x_{2n,U} = \frac{(1 - d_L)(1 - d_U)(1 - (d_U d_L)^n)}{1 - d_U d_L} \tag{4.A14}$$

The right-hand side of (4.A14) is always positive. This difference is independent of the stopping rule (x_0) and increases with the number of rounds. Its maximum is

$$\frac{(1 - d_L)(1 - d_U)}{1 - d_L d_U}$$

which is the advantage of the first reader in case of an infinite number of rounds (no stopping rule).

5

A model of conference committees and their proposals

As we discussed in Chapter 2, conference committees are frequently employed to reconcile intercameral differences. Conference committees are important because, in most cases, they are the last stage where legislative compromises are worked out and legislation is forged. The outcome of conference committee deliberations is then introduced to the parent chambers for approval under closed rule, that is, without possibility of amendment. Consequently, a strategic conference committee can select, from among all the proposals that the parent chambers prefer over the status quo, the one that is closest to its own preferences. The parent chambers may dislike one provision or another of the compromise bill, but they cannot alter the specifics; they can only reject the whole bill and start the legislative process again. Consequently, if a bicameral legislature resolves its differences through a conference committee, the compromise elaborated in this committee usually becomes the law.

In all countries where the institution exists, except for the United States, the committee is composed of an equal number of members from each chamber, and it decides as a unicameral institution. In the U.S., the size of the conference committee varies as does the number of delegates from each house. Decisions are made by the so-called unit rule, that is, by concurrent majorities of each chamber's delegation. In countries where committees decide as unicameral institutions, the decision-making rule is by majority, with the exception of Japan, which requires qualified majorities.

To analyze the U.S. conference committee, we refer the reader to Chapter 3, since the unit decision-making rule is the same as bicameral decisions. However, before proceeding, we point out one aspect of the unit rule that we will refer to subsequently. As we demonstrated in Chapter 3, bicameral legislatures have a larger uncovered set than unicameral ones. The same holds true for conference committees. Committees deciding by the unit rule (bicameral committees) have a larger set from which they select the compromise solution and, consequently, have more leeway than committees deciding by majority rule (unicameral committees).

In this chapter, we focus on conference committees with a unicameral structure and examine the problem facing a conference committee composed of strategic legislators with a majority decision-making rule. Unfortunately, knowledge about conference committee decision making is limited. Committee deliberations are often secret.[1] Furthermore, conference committee rules, if they exist, are very informal and flexible, facilitating compromises among the legislators. However, some aspects of conference committee decision making are explicitly addressed in the relevant literature. In some of the countries, political parties or their committee representatives are in control of the process, as in Germany. In other countries where parties are weak, the committee members know each other from previous meetings of other conference committees and enter a long-term interaction, as in the United States (Longley and Oleszek 1989). We interpret this information to mean that conference committees decisions are cooperative; that is, they entail decision making with enforceable agreements. In this case, exactly as in Chapter 3, we can apply concepts from cooperative game theory (the uncovered set and tournament equilibrium set). The first section of this chapter locates the uncovered set of the conference committee itself, based on conference committee membership. The second section analyzes the logic of strategic conference committee deliberations. Conference committees attempt to locate their proposals within parameters acceptable to the parent chambers while remaining as close to the committee's preferences as possible. The reader will see that the conference committee selects a proposal from the set of feasible outcomes that is closest to its own "policy preferences." This finding will be discussed in the conclusions.

1. PREFERENCES OF CONFERENCE COMMITTEES

Consider for a moment a conference committee that faces no constraints from the parent chambers, a case where any compromise negotiated by the conference committee is automatically ratified by the parent chambers. Where would its legislation be located? Obviously, it would be a point in space that defeats the status quo according to the appropriate decision-making rule. However, this restriction is not very significant because, unless the status quo is centrally located within the committee, the winset of the status quo is quite large.

The cooperative decision-making assumption leads us to the uncovered set and the tournament equilibrium set of the committee itself. Here

---

[1]See Chapter 8 for further details and citations.

we have restricted the outcome significantly because, if the committee decides by majority rule, the outcome will be located within the uncovered bound sphere, that is, a sphere whose center is the center of the yolk and whose radius is four times the radius of the yolk. In fact, if the conference committee decides as a whole by mixing the votes of the two delegations, the outcome of deliberations will still be located within the same sphere or will be the status quo itself (as qualified majorities become more demanding, it is possible that nothing defeats the status quo). If the conference committee decides by the unit rule (as in the United States or in the European Union), the outcome will be located within the uncovered set calculated in Chapter 3 and depicted in Figure 3.6.

In all cases, the conference committee would prefer to promote a compromise centrally located within the preferences of its members. If the committee members faithfully reflect the preferences of the parent chambers, even unconstrained conference committees will produce legislation similar to outcomes achieved in their absence. If conference committee members have preferences that are outliers vis-à-vis the parent chambers, the suggested compromise may be quite different. Understanding the conference committee decision-making process, the parent chambers may decide to shape the outcome by appropriate selection of conferees. They may include certain members who will skew the majority one way or another. Or they may include "experts" that disproportionally influence their colleagues on one particular dimension. In Switzerland, for example, standing committee members become conference committee members, but because the Senate standing committee is smaller than its counterpart in the lower house, additional delegates are added when a conference committee is called. Selection of these delegates is a political decision that ultimately affects the conference committee compromise.

Parent chambers limit the discretion of conference committees in other ways as well. They may issue directions or constraints or declare certain outcomes to be "unacceptable." In both Switzerland and France, the jurisdiction of the conference committee is limited to those aspects of the legislation where disagreement remains; issues already resolved by the parent chambers remain closed, even though reopening the issues may facilitate compromise on other dimensions. In the U.S., it is common for each chamber to give "instructions" to its conference committee delegation, although the instructions are not binding. Conference negotiations may be interrupted so the delegations can receive additional instructions from their parent chamber.

Ultimately, however, conference committee compromises are subject to parent chamber approval. And in a presidential system, like the U.S., conference committees also have to consider constraints imposed by the president, if they want legislation to be enacted into law and if the legisla-

A model of conference committees

ture does not have the necessary majorities to override a presidential veto. We call the set of restrictions imposed on conference committees by the parent chambers, and when applicable, the president, *bicameral restrictions*. In the next section, we study the outcomes of conference committee deliberations when there are bicameral restrictions.

2. PROPOSALS OF STRATEGIC CONFERENCE COMMITTEES

Even if there are no explicit restrictions from the parent chambers, the conferees still must make a proposal acceptable to both chambers, that is, a proposal contained within the intersection of the winsets of the status quo of each chamber (and the president when applicable). Consequently, conference committees face a set of constraints that vary significantly. The minimal constraint is provided by the intersection of the winsets of the status quo in each chamber; that space can be further restricted by additional rules and instructions.

In the remainder of this section we employ the uncovered set solution concept for reasons similar to those outlined in Chapter 3 (we remind the reader that the tournament equilibrium set is a subset of the uncovered set). If the parent chambers have imposed bicameral restrictions (BR), the problem for a sophisticated conference committee is to consider only the points within BR and to find the most appropriate point. If the uncovered set and tournament equilibrium point are the appropriate solution concepts, then we label the area within which the conference committee must offer a solution the *induced on bicameral restrictions* (IBR) uncovered set.

The real question for a conference committee is to locate its IBR uncovered set; in other words, the committee must locate the restricted uncovered set from the available set of points and make a proposal in this area. In the appendix to this chapter we define the terminology in a precise way and calculate where the IBR uncovered set of the conference committee lies in an *n*-dimensional Euclidean space. The uncovered set is located at the intersection of bicameral restrictions and a sphere concentric to the yolk of the conference committee.

The logic of the calculations is similar to that in Chapter 3. From the set of points defined by bicameral restrictions, consider point C', which is the point closest to the center of the yolk of the committee, with d being the distance between C' and the center of the yolk. From Chapter 3, we know that all points located at a distance of $d + 2r$ from the center of the yolk can be defeated by C' by majority vote of the committee. However, the only viable solutions are within the bicameral restrictions because any other proposal will be defeated by the parent chambers. Therefore, the area of points defeated by C' can be enlarged considerably (in the appendix to this chapter we show how). We repeat the calculation once more and we find the points that can be defeated by the points that can be defeated by C' (points that can be indirectly defeated by C). All these points are excluded from the induced uncovered set of the committee.

The appendix to this chapter produces two different conservative estimates of the radius x^{**} of a sphere that contains the IBR uncovered set, in the case where bicameral restrictions are on one side of the yolk of the conference committee. If BR intersect with the yolk of the committee or if they surround it, the committee's uncovered set is a good approximation of the induced uncovered set.

Proposition 5.1: *Under the assumptions of cooperative decision making and Euclidean preferences, a conference committee deciding by majority rule will make a proposal in the intersection of BR and a circle (C, x^{**}), where C is the center of its yolk and x is calculated by (5.A5').*[2]

Corollary 5.1: *Under the assumptions of cooperative decision making and Euclidean preferences, a conference committee deciding by qualified majority rule will make a proposal in a subset of the area defined in Proposition 5.1.*

This is because any proposal by qualified majority requires a majority of committee members and some additional members.

Corollary 5.2: *Under the assumptions of cooperative decision making and Euclidean preferences, if bicameral restrictions include the yolk of the conference committee, the committee deciding by majority rule will make a proposal in an area included in a circle centered at the center of the committee's yolk with radius 4r (where r is the radius of the yolk).*

The proof is straightforward from (5.A5'') if we consider $d = 0$.

Three figures will make these points clearer. Figure 5.1A presents the location of the conference committee report when the two chambers insist on a linear combination of the bills reported out of the two houses. According to Proposition 5.1 the proposal will be located around the projection of the center of the yolk on the BR line. Consequently, this projection of the center of the yolk of the conference committee is a good approximation of the location of the committee report.

Figure 5.1B presents a different (and unlikely) stylized story, where the committee is composed by preference outliers. In the figure, BR are defined by the indifference curves of one member of the upper house and one of the lower house, U and L, respectively. Since the majority of

[2]See the appendix to this chapter.

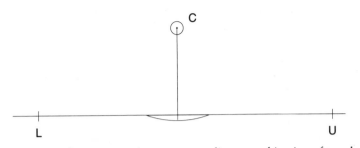

Figure 5.1A. Conference committee report on linear combination of two house bills

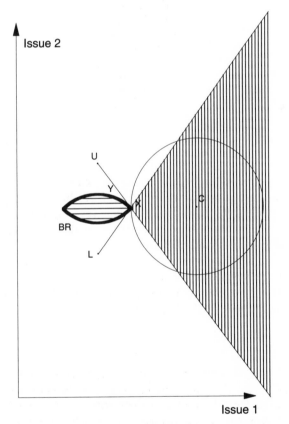

Figure 5.1B. Location of proposal of outlier committee

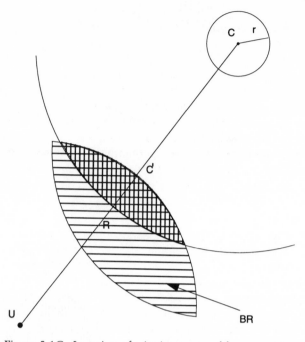

Figure 5.1C. Location of winning proposal by committee

committee members are located inside the shaded area, far away from *BR*, the committee proposal will be at point *X*, the intersection of two of the indifference curves generating *BR*. It is easy to demonstrate that, in this case, point *X* is the only point of the uncovered set, and consequently the committee would make this unique proposal *X*.

Finally, Figure 5.1C presents the most frequent story, where the bicameral restrictions permit leeway for the committee, and the committee is not composed of extremists. In this case, the induced uncovered set of the committee is the best prediction for the outcome.

CONCLUSIONS

The formal analysis allows us to draw several conclusions. In a multidimensional space, the policy preferences of conference committees can be approximated by the center of their yolk. Because decision making inside the committees is cooperative (agreements are enforceable), the uncovered set of *the conference committee itself* is likely to be the outcome of the committee decision-making process and, therefore, of the final bill. If bicameral constraints are very effective, the committee bill will be located around the projection of the center of the committee's yolk on the privileged dimension of bicameral conflict *UL*.

Conference committees have extraordinary powers, stemming from the fact that generally their proposal cannot be amended.[3] Consequently, the location of the final outcome depends on two factors: the bicameral restrictions and the committee yolk (center and radius). The bicameral restrictions are a function of how much the parent chambers decide to rein in the committee. However, when *BR* are weak, the committee features (yolk) increase in significance. The committee yolk is a function of the *composition* of the conference committee, whether the delegation of each chamber is a faithful agent of the parent chamber *or* whether the set of conference committee members is a faithful representative of the bicameral legislature.[4]

This analysis concludes Part II of the book, models of bicameral legislatures. In the next part, we test the propositions generated here, and we will compare our expectations with analyses presented in Chapter 1. It is therefore important at this point to remind the reader of our findings.

In the introduction to Part II and in Chapter 3 we came to two conclusions. Bicameralism preserves the status quo (Proposition II.1) and selects one predominant dimension of conflict and compromise (Proposition 3.1). Whether it is the core that is unidimensional or the uncovered set that is cylindrically symmetric, the line that connects the centers of the yolks of the two chambers is the line on which the major compromises must be struck. A fortunate consequence of this point is that one-dimensional models are quite appropriate for the study of bicameral legislatures.

In Chapter 4 we employed a one-dimensional bargaining model to produce a series of predictions concerning the effects of different institutions for the resolution of intercameral differences. In particular, we demonstrated that where power is distributed asymmetrically, the power of the least-powerful house increases with the number of negotiating rounds (Propositions 4.1 and 4.2) and that there is a first-reading advantage (Proposition 4.3). Our incomplete information models produced the expectation that the actual number of negotiating rounds will increase with the level of uncertainty (Conjecture 4.1) and with the time discount factor of both houses (Conjecture 4.2).

---

[3]In fact, the procedure that most fully constrains the conference committee is the rule of the U.S. Congress that permits the first chamber that reads the bill to recommit it to committee; in other words, recommitting the bill to committee permits an entirely new compromise to be negotiated.

[4]In fact the second condition is much more general than the first, because it is possible that the delegation of each chamber is extreme with respect to the chamber, but the direction of their deviations cancel each other out.

Finally, in the Chapter 5 we returned to cooperative game theory to examine conference committee proposals and we discovered that, under cooperative decision making, such a committee will make a proposal inside the set of bicameral restrictions, and in the area that is closest to the center of its yolk (Proposition 5.1). As a result, we concluded that the composition of the conference committee, its decision-making rule, and the set of bicameral restrictions are critically important to the results of bicameral bargaining.

Location of the induced (on bicameral restrictions) uncovered set

Definitions 3.B1–3.B4 from Appendix B of Chapter 3.

Definition 5.A1 (Induced [on BR] uncovered set): IUC = $\{x/x \in$ BR and $\forall y \in BR$, not $yCx\}$ (read: the induced (on BR) uncovered set is the set of points in BR not covered by any point in BR).

Consider BR and the yolk of conference committee with center C (Figure 5.A1). Call C' the point of BR closest to the center of the yolk. Call r the radius of the yolk and d the distance of the center of the yolk from BR. Call R the radius of BR at C' (R is the radius of the indifference surface of some member of the bicameral legislature; call her U).

We know that this winset of C' is included inside a cardioid which is given in polar coordinates by the equation $2(r + d \cos \vartheta)$ (Ferejohn et al. 1984). Call x the distance of the center of the yolk from the point Y of the cardioid at angle ϑ from C'.

The distance x is given by the formula

$$x^2 = d^2 + 4r^2 + 4dr \cos \vartheta \qquad (5.A1)$$

Proof: Line x is the third side of a triangle with sides d, $2(r + d \cos \vartheta)$ and angle ϑ in between. Applying the Pythagorean theorem to the triangle CYY' we get $CY^2 = CY'^2 + YY'^2$, which, after substitutions and simplifications, reduces to Equation (5.A1).

Note from Equation (5.A1) that x is a decreasing function of ϑ since $\cos \vartheta$ is a decreasing function of ϑ. Consequently, if instead of examining the sphere that includes the whole winset of X we are concerned with a sphere including some part of it, it is possible that ϑ has a lower bound ϑ^* that would produce a smaller sphere surrounding the part of $W(C')$ in which we are interested. The radius of this sphere would be

$$x^{*2} = d^2 + 4r^2 + 4dr \cos \vartheta^* \qquad (5.A2)$$

Consider now the outer cardioid associated with point C' (call it first-generation cardioid) and its intersection with BR. Call ϑ^* the angle of the cardioid. The winset of C' for the conference committee is included in the

119

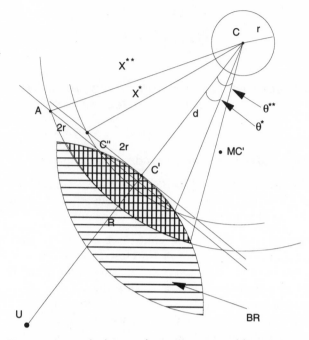

Figure 5.A1. Calculation of winning proposal by committee

intersection of two spheres: one with center *MP* and radius *R* (which is the relevant part of *BR*) and one with center *C* and radius x^* (given from (5.A2)). Call C'' the point where the two spheres intersect in Figure 5.A1. Repeating the same enterprise with the outer cardioid of point C'' produces another angle ϑ^{**} and associated radius x^{**}. The induced uncovered set is included in the intersection of the spheres (U, R) and (C, x^{**}).

The cardioid of point C' (first-generation cardioid) intersects with the sphere (U, R) for $\vartheta^* > \pi/2$. Consequently, the intersection of the cardioid and the sphere (U,R) is included inside the sphere (C, x^*) where

$$x^{*2} = d^2 + 4r^2 \tag{5.A3}$$

In order to find a sphere that includes the second-generation cardioids, it is sufficient to calculate a sphere that includes the cardioid of point C''. Indeed any other point of the intersection of the two spheres (U,R) and (C, x^*) produces either a smaller distance from C' or a bigger angle ϑ^{**}, which according to Equation (5.A2) produces a smaller radius x^{**}.

As Figure 5.A1 indicates, point *A*, which is in distance $2x^* \cos \vartheta^{**} + 2r$ from C'', is not included in the sphere (U,R); consequently, distance

120

Appendix 5.A

x^{**} is a conservative estimate of the radius of a sphere that includes the induced (by the winset of the status quo) uncovered set.

Angle ϑ^{**} can be calculated indirectly, since angle $C''CC' = (\pi/2 - \vartheta^{**})$ and the sides of the triangle are known to be R, $R + d$, and x^*. Consequently,

$$\cos\left(\frac{\pi}{2} - \vartheta^{**}\right) = \frac{d^2 + 2r^2 + Rd}{(R + d)\sqrt{d^2 + 4r^2}} \tag{5.A4}$$

or

$$\cos\vartheta^{**} = \frac{2r\sqrt{R^2 + Rd - r^2}}{(R + d)\sqrt{d^2 + 4r^2}} \tag{5.A4'}$$

Now the distance x^{**} can be calculated as the third side of a triangle for which the other sides are x^*, and $2x^* \cos \vartheta^{**} + 2r$ and the angle in between ϑ^{**}.

From Equation (5A2) we get

$$x^{**2} = x^{*2} + 4r^2 + 4x^*r \cos \vartheta^* \tag{5.A5}$$

or

$$x^{**2} = d^2 + 8r^2 + \frac{8r^2\sqrt{R^2 + Rd - r^2}}{R + d} \tag{5.A5'}$$

And since $\sqrt{R^2 + Rd - r^2} < \sqrt{(R + d)^2 - r^2} < R + d$

$$x^{**} < \sqrt{d^2 + 16r^2} \tag{5.A5''}$$

Empirical studies of bicameralism and implications

Introduction to Part III

In the next four chapters we empirically investigate the predictions developed in Part II and compare our findings with alternative theories of bicameralism outlined in Chapter 1. In Chapters 6 and 7, we draw on data from the French Fifth Republic. The prominent position of France is attributable to the complexity of its institutions: the two houses may be equal or, upon decision of the government, unequal; the deliberation may involve a conference committee or not; the navette may conclude after a single round or last indefinitely. With the exception of the United States and the European Union,[1] no other country or institution has bicameral procedures that vary so extensively. Thus, France presents an opportunity to test various dimensions of our models and to evaluate institutional features of the bicameral systems described in Chapter 2 within a single country, so that we can hold a variety of conditions constant.

Chapter 8 relies more heavily on data from other countries in order to capture the variations in conference committee composition, decision-making rules, and constraints imposed by the parent chambers – the characteristics of conference committees that are important independent variables in our theoretical models. The tests presented here are far from exhaustive. We strongly believe our models should undergo additional evaluation employing data from a wide variety of countries. Nonetheless, the evidence presented here helps to establish the plausibility of the models developed in Part II.

In Part III, we employ both statistical analysis and case studies to

[1]For references on the U.S. literature, see, among others, Fenno (1982), Ferejohn (1975), Gladieux and Wolanin (1976), Ippolito (1981), Kanter (1972), Krehbiel (1987), Longley and Oleszek (1989), Manley (1970), Shepsle and Weingast (1984, 1987a, 1987b), Steiner (1951), Strom and Rundquist (1976, 1977), and Vogler (1970, 1971). This list is not exhaustive of the literature on the U.S. House of Representatives and the Senate; it includes citations treating the bicameral nature of the U.S. Congress. With respect to the European Union, see Tsebelis (1994, 1995b) and references therein.

evaluate our theoretical arguments. Undoubtedly, it would be helpful to extend statistical analyses further than we have done in this book. But our use of case studies is not based on the lack of machine-readable data alone. Because we examine the impact of deliberations involving two distinct chambers, our primary material is, as it should be, legislative outcomes. There is no other way to test theories about legislative outcomes than to examine closely the legislative product, the laws themselves and the history of their passage through the legislature.

There is another important reason to use case studies. Frequently, research literature takes the form of a theory and an aggregate empirical test that corroborates the theory; very little attention is paid to whether the mechanisms that actually produce the aggregate outcomes are the ones posited by the theory. In this book we combine aggregate empirical tests with an alternative approach, an analysis of the legislative process. We believe that testing empirically the micromechanisms that produce the aggregate outcomes, that is, testing empirically the assumptions of the theory, is an additional step of empirical research that ultimately increases confidence in the theory.

Finally, Chapter 9 presents the implications of our analysis for the study of bicameral legislatures. On the basis of our empirical analyses we evaluate the various arguments presented in the relevant literature. We qualify some of the arguments, revise some others, and provide new directions for research on bicameral legislatures.

6

The outcomes of intercameral bargaining

This chapter is designed to test the model developed in Chapter 4. Consequently, we retain the assumption that bicameral negotiations are driven by impatience to reach agreement. We operationalize impatience in terms of the strength and breadth of the governing political coalition. The reader should suspend judgment about the adequacy of our choice until the following chapter, where we take time to examine the impatience assumption critically.

The complete information model developed in Chapter 4 connects different institutional features of the navette system with outcomes. The incomplete information model of Chapter 4 predicts that under conditions of one-sided incomplete information, the number of negotiating rounds in bicameral legislatures increases with one house's uncertainty about the other house's impatience (time discount factor). In more common political terminology, relations between the chambers should be more acrimonious under conditions of uncertainty; it will take longer for the two houses to reach agreement.

We test these predictions with data from the French legislature under the Fifth Republic. France represents a natural test of the model of one-sided incomplete information because the composition of the Senate remained relatively constant while the composition of the National Assembly varied widely – from a Gaullist to a Socialist majority, by way of a centrist–Gaullist coalition. We argue first that the composition of the National Assembly affects the impatience of that legislative body to reach agreement. We argue second that the changing composition of the National Assembly introduces uncertainty about the impatience of the legislative body in a nonlinear fashion. When impatience of the National Assembly is high or low, the uncertainty about this impatience is low; in between, uncertainty rises, and following from the model, the length of the navette rises. The evidence presented supports our conclusions regarding the length of the navette process. In addition, the predictions of the complete information model provide an alternative interpretation of recent French legislative history.

In the first section, the contours of the French bicameral system are described in some detail. We then outline our empirical referents for the concepts of "discount factor" and "uncertainty" and develop specific hypotheses to be tested. Because we examine the French case in detail, we make an effort to pitch our hypotheses against alternative explanations developed by French legislative analysts. Our model should be able to hold up against both general explanations and explanations specific to France. In Section 3, we compare the results of our model with alternative explanations of bicameral negotiations and demonstrate the superiority of our model. In the fourth section, we reinterpret French legislative history in light of our model.

1. THE LEGISLATIVE PROCESS

According to the Constitution of the French Fifth Republic, a bill becomes law if it is voted in identical terms by both chambers or if the National Assembly, upon the request of the government, makes the final decision. The process by which the two houses review and approve new legislation is complex.[1] Article 34 proclaims, "The law is voted by Parliament," and until the last stage of the decision-making process, legislative responsibilities of the National Assembly and the Senate are almost identical. Bills can be proposed either by the executive (projects) or by the legislators themselves (propositions). Whereas members of Parliament introduce bills in their respective houses, government bills, with the exception of the annual budget,[2] can be introduced in either house. Bills passed by the originating house are then forwarded to the second house for review, a process labeled *navette* (shuttle). If the second house amends the legislation, it returns to the first house for repassage. Discussion is limited to those articles of legislation remaining in dispute;[3] if disagreement con-

---

[1] See Maus (1987) for the constitutional provisions and Bourdon (1978: 109–45), among others, for a detailed description of the process.

[2] The budget is always introduced first in the lower house. The budgetary powers of both the National Assembly and the Senate are curtailed by the executive branch of government. The National Assembly has a mere 40 days to review financial legislation; the government can then refer the budget to the Senate, which has an additional 15 days to respond. In case of disagreement, procedures for normal legislation are followed with the proviso that Parliament has a maximum of 70 days from the initial deposit of the bill to reach agreement. After 70 days, the government can enact the budget by ordinance (see Article 47 of the constitution; Luchaire and Conac 1987: 914).

[3] According to internal National Assembly and Senate regulations Article 108, paragraph 3, and Article 42, paragraph 10, respectively (Luchaire and Conac 1987: 871).

tinues, the navette is prolonged indefinitely unless the government chooses to intervene.

After the legislation has been reviewed twice by each chamber (or after a single reading if the government determines that the legislation is "urgent"), the government can intervene in the navette. By intervening, the government calls into play a conference committee (*commission mixte paritaire*), composed of an equal number of senators and representatives.[4] The conference committee deliberates on only those articles in dispute and attempts to draft legislation acceptable to both houses. If a compromise is reached, the new version is resubmitted to both houses for approval.[5] Amendments, at this point, require the approval of the government.[6] If a compromise cannot be negotiated or if either house rejects the conference committee version, the government can ask the National Assembly to vote in last resort (Article 45.4 of the constitution).

The government can introduce amendments reinstating its preferred version of the text and can limit parliamentary amendments by calling for a vote under closed rule (*vote bloqué*) at any point in time.[7] The government can even apply Article 49.3, according to which a bill is transformed into a question of confidence and is adopted by the National Assembly unless the government is voted down through a censure motion.

After a bill is voted by Parliament (whether by both houses or by the National Assembly alone) and before it is implemented, it can be challenged before the Constitutional Council. The challenge can originate from the President of the Republic, the prime minister, the president of one of the houses of Parliament, or, since 1974, from 60 members of Parliament. The provision for the 60-member parliamentary challenge was introduced by the Giscard government, and its impact was underestimated at the time (it was called a *reformette,* or "little reform"). However, since it provides any major party the possibility of challenging legislation, the reform has been responsible for a substantial increase in power of the Constitutional Council since 1974 and a spectacular rise in prominence since 1981 (Stone 1992).

Figure 6.1 illustrates the various stages of the French legislative pro-

---

[4]In practice, the Senate selects its own representatives through proportional representation, while the National Assembly is represented by its own majority. After the victory of the Left in 1981, the National Assembly regulations were modified to resemble those of the Senate (Grangé 1984).

[5]The government, if displeased with the conference committee compromise, is not required to submit the joint text to Parliament for final approval. After fifteen days, the house that last read the bill can restart the legislative process (Bourdon 1978: 125).

[6]According to Article 45, paragraph 3, of the constitution (Luchaire and Conac 1987).

[7]Article 44, paragraph 3, of the constitution (Luchaire and Conac 1987).

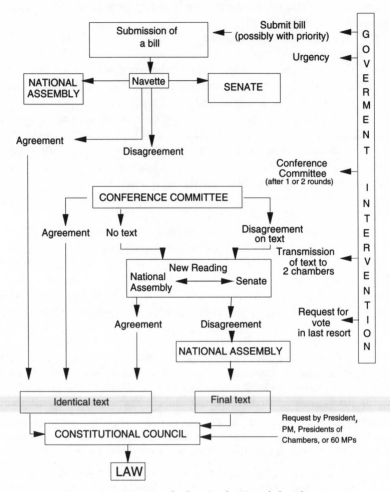

Figure 6.1. Passage of a law in the French legislature

cess. The main body of the figure represents the interaction between the two houses, while intervention by the government and Constitutional Council is indicated at appropriate points.

The formal process of bicameral interaction indicates that the French navette system is composed of several different games. One is a bargaining game between the two houses; a second is the intervention of the government, which chooses the rules and/or permits the National Assembly to ultimately decide; and a third involves the possible intervention of the Constitutional Council. John Huber (1992; 1996) has examined the

The outcomes of intercameral bargaining

second game in detail; Alec Stone (1992) deals with the third; we focus on the first, the game between the two legislative houses.

2. EMPIRICAL PREDICTIONS

Table 6.1 presents the number of laws enacted by the French Parliament each year between 1959 and 1985, divided into three categories: laws that were adopted in the first two rounds of the navette system; laws that were adopted after convening a conference committee of the two houses; and laws that were adopted by the National Assembly alone (Article 45.4 of the French constitution).[8] The table also presents the number of government bills introduced first in the National Assembly. Finally, the table presents data relevant to the composition of the National Assembly (Gaullist allies,[9] Left opposition, and total number of seats).

According to Conclusion 4.2, the length of negotiations increases with uncertainty of one chamber about the time discount factor of the other. In order to operationalize this proposition, we first have to find empirical referents for time discount factors, that is, the legislative houses' level of impatience to see legislation passed. We operationalize *time discount factors*[10] of the two houses *as a function of their composition.*[11] *A large and cohesive ruling majority exhibits high levels of patience (high dis-*

---

[8]It would have been desirable to have data concerning bills which were not voted into laws broken down into similar subgroups (bills aborted before, during, or after the joint committee). Unfortunately such data are costly to collect.

[9]The major part of these allies belong to the party of Valéry Giscard d'Estaing. In 1958 he was a young but prominent leader of the Centre National des Indépendants et Paysans (CNIP). In subsequent elections Giscard became the leader of the Independent Republicans (RI), who were allied with the Gaullists. In 1978 the Independent Republicans merged with other center-right parties and formed the Union for French Democracy (UDF). There were other center-right parties that joined the Gaullist majority over time. The party names change while leadership and political platforms are more stable, so we refer to all the parties that joined the Gaullist majority as *allies*.

[10]Obviously this is a simplification because discount factors are also bill specific. As the last three cases in Chapter 7 indicate, the same National Assembly facing the same Senate may be in a big hurry to adopt one bill and indifferent about another; or one particular project may be very important for the Senate, while another may not be. However, considering discount factors as a function of the composition of the two houses will give us some information about the average interaction between the two houses in the course of the legislative period.

[11]As noted in Chapter 4, an alternative conceptualization of the process involves the preferences of the two houses, the distance between their preferences, and uncertainty over preference structures. In the case of one-sided incomplete information, the preferences of the Senate are considered known, while the preferences of the National Assembly are known only by the National Assembly itself, while the Senate has a probabilistic assessment: a uniform distribution over the range of possible policy preferences.

Table 6.1. *Early agreement in the navette system and composition of the National Assembly*

Year	Agreement before joint committee	Agreement in joint committee (2-3 rds.)	Decision by National Assembly	Bills in National Assembly	Allies	Opposition[a]	Total seats
1959	51	1	0	41	181	57	579
1960	84	2	3	65	181	57	579
1961	98	4	1	61	181	57	579
1962	50	1	1	30	35	107	482
1963	85	6	5	72	35	107	482
1964	107	5	6	72	35	107	482
1965	63	5	7	55	35	107	482
1966	129	9	5	119	35	107	482
1967	68	8	4	49	42	194	486
1968	58	7	5	53	61	91	487
1969	70	8	0	67	94[b]	91	487
1970	79	16	2	70	94	91	487
1971	94	17	4	85	94	91	487
1972	115	9	7	81	94	91	487
1973	60	6	4	41	85	175	490
1974	57	13	0	41	85	175	490
1975	121	28	0	78	85	175	490
1976	86	23	1	58	85	175	490
1977	134	32	0	90	85	175	490
1978	60	29	1	43	123	199	491
1979	64	13	2	57	123	199	491
1980	71	14	2	54	123	199	491
1981	40	6	10	51	50	150	491
1982	68	12	32	86	50	150	491
1983	81	13	26	65	6[c]	150	491
1984	78	16	27	74	6	150	491
1985	63	15	45	90	6	150	491

[a]Between 1959 and 1980 the Left political parties were in opposition; in 1981 the conservative parties moved into opposition in the National Assembly.
[b]The centrist party joined the coalition when Pompidou was elected president in 1969.
[c]The Communist Party left the coalition in 1983.
Sources: The data concerning the navette system (columns 2, 3, 4 and 5) from 1959 to 1980 are from Grangé (1981); the data concerning composition of the National Assembly and parties participating in majority from 1959 to 1980 are from Colliard (1978); all data from 1981 to 1985 are from Maus (1987).

count factor), whereas internal divisions as well as external opposition raise the level of impatience (low discount factor). For example, the Gaullist party captured a large majority in the 1968 National Assembly elections, 293 of 487 seats, or 60 percent. Defections by its coalition partner, the Independent Republicans, would not undermine its ability to rule. Even unruly backbenchers within its own ranks represented little threat that the Left, with only 91 seats, would come to power. We describe this coalition as patient. In contrast, the coalition elected in 1978 was much less cohesive. The Gaullist strength was reduced to 154 seats (31 percent) while its centrist coalition partner captured 123 of the seats (25 percent). Moreover, the Left began to represent a real threat to the Gaullists' ability to govern, with 199 seats in the National Assembly. The governing coalition in this legislature was more impatient to produce legislative outcomes.

Let us turn now to uncertainty about time discount factors. Under the Fifth Republic, the Senate's composition has remained relatively constant over time. The majority of senators represent the center-right parties that are ideologically close to the different incarnations of the Giscardian party. In contrast, political representation in the National Assembly varies considerably over time. The Gaullist party (under different names) grew from having 35 percent of the seats in 1958 to having 60 percent in the landslide victory that followed May 1968; its allies (under different names) were numerous and heterogeneous in 1959 (31.5 percent) and became more homogeneous over time, while their strength increased from 7 percent in 1962 to 25 percent in 1978. The Left (Socialist–Communist coalition) expanded from 8 percent of the seats in 1958 to 40.5 percent in 1978. In 1981, the Socialist François Mitterrand was elected president and the subsequent election provided a Socialist majority in the National Assembly. At this point in time, the Senate became the core of the political opposition that preferred to oppose legislation. For purposes of testing the model, we divide the data set into two periods, the 1959–80 period of conservative domination and the 1981–85 Socialist period.

Since the Senate has essentially constant composition over time, we can assume its discount factor is common knowledge. In contrast, we hypothesize that *uncertainty* about the National Assembly's discount factor *varies according to its composition. When the strength of the allies is either high or low, uncertainty about the discount factor is low; when the allies have an intermediate level of strength, uncertainty about the National Assembly's discount factor will be high.*[12]

---

[12]An alternative and, in our opinion, less convincing hypothesis would be that intermediate levels of strength would not increase uncertainty about the National

When the percentage of allies is high, the National Assembly will be known to be impatient (low discount factor). The idea is that the Gaullists will cater to their allies when they are an important part of the government majority. Conversely, when the majority in the National Assembly is known to be cohesive, that is, when the allies are weak, the Senate knows that any further delay will not produce significant results. So, high (low) percentages of allies in the National Assembly indicate that the National Assembly is impatient (patient) and that their level of patience (discount factor) is readily understood by the Senate. Intermediate levels of strength of the allies make the Senate unable to assess exactly the discount factor of the National Assembly. The Senate believes that the National Assembly's discount factor may be high or low or anywhere in between.[13]

Our model predicts that when uncertainty about the National Assembly's discount factor is high, the length of the navette will increase; as uncertainty decreases, the navette concludes more quickly. Therefore, when the majority in the National Assembly is cohesive (weak allies), the Senate knows that the National Assembly is strong; consequently it will compromise in the negotiating process. When the majority is noncohesive in the National Assembly (strong allies), the Senate knows that the (Gaullist) National Assembly is impatient to reach an agreement, and it will not settle without substantial concessions. In both cases, the navette should be short. In between, uncertainty about the National Assembly's discount factor increases; according to our model, the length of the negotiating process increases. Consequently, when the allies are strong or weak (ceteris paribus), there will be fewer iterations; when they are at some intermediate level of strength (to be specified empirically) it is not known whether they are strong or weak and the number of iterations increases. This interpretation leads to a *quadratic specification* of the actual number of negotiating rounds (low when the National Assembly is

Assembly's discount factor but produce an intermediate discount factor. Although we find the reasoning developed in the text more convincing, we test this hypothesis too. It produces expectations identical with the "linear composition models."

[13]For this period of French legislative history, the negotiation process between the two houses may also be understood as negotiations between parties of the majority. Given that the majority in the National Assembly is mainly Gaullist, while the majority in the Senate is composed of allies, it can be argued that the two houses are surrogates for the negotiations between the two partners of the right-wing majority. This point of our analysis is similar to Huber's (1996) findings. For example, as described in Case 4, Chapter 7, Prime Minister Chirac introduced legislation regulating radio and television in an extraordinary session of Parliament in July 1974. The final bill was passed by both houses in ten days. The government wanted to pass the bill quickly, so it accepted the compromise even though it was unhappy with some of the senatorial amendments.

known to be strong or weak and high when the National Assembly is in between). We will call this the *quadratic composition* model. In algebraic terms

$$\text{pagree} = C - c(\text{allies}) + d(\text{allies})^2 + e \qquad (6.1)$$

where *pagree* is the percentage of bills adopted prior to a joint committee (indicating a short navette),[14] *allies* is the percentage of allied seats, *c* and *d* are *positive* coefficients, and *e* is an error term.[15]

Similar arguments can be made about the strength of the Left. When the Left is strong or when the Left is weak, agreement will be reached faster (for different reasons) than when the Left has intermediate strength. This argument leads to the following model:

$$\text{pagree} = C' - a(\text{Left}) + b(\text{Left})^2 + e \qquad (6.2)$$

where Left is the percentage of Left seats, *a* and *b* are positive coefficients, and *e* is an error term.

Estimation of Equations (6.1) and (6.2) produces the correct signs for *a*, *b*, *c*, and *d*, but only Equation (6.1) produces statistically significant coefficients.[16] The estimated coefficients can be used to calculate the strengths of the Left and the allies that generate the maximum uncertainty about the National Assembly's discount factor.[17] Such calculations indicate that the maximum uncertainty occurs when the allies control around 20 percent of the seats, while the corresponding percentage for the Left has never been reached in the period we examine.[18] On the basis

[14]In other words, the Senate and the National Assembly agree on the legislation after one or two rounds of the navette, making government intervention and further negotiations unnecessary. We resort to this indicator because the data on French legislation do not indicate the number of rounds of the navette. Rather they indicate whether agreement was reached fast (in one or two rounds), whether the legislation was referred to a joint committee (two or three rounds), and ultimately whether the joint committee failed to reach an agreement and the government asked the National Assembly to make the final decision. While these distinctions do not replicate the actual number of rounds in the navette, they are an indicator of the length of the process ranging from few to many rounds. See Table 6.1 for actual data.

[15]The dependent variable in all the subsequent models is not dichotomous, but continuous (frequency of early agreement). The results reported subsequently are calculated by OLS. However, logit models produced similar findings.

[16]In a previous draft we considered only the MPs of the Giscardian party as "allies" and found all four coefficients with the correct sign and statistically significant. However, we consider that because of the ideological similarities of the other allies with the Giscardians (a similarity that led them to merge under the umbrella of the UDF in 1978), we should include all parties that enter into government coalitions with the Gaullists as "allies."

[17]The minimum of a quadratic function $y = ax^2 - bx + c$ is at the point $x = b/2a$.

[18]Depending on the estimated model, this percentage is 67 percent (calculated from the estimated coefficients of Equation (6.3)) or 44 percent (calculated from the esti-

of these observations we combine Equations (6.1) and (6.2) into the following equation, which we refer to as the *quadratic composition with Left* model. Since the Left is always in the declining part of the quadratic, we use a linear specification:

$$\text{pagree} = C - a(\text{Left}) - c(\text{allies}) + d(\text{allies})^2 + e \qquad (6.3)$$

where a, c, and d are positive coefficients.

Equation (6.3) makes two simplifying assumptions. First, it assumes that the Senate fails to learn from its negotiating experience with the National Assembly throughout the life of the legislature, that it is no more able to discern the National Assembly's impatience toward the end of the five-year legislature than at the beginning. However, if the time discount factor of the National Assembly comes from the same distribution, it is possible for the Senate to use information from previous iterations in order to make more accurate predictions of the National Assembly's strength; in this case, the use of the joint committee should decline over time inside each legislative period. This is called the *learning hypothesis*.

Equation (6.3) also assumes that the discount factor of the National Assembly is uniform during each legislative period. A more realistic approach would assume that the discount factor of the National Assembly may not come from the same distribution. It may change with the life cycle of the National Assembly. A newly elected National Assembly may be stronger (it is less impatient or has a higher discount factor) than one that is about to be reelected (for a more detailed discussion, see Chapter 7). If this is correct, joint committee referrals will be highest in the middle of the legislature's life. Consequently, the frequency of agreement will reach its minimum in the middle of the life of the legislature. Note that the argument is similar in nature to the quadratic composition hypothesis and is congruent with our bargaining model. We call this the *cycling hypothesis*.

In order to test the learning and cycling hypotheses, one additional variable is introduced: age of the legislature. This variable has the value 0 in an election year and a maximum value of 4 (since elections occur normally every five years). Two additional equations are estimated:

$$\text{pagree} = C - a(\text{Left}) - c(\text{allies}) + d(\text{allies})^2 + f(\text{year}) + e \qquad (6.4)$$

$$\text{pagree} = C - a(\text{Left}) - c(\text{allies}) + d(\text{allies})^2 - f(\text{year}) + g(\text{year})^2 + e \qquad (6.5)$$

where all variables are as in Equation (6.3), year is the age of the National Assembly, and f and g positive coefficients.

---

mated coefficients when (6.2) and (6.3) are merged into the same equation) or 52 percent when one includes time in the equation (see below). The maximum strength of the Left during the examined period was 40.5 percent in 1978.

The outcomes of intercameral bargaining

Equations (6.1) through (6.5) represent various hypotheses originating in the model of bicameral bargaining developed in Chapter 4. However, attributing the relations between the legislative houses to the strength and breadth of the ruling coalition is not original. French legislative analysts have also hypothesized about such a relationship. However, they differ on the nature of that relationship.

Grangé (1984: 970) argues that, in general, a weak majority in the National Assembly is more intransigent in its negotiations with the Senate, because the government cannot afford to lose the fragile compromise obtained in the National Assembly. When the ruling coalition is fractionated and its margin of victory narrow, it will tend to ignore senatorial input, decreasing the speed and likelihood of agreement. His rationale suggests a positive linear correlation between size and cohesion of majority in the National Assembly and speed of agreement (see also Marichy 1969: 431). Consequently, the stronger the Left and the allies in the National Assembly, the more iterations will be needed to make a decision.

In contrast, Georgel (1968: 102) argues that when the National Assembly majority is large, ministers are no longer preoccupied with the opposition and refuse to negotiate. The working hypothesis here suggests a negative linear relationship between size and cohesion of the majority in the National Assembly and speed of agreement (see also Mastias 1980: 49). We label these models the *linear composition model*. In algebraic terms, the model is defined as follows:

$$\text{pagree} = C + a(\text{Left}) + c(\text{allies}) + e \tag{6.6}$$

where a and c are coefficients that are *both* positive or *both* negative (depending on the hypothesis), C is the intercept, and e is an error term.

3. EMPIRICAL RESULTS

To summarize, we test six distinct models, five of which represent variations of our hypotheses and a sixth that tests hypotheses developed in the French literature. In the first model, the length of the navette process is attributed to uncertainty about the strength of the majority in the National Assembly, where uncertainty is highest at intermediate levels of strength of the Gaullist allies. The second model tests the same hypothesis for the Left opposition. The third model combines the first two models and the fourth and fifth add learning and electoral cycles to the equation. The sixth model tests the proposition that the strength of the Gaullist allies and the Left opposition affect the length of the navette process in a linear fashion.

Table 6.2 demonstrates the goodness of fit of the competing hypothe-

Table 6.2. *Estimation of frequency of early agreement (without use of joint committee): 1959–80*

	(1) Quadratic composition (allies)	(2) Quadratic composition (Left)	(3) Quadratic composition (+ Left)	(4) Quadratic composition (+ Left + learn)	(5) Quadratic composition (+ Left + cycles)	(6) Linear composition
Constant	1.05*** (17.6)	1.01*** (12.81)	1.08*** (21.59)	1.08*** (20.45)	1.08*** (19.48)	1.00*** (24.0)
Left		-.79 (-1.17)	-.35*** (-3.16)	-.36*** (-3.04)	-.36*** (-2.94)	-.49*** (-4.60)
Left²		.58 (.46)				
Allies	-2.69*** (-3.77)		-1.67** (-2.48)	-1.63** (-2.32)	-1.62** (-2.25)	-.09 (-.66)
Allies²	7.33*** (3.88)		4.35** (2.39)	4.24** (2.28)	4.24** (2.16)	
Year				-.002 (-.301)	-.003 (-.14)	
Year²					.003 (.05)	
R^2	.44	.52	.64	.64	.64	.53
Prob>F	.004	.0009	.0003	.001	.003	.0008

Coefficients indicated *** are significant at the .01 level or higher; coefficients indicated ** are significant at the .05 level or higher; coefficients indicated * are significant at the .10 level or higher in two-sided tests; t-statistics in parentheses.

ses. Model (1) introduces quadratic specification and finds that the coefficients reflect the predicted sign and are highly significant (at the .01 level). Model (2), which replicates the same hypothesis for the Left, does not do well in terms of significance. The quadratic specification produces the correct sign of coefficients, but Left and Left² are collinear ($r = .99$), so the significance of both coefficients declines. Model (3) provides a better fit than all previous models. All three coefficients have the predicted sign and are highly significant. Comparison of the cycling and the learning models with the quadratic composition model indicates that the coefficients of the composition variables remain virtually the same,[19] and the coefficients of the legislature's life are statistically insignificant. The R^2 of Models (4) and (5) does not improve. Finally the linear composition model (Model 6), derived from French legislative analyses, finds that the size of the Left decreases the probability of an early agreement; however, the size of the allies does not affect the probability of early agreement. This partially supports the Grangé hypothesis and undermines Georgel's argument.

Closer examination of the frequency distribution of cases of prolonged bargaining (use of the joint committee) indicates that the year 1978 is an outlier. The annual average use of joint committees is 11.5 percent, while its value in 1978 reached 32.2 percent; the next highest value is 20.9 percent.[20] Consequently, a good statistical argument can be made for the elimination of 1978 from the data set. However, a substantive explanation for the peculiarity of 1978 must be provided. The number of important political bills introduced in 1978 was very high.[21] The quantity of politically important laws in 1978 was affected by the parliamentary elections scheduled that year. Giscard had postponed significant pieces of the conservative legislative agenda fearing a political backlash that would strengthen the Left and increase political support for the common electoral program signed by the Socialists and Communists in 1972 (Lange, Ross, and Vannicelli 1982: 39 and 57). The March elections defused the leftist threat and positioned the allies more favorably within the conservative coalition. Giscard seized the opportunity created by friendly majorities in both houses to promote the program described in his book *Démocratie française*.[22] If one assumes that the discount factors of both houses increase when an important bill is introduced,[23] that is, neither is

[19]Since the correlation between the age of the National Assembly and its composition is zero, the estimated coefficients of Equation (6.2) are unbiased even if one assumes that the fully specified model is (6.3) or (6.4).

[20]Without 1978 data the mean is 10.5 percent, the standard deviation, 6.3. It can be calculated that the point 32.2 percent lies 3.44 standard deviations away from the mean, and, therefore – assuming a normal distribution, with a probability of more than 95 percent – 1978 lies outside the area where at least 99 percent of the points of the distribution are (see Walpole and Myers 1985: 223, on tolerance intervals).

[21]In 1978 the Parliament voted the annual budget and two additional financial laws; two laws modifying the penal procedure and penalties; one law reorganizing radio and television; one law regulating the relations between citizens and the bureaucracy; one law on financial reorganization of local government; laws on unemployment, employment of youth, businesses; laws concerning savings and investment; one law on rents; laws on ocean pollution; etc. (Jean Grangé, personal communication).

[22]Jean Mastias, personal communication.

[23]This is only one possible assumption. One could argue that discount factors decline with the importance of bills, because the two houses are under stronger pres-

Table 6.3. *Estimation of frequency of early agreement (without use of joint committee): 1959–80, excluding 1978*

	(1) Quadratic composition (allies)	(2) Quadratic composition (Left)	(3) Quadratic composition (+ Left)	(4) Quadratic composition (+ Left + learn)	(5) Quadratic composition (+ Left + cycles)	(6) Linear composition
Constant	1.04*** (25.36)	1.05*** (16.14)	1.05*** (29.05)	1.06*** (29.67)	1.08*** (31.67)	.96*** (25.6)
Left		-1.14** (-2.05)	-.22** (-2.58)	-.24** (-2.92)	-.24*** (-3.08)	-.39*** (-4.08)
Left²		1.43 (1.36)				
Allies	-2.43*** (-5.01)		-1.83*** (-3.81)	-1.71*** (-3.62)	-1.73*** (-3.92)	-.0006 (-.0005)
Allies²	6.90*** (5.38)		5.11*** (3.88)	4.80*** (3.73)	5.01*** (4.15)	
Year				-.008 (-1.48)	-.04** (-2.22)	
Year²					.008* (1.84)	
R^2	.62	.54	.73	.76	.81	.49
Prob>F	.0001	.0009	.0000	.0001	.0001	.002

Coefficients indicated *** are significant at the .01 level or higher; coefficients indicated ** are significant at the .05 level or higher; coefficients indicated * are significant at the .10 level or higher in two-sided tests; t-statistics in parentheses.

willing to give in easily to the demands of the other, then Conclusion 4.2 indicates that the number of negotiation rounds will increase. We claim that the high number of politically significant bills is a plausible explanation for the high frequency of joint committee use in 1978.[24]

Table 6.3 tests the same models without 1978 data. The omission of 1978 improved the fit of all models except for the linear composition

sure. However, we defend our assumption not only because it is reasonable ("good" results for each house are more important than expedience), but also because it is congruent with experiences in other countries. For example, in the U.S., the joint committee is used more frequently for important bills (Krehbiel 1990).

[24] A strict test would require the introduction of one additional variable (percentage of politically important bills) to our model.

model. With respect to the quadratic composition model with Left, both the R^2 and the t-statistics have improved significantly: now most coefficients are significant at the .01 level. The improvement of fit of the other two models is more impressive. Now, the learning hypothesis can be safely rejected, since the coefficient has the opposite sign (significant at the .16 level). The cycling hypothesis is corroborated; the R^2 rises to .81 and all coefficients have the correct sign and are significant. It is only the comparison with a more complete theory that demonstrates the inadequacies of the linear model. Moreover, once 1978 is eliminated, the fit of the linear model and the significance of the coefficients decline.

The model provides different expectations for the 1981–85 period. During these years the Left dominated the National Assembly, while the composition of the Senate remained the same. The Senate preferred the status quo ante over many projects introduced by the government. In other words, the Senate was infinitely patient. Under these circumstances our model predicts a high number of disagreements. For the 1981–85 period our model generates the same predictions as the existing literature. Empirically, we find that the use of Article 45.4 (request to the National Assembly to make the final decision) was higher than ever before. It increased from 2.8 percent on average in the 1959–80 period to 26.2 percent in the 1981–85 period (Tardan 1988: 100).

4. INTERPRETATIONS OF FRENCH LEGISLATIVE HISTORY

Indirect support for our model can be gleaned from French legislative history. If we are correct in Conclusion 4.1 that the relative power of each house in bicameral legislatures is a function of institutional constraints (number of possible iterations, stopping rules, and where the legislative process is initiated), these institutional tools should be used as political weapons.

France is usually described as a semipresidential system. However, as the relationship between the president, the cabinet, and the legislature has been elaborated since 1958, it is more correct to understand the system as a parliamentary one, except in the area of foreign policy, where the president retains substantive control (Tsebelis 1995a). Although the president nominates the prime minister and the cabinet, the government is responsible to the National Assembly and must retain its confidence.[25] Thus,

---

[25]The president is granted the power to dissolve the National Assembly, but if new elections do not return a politically more sympathetic audience, the government must still retain National Assembly support. New dissolutions are forbidden for at least 12 months. In practice, the National Assembly is rarely dissolved. An example is the dissolution after Mitterrand won the presidency in 1981 (and again in 1988); the

President Mitterrand, after losing his Socialist majority in the National Assembly in 1986 and again in 1993, appointed cabinets that were politically foreign to him but nonetheless retained the confidence of the National Assembly. The government, then, is the cabinet, led by the prime minister, who is supported by a governing coalition in the National Assembly. In France it is the government that decides where to introduce a particular bill, the number of rounds (two or three) the navette will last, as well as whether it will ask the National Assembly to make the final decision.

The government can be expected to employ the institutional tools that control the navette both to shift power between the National Assembly and the Senate and to negotiate with its own coalition in the National Assembly. Evidence indicates a positive correlation (.34) between the bills the government introduces in the National Assembly and the bills where the government applies Article 45.4 (final decision to the National Assembly), both of which reduce the power of the Senate. In the 1959–80 period the actions of the governments appear consistent with their attitudes toward the Senate. De Gaulle was against the Senate, Giscard promoted its role through these institutional tools. In this sense, as suggested by French legislative analysts, the government affects the power of the Senate; our model specifies the means through which the government is able to vary senatorial power, as well as the limits of this manipulation.

Further investigation leads to the conclusion that the stronger the Gaullist Party, the more the government stacked the cards in favor of the National Assembly: the correlation between the percentage of bills introduced in the National Assembly first and the percentage of the Gaullist Party is .52, the correlation with the percentage of allies is −.15, and the correlation with the percentage of the Left is −.59. Similarly, the correlation between the percentage of bills where the National Assembly had the final word and the percentage of the Gaullist Party was .38, the correlation with the percentage of the allies is −.51, and the correlation with the percentage of the Left is −.14. The government appears to use the less significant weapon (introduction of the bill in the National Assembly) more frequently against the Left, and the more important one (final decision by the National Assembly) more often against the allies. These results jibe with Huber's (1996) finding that the government uses important legislative weapons (vote of confidence) to target the government

following elections provided a Socialist parliamentary majority. Subsequent, less favorable National Assembly electoral results in 1986 (and 1993) did not end in dissolution since these results were understood as reflecting the preferences of the French electorate. Thereafter, Mitterrand "cohabited" with a conservative cabinet and conservative majority in the National Assembly.

majority itself rather than the opposition. However, in regressions the statistical significance of the corresponding coefficients is low.

The strategy of the government changed in the 1981–85 period. For example, while the government applied Article 45.4 more frequently than ever before, it also introduced an unusually high number of bills in the Senate first, 32.8 percent. Maus (1988: 122–23) explains this apparent inconsistency by reference to rationalization of legislative work. He claims that the government introduced bills in both houses to speed the legislative process. In fact expediency was an important consideration of the Left in power because, since the Right was blocking the legislative agenda through the Senate and through frequent recourse to the Constitutional Council, the Left had to ask for 17 extraordinary sessions of Parliament.[26]

Existing literature attributes such institutional decisions exclusively to the desire to improve legislative efficiency. For example, Grangé (1984) notes that the use of the conference committee, as well as the declaration of urgency, by the government increases over time. He claims that both measures economize time. However, if time alone were the issue, it is not clear why members of Parliament and governments alike would not want to economize time in the beginning of the period as well as in the end. Our analysis indicates that all these decisions, in addition to their technical dimension,[27] transfer power from the Senate to the National Assembly and are used as political weapons as well.

5. CONCLUSIONS

The navette system is the primary mechanism for resolving disagreement between the two houses in bicameral legislatures. In France, the ability of the two houses to reach accommodation, rather than resort to a definitive vote of the National Assembly, is explained by reference to the strength and breadth of the ruling political coalition. Moreover, French political analysts provide organizational explanations for the use of different institutional provisions. For example, governments choose where to introduce a bill or whether to declare urgency and reduce the number of rounds of the navette to gain time; similarly, parliaments refer bills to conference committees to increase legislative efficiency.

We adopted a different approach. The model developed in Chapter 4

---

[26]The French Parliament cannot sit in normal sessions more than six months a year. The extraordinary sessions cannot last more than two weeks each (Wright 1989).

[27]The technical dimension includes time constraints that lead the government to declare urgency and reduce the number of rounds and excess load of the lower house that leads the government to introduce a bill in the upper house first.

suggests that the relations between the two houses are based on impatience to conclude the bargaining and on the level of uncertainty about this impatience. If the ruling coalition in the National Assembly is either weak or strong, the Senate understands that it can obtain either minimal or maximal concessions and concludes the negotiations quickly. It is only when the Senate is unsure of the National Assembly's level of impatience, when the ruling coalition is neither weak nor strong, that the relations between the chambers are acrimonious. As a result of Conclusion 4.1 we paint a much different picture of French legislative politics than do French political analysts and can explain some puzzling facets of French legislative history, such as the ability of the Gaullist government to reach early agreement with the Senate despite the animosity between de Gaulle and the Senate, as well as the rise in joint committee use under Giscard d'Estaing despite an ideologically compatible Senate. The first case is attributed to the certainty associated with the majority under the Gaullist rule, the second with the uncertainty under the Giscardian centrist–Gaullist coalition. Of course, once the Socialists won a majority in the National Assembly and the opposition controlling the Senate preferred the status quo ante to any new legislation, our predictions coincide with the predictions of French legislative analysts. Our results also stress the political as opposed to the organizational consequences of different institutional arrangements or choices by governments or parliaments.

This quantitative analysis lends support to the model of bicameral negotiations developed in Chapter 4. It performs better than alternative hypotheses developed by French legislative analysts, tested here systematically for the first time. The model is based on the assumption that impatience is driving the legislative process, that the two legislative houses prefer legislation today rather than tomorrow, and that the primary reason for this impatience is the concern with maintaining a governing majority. Hence, we have operationalized impatience in terms of the cohesion of the ruling majority and the strength of the political opposition. Given that the quantitative analysis supports our model, we turn now to examine more closely the assumptions underlying the model by investigating the process of intercameral bargaining.

7

The process of intercameral bargaining

In this chapter we evaluate the assumptions underlying the model of intercameral bargaining developed in Chapter 4. We do so by analyzing six laws passed by the French legislature between 1971 and 1981. In Chapter 4 we argued that impatience to reach agreement drives bicameral bargaining and that impatience is generated by a number of factors: the desire of legislators to be viewed as efficient, the need to resolve fiscal or political crises, and the concern that legislators will defect from the political coalition supporting the bill. Moreover, we concluded that the relative power of each house in bicameral legislatures is a function of institutional constraints and the impatience of each legislature to reach a deal. In this chapter, we examine the assumption that impatience for legislative outcomes (1) drives the negotiating process *and* (2) determines the outcomes of bicameral negotiations in France (within the limits set by institutional constraints). As in Chapter 6, because we focus such attention on a single country, we also address the relevant French legislative analyses on relative house power. One explanation of senatorial power, expertise, is common to many countries, as noted in Chapter 1. The second explanation, presidential politics, is peculiar to France.

We proceed by defining the concept of impatience and our approach to operationalizing that concept. We then briefly present the two alternative models of French legislative behavior against which we pitch our own. In the third section, we evaluate the three competing hypotheses in light of six pieces of legislation. The detailed examination of the bills as they shuttle from one chamber to the other allows us to focus on the *process* of bicameral negotiations.

1. IMPATIENCE

By *impatience* we mean the desire of the governing party or coalition to strike a legislative deal sooner rather than later (everything else being

145

equal). Impatience for agreement can be generated by a series of factors. We distinguish three types of impatience that drive the bargaining game between the Senate and the National Assembly: systemic impatience, bill-specific impatience, and impatience associated with the electoral cycle. Each is defined and justified in turn.

The most general type of impatience, what we label *systemic impatience,* arises from concern with maintaining a governing majority. Each law must be approved by a majority of the legislators, and a certain majority today becomes an uncertain majority tomorrow. The strength of the majority is based on a number of factors, including the level of party discipline. On a cross-national basis, coalitions in systems with greater party discipline, such as the British system, are more patient than in systems with less party discipline, such as the United States. Fewer legislators in Britain cross party lines than in the U.S., making retention of a legislative majority more certain in Britain than in the U.S. However, impatience – when holding party discipline constant, as we do when studying legislative processes in France – varies with the size of coalition partners and the size of the opposition. Where coalition partners are large, defections become more likely, and where opposition parties are large a few defections may prevent the passage of the desired legislation and force the majority coalition to modify its proposal in order to obtain passage.

Why would individual members of the political majority defect from supporting the ruling coalition's ideal position? Most straightforwardly, legislators may change over time, even within a specific legislature. A legislator may be incapacitated at the time of the vote. Or a legislator may die and be replaced through interim elections by a legislator from another party. Or a legislator may change his or her party affiliation. John Major's conservative majority in Britain dwindled from 21 in 1992 to a single vote at the beginning of 1996 through these types of "defections."[1]

More frequently, though, legislators may defect from supporting the majority coalition's ideal position because their preferences are not identical to those of the party leaders. In a multidimensional issue space, although the majority-supported legislative proposal must be centrally located, it is indeterminate. Therefore, when the other legislative chamber proffers via the navette a new proposal that is closer to the legislator's ideal point, the legislator may defect. This type of defection does not represent a change of preferences on the part of the legislator; it represents an alternative law that is closer to the legislator's preferences. Party leaders are concerned that another majority-preferred alternative will be

[1]The California state legislature represents another example where, in 1995 and 1996, recall elections were used as a technique to shift the legislative majority, some of which succeeded, others of which failed.

located that promotes defection from their alternative and prevents passage of the proposed legislation. Therefore, to obtain legislation that depends on support from the members of the majority coalition, the sooner the deal is concluded, the better.

However, governing parties or coalitions are not equally vulnerable to defection. A single governing party with a large majority is less vulnerable and therefore more patient than a governing party with a large coalition partner and a narrow parliamentary majority. Therefore, we operationalize *the level of systemic impatience in terms of the breadth and strength of the current political coalition.* If the dominant party (coalition) has a large majority, defections have little effect on the ultimate passage of legislation; it can afford to be patient. Similarly, if one party dominates the political coalition, defections from coalition members are less threatening. In the opposite case, where the political opposition is strong and the coalition partners large, defections threaten the passage of legislation and the dominant party is impatient to see legislation passed. In other words, internal divisions as well as external opposition raise the level of impatience.

The second type of impatience is *bill specific.* Some bills are more urgent than others. For reasons of fiscal or political expediency, some problems require immediate solutions and therefore immediate legislation. Urgent legislation is not synonymous with important legislation. As discussed in Chapter 6 with regard to the heavy load of important legislation in 1978, important legislation often takes more time rather than less, although some important legislation may be urgent as well.[2] Where one legislative house perceives a more urgent need for legislation than the other house, it will grant more concessions in order to obtain agreement and quick passage of the legislation. *Bill-specific impatience is normally associated with some type of fiscal or political crisis* that, if left unresolved, threatens government stability.

The third type of impatience stems from the *election cycle.* A newly elected National Assembly has a full term in office (five years) before it is held responsible for its actions or lack thereof. A newly elected National Assembly can therefore afford to be patient in pursuing its legislative agenda. In contrast, at the end of the electoral period, members face reelection and desire a positive legislative record to present to their constituencies; they are eager to achieve their legislative program before the

---

[2]One way to think about urgency is to think of the terms of an outstanding $10 loan when your house is burning and you need a quarter from the debtor to call the fire department. In these urgent circumstances, he may force you to accept a quarter (2.5 percent of the principal) as total repayment of the debt. Urgency is thus distinct from importance: in this example, importance increases with the size of the loan. A $10 loan is less important than a $1 million loan.

elections. Thus, the election cycle introduces a third type of impatience that drives the legislative process. This type of impatience is addressed in Chapter 6 but ignored here, given the small number of cases and the lack of variance in terms of the electoral cycle.

A reasonable approximation of the conditions prevailing in the French legislature would be to consider that both systemic and bill-specific impatience vary in the National Assembly but remain constant in the Senate.[3] In the case of systemic impatience, the strength and breadth of the National Assembly varies substantially over time, while the composition of the Senate remains relatively constant (Maus 1987). In the case of bill-specific impatience, the institutional provisions of the French Fifth Republic make the National Assembly more accountable to the electorate than the Senate: under specified circumstances, the National Assembly can be dissolved.[4] The Senate, on the other hand, is never dissolved; senators are elected indirectly and have long (nine-year) terms of office. For the National Assembly, legislation that threatens governmental stability in some fashion is more urgent than other pieces of legislation. The Senate, by constitutional provision, is much less affected by political crisis and public opinion and therefore can be considered to debate each piece of legislation with the same level of patience.

To recapitulate, the model of intercameral negotiations developed in Chapter 4 assumes that impatience drives the bargaining process and that the greater relative impatience of one legislative chamber, the less power it has over the legislative outcome. We define three types of impatience, two of which, systemic and bill-specific impatience, will be evaluated empirically through an analysis of six cases of legislation. We remind the reader that bargaining proceeded under conditions of incomplete information. Had there been complete information, the deal would have been struck and the legislation passed immediately. Of the six cases analyzed here, all took two or more rounds. Because of the small number of cases, we have not been able to control for variation in the institutional rules that shift power between the houses. The outcomes described in the six cases below reflect both the impatience (discount factors) of the legislative chambers and the institutional setting within which the navette takes place. Nonetheless, because strategic actors understand that some institutional rules will be applied uniformly, such as the government's willingness to request a National Assembly decision at least for important government bills, most of the variation seen in our cases can be attributed to variation in the

---

[3]This is not necessarily true of other bicameral legislatures.

[4]See Article 12 of the constitution, which permits the president to dissolve the National Assembly upon appropriate consultations. However, the president's power is limited by the provision that ensures the new National Assembly a minimum one-year life.

levels of impatience. Before proceeding to analyze the legislative process and outcomes, we refer to the contending explanations of French legislative analyses of relative house power.

2. COMPETING HYPOTHESES

Although the National Assembly is constitutionally endowed with the ultimate power of legislation, the Senate was originally expected to support the president of the Republic against a divided National Assembly (Luchaire and Conac 1987: 637). The 1958 Constitution called for senators and the president to be elected indirectly from analogous electoral colleges. The Constituent Assembly anticipated an upper house that was ideologically compatible with the president and that, in alliance with the executive, could veto legislation initiated by the National Assembly. The framers of the new constitution hoped thereby to bypass some of the divisive and fractionated party politics characteristic of both the Third and Fourth Republics and to reinforce the power of the presidency. However, the reality of the Fifth Republic proved much different. The 1962 parliamentary elections provided a Gaullist (near-)majority in the National Assembly, and a referendum that same year transferred the presidential elections from the electoral college to the general public. Given the changed circumstances, French political scientists began to question both the role and effectiveness of the Senate in the legislative process.

To explain continued senatorial influence on legislative outcomes in the context of a majoritarian National Assembly that was granted ultimate power of decision, legislative analysts proposed two alternative hypotheses, which we label (1) the *wisdom and expertise approach* and (2) the *presidential attributes approach*. In much of the literature these two hypotheses are intertwined, but for purposes of comparing the explanatory value of these hypotheses against our own, we analyze them separately.

According to the first line of analysis, senatorial influence can be explained by its expertise, wisdom, and representation of specific interests. This approach can be interpreted in either a broad or a narrow manner. Broadly speaking, the Senate differs structurally from the National Assembly. Its members, drawn from a pool of distinguished individuals, are more knowledgeable about all types of legislation and more insulated from the whims of public opinion. Their input is useful in all areas of legislation. Thus, Maus (1985) cites "traditional senatorial wisdom"; Tardan (1988) labels the Senate a "house of reflection" that exerts its influence through "a perfect understanding of the subject"; and Grangé (1984) refers to the "normative" influence of the Senate.

A narrower interpretation suggests that Senate expertise is not uniform

149

but concentrated in specific areas that reflect the training and interests of the senators themselves. Following this line of reasoning, Lassaigne (1968), Marichy (1969), Mastias (1980), and Grangé (1981) identify specific areas of senatorial interests and expertise: family law, civil liberties, local government, and agricultural policy, among others.

Both the wider and the narrower interpretations claim that wisdom is the *sole* reason for senatorial influence (other than veto power). Here is how Grangé (1981: 956) presents his argument:

As the Roman senate illustrates, the senate of the 5th Republic has no power but may have authority. This was the lot of a good number of senates, notably in democratic regimes, as soon as they differed from the popular chamber. This then is their servitude but their prestige is even more enhanced when they come to impose [their ideas] *solely* by the merit of their judgements. (Emphasis added.)

Since the French Senate has no veto power, it is left with wisdom as its only means of influence. Consequently, according to this theory, in our six pieces of legislation, senatorial influence should be constant as long as expertise and wisdom remain constant.[5] Moreover, if the Senate's opinion is expert, the National Assembly should adopt immediately or very quickly the improvements offered by the Senate. Because all six cases of legislation examined below fall under widely acknowledged areas of senatorial expertise, senatorial amendments should not only have a consistently high success rate, but also should be accepted immediately (in the first round) or soon thereafter (second round), with infrequent use of the conference committee.

Alternatively, French legislative analysts have referred to the relations between the president of the Republic and the Senate to explain the degree of senatorial influence. Discussions of the legislative process in France are invariably distinguished according to the presidential term of office.[6] This is because, until 1986, the president, the government, and the

---

[5]One might argue that expertise is a continuous rather than a dichotomous variable. Instead, we believe that "expert opinion" presents a solution that makes all parties better off and, as such, is easily recognizable. The problem, of course, is that much partisan debate is cloaked in efficiency terms; however, the redistributive consequences of the so-called efficient solutions are generally understood, giving rise to extended debate. Thus, the efficiency cloak is a relatively transparent one: if the amendments bring both houses closer to their preferred positions, they represent "real" efficiency. If amendments move the outcome away from one house's ideal point toward the other's, they do not represent efficiency gains, despite the political rhetoric, and comprise what we have labeled the *political, or redistributive, dimension* of bicameralism. We thank two anonymous reviewers for bringing this point to our attention. A more generous interpretation of the theory would make senatorial wisdom *one*, but not the sole factor affecting outcomes. We discuss this broader interpretation in our conclusions.

[6]Two alternative ways of analyzing the legislative process are by the government (by the prime minister) and the legislature (by legislative elections). These breakdowns

The process of intercameral bargaining

National Assembly had similar ideological tendencies. When combined with the semipresidential institutional structure (long term of office, ability to appoint the government, ability to dissolve the legislature), this allowed the president to dominate the legislative process.[7] There are two variants of this approach, which we label the *presidential attributes* approach.

The first variant emphasizes the willingness of the president to work with the Senate. It analyzes the president's conception of legislative institutions, from de Gaulle's preferences for a functionally designated advisory body, to Pompidou's expectation of senatorial oversight, to Giscard d'Estaing's desire for political support. The second variant focuses on the degree of ideological or political congruence between the president, as representative of the executive branch, and the Senate. According to this line of reasoning, the degree of congruence decreases the divergence in preferences and enhances the level of influence.

Both variants provide a similar analysis of senatorial influence, emphasizing the presidential terms of office. The 1958 to 1962 period was one of political uncertainty and constitutional elaboration. But beginning in 1962, when de Gaulle's power and prestige were enhanced, the centrist Senate began to be systematically excluded from the legislative process. Ultimately, de Gaulle proposed a referendum (1969) for an institutional reform of the Senate, modifying its traditional membership and responsibilities. When the referendum incorporating these reforms failed, de Gaulle resigned from the presidency. His successor, Pompidou, normalized relations with the Senate, although he remained ideologically distant. The presidential victory by Giscard d'Estaing in 1974 brought with it a period of close collaboration. Mitterrand's victory brought the Senate a mixed but mainly negative bag. On the positive side, more bills were introduced in the Senate (relative to de Gaulle) and declarations of urgency were less frequent; these factors tended to improve the legislative

---

were rarely, if ever, used until 1986, when a conservative legislature and government "cohabited" with a Socialist president. Now, analyses invariably include a dual breakdown, by president and by government.

[7]According to these arguments, the power of the presidency lies in the personality of the president and, more importantly, in the institutional structure associated with his role. In France, members of the National Assembly are elected to five-year terms, while the president is elected for a full seven years; the president will still be presiding over the executive after the members of the legislature have come and gone. The president also appoints the prime minister and other cabinet ministers. Although the National Assembly has the ability to reject the recommendations, it does not have the ability to nominate individuals. Finally, the president has the power to dissolve the National Assembly, whereas the National Assembly cannot unseat the president. These combined powers tend to reinforce the president of the Republic at the expense of the legislature.

dialogue. On the negative side, the growing failure of conference committees to reach agreement and the resort to National Assembly definitive votes decreased Senate input.

This theory attributes variable senatorial influence to the occupant of the presidency. Greater senatorial influence occurred during the Giscard presidency; at the other extreme, the smallest senatorial influence was during the de Gaulle and the Mitterrand (first part: 1981–86) presidencies, while the Pompidou presidency is located in between.

In the following section, we pitch the model of senatorial influence presented in Chapter 4 against these two competing explanations. As developed in the preceding section, we hypothesize that senatorial influence is a function of the institutional rules governing the navette and the degree of impatience of each chamber to see the legislation passed. According to this theory, legislators will tend to defect over time, reducing the likelihood of successful passage; the narrower and less cohesive the governing coalition, the greater the concessions. The relative urgency of some bills produces bill-specific impatience that also increases the level of concessions. Finally, the National Assembly invariably offers concessions to the Senate despite its ability to prevail ultimately.

3. THE MECHANICS OF BICAMERAL NEGOTIATIONS

Here we describe intercameral negotiations over six significant pieces of legislation. The selection was made in order to maximize variance in dependent and independent variables involved.[8] The first three cases are those where the systemic level of impatience varies, that is, where the size of the coalition allies and opposition vary. In the second three cases, the systemic level of impatience is held constant by selecting legislation passed by the same National Assembly, elected in 1973; the cases vary in terms of bill-specific impatience associated with political controversy and fiscal crisis. All the bills deal with areas of senatorial expertise. Two of the cases occurred under the presidency of Pompidou, two under Giscard d'Estaing, and one under Mitterrand, and one was initiated under Pompidou but concluded by the same Parliament under Giscard. For each of the six cases, we delineate (1) the independent variables of each theory, the level of senatorial expertise, the presidency, and indicators of the

---

[8]The first cut involved selecting six cases that varied on the dependent variable, Senate influence. Our selection was guided by the list provided in Grangé (1984). We then sought to ensure variation on the independent variables: systemic impatience, bill-specific impatience, presidency, and Senate expertise. Unfortunately, given the number of criteria governing our choice of cases and the small number of cases, we were unable to ensure variation in Senate expertise.

National Assembly's level of impatience;[9] (2) the issue at stake; (3) the initial positions or policy preferences of the National Assembly and the Senate; (4) the negotiation process; and (5) the legislative outcome. The distance between initial position and outcome indicates relative house power.[10]

Case 1: Penal code reform, 1977–78. This legislation was introduced under the presidency of Giscard d'Estaing during the second legislative session of 1977. The debate continued after the March 1978 National Assembly elections, which produced a conservative coalition. The impatience of the National Assembly was high because the coalition was threatened by potential defections by coalition partners and by the strength of the Left opposition, despite the fact that it was newly elected. The two parties of the Right, the RPR (Rassemblement pour la République) and the UDF (Union pour la Démocratie Française) were closely matched in strength – 154 RPR seats and 123 UDF seats – and the Left reached its second strongest position in the history of the Fifth Republic – 199 seats.[11] Senatorial expertise was also high; penal code reform falls into an area of traditional senatorial interest in civil liberties (Grangé 1984). Giscard d'Estaing was ideologically close to the Senate's centrist majority, and he viewed the Senate as an appropriate partner in the legislative process.

The legislation dealt with a number of issues confronting the judicial system at the time: access of the press and the public to information concerning ongoing criminal investigations; the speed of the judicial process; and prison reform (*Journal officiel* 1977–8, Sénat No. 9). The government, supported by the National Assembly, drafted legislation comprising four chapters. The first chapter opened criminal investigations to the press under specific conditions. The second expanded the number of investigating officers (*police judiciaire*) by lowering the criteria for appointment and enlarging the job responsibilities of traffic officers to include investigation. These measures expanded the investigative corps from 14,000 to 35,000. The third chapter of the legislation reformed the jury selection system, transforming it from a quasidiscretionary system to one based on random selection. The fourth chapter, introduced via gov-

[9]The level of senatorial impatience is not discussed because it remains constant throughout the period; see Maus (1987) for the breakdown of political parties in the Senate.

[10]We do not deal here with strategic misrepresentation of initial preferences. Although this is possible, there is no way to assess empirically whether the initial position of a chamber is "sincere" or not.

[11]See Maus (1987) for electoral outcomes. The total number of seats was 491, requiring a majority of 246.

ernment amendment after the initial reading in the Senate, transferred control of prisoner movement through different levels of prison security from the courts to prison administrators. This last provision was an effort to reconcile the law with the de facto system already in place.[12]

The Senate, although sympathetic to the need for reform, was concerned about the contents of the reform. Senators weighed the criminal suspects' rights of privacy more heavily than the public's right to information and opposed opening criminal investigations to public scrutiny. They favored expansion of the officer corps but argued that it should be achieved through increased training rather than lowered standards. They also opposed the reclassification of traffic officers, perceived as a threat to individual rights via unwarranted vehicle searches, among other things. They supported the reform of jury selection but remained concerned about the potential for abuse and the size of the jury pools. And they firmly rejected the transfer of control over prisoners from the courts to prison administrators. This transfer undermined prisoner rights and the principle of equal punishment for equal crimes.

The government introduced the bill, initially comprising three chapters, to the Senate. In keeping with the positions described above, the Senate voted to delete Chapter 1 altogether and to delete those provisions in Chapter 2 that lowered officer standards and reclassified traffic officers. The provisions for jury selection were modified to increase the size of the jury pool and to restrict excuse from jury service to medical reasons.

The bill then shuttled to the National Assembly, where the government introduced Chapter 4 on prison reform. The National Assembly adopted Chapter 4 but made concessions to the Senate in the other three chapters. They agreed to the complete deletion of Chapter 1. In Chapter 2, they adopted the initial government provisions to modify appointment criteria and job classifications. However, they promised additional funds for training to ensure the quality of the investigative corps and inserted provisions to delimit the investigative reach of traffic officers. In Chapter 3, they adopted Senate recommendations on the size of the jury pool but reintroduced broader criteria for excuse from jury service.

The bill shuttled back to the Senate for the second reading. The Senate

[12]In 1945, the prison system had been structured to provide digressive security levels for the inmates *within* a single institution. The sentencing judge followed the inmate's progress and transferred the inmate from one category to another based on rehabilitation. A 1975 administrative reform of the prisons provided digressive levels of security *between* institutions, requiring the inmate to move from facility to facility throughout his rehabilitation. The constitutionality of this administrative reform had been challenged and a case was pending in front of the Conseil d'État (the highest administrative court in France). The government hoped to avoid this challenge by modifying the prison statutes through legislation. See the Senate and National Assembly reports and debates as listed in the published law No. 78-788 of July 28, 1978.

remained concerned with lowered standards for investigative officers and, agreeing to the modified standards of appointment, raised the experience requirement for particular officers from two years to three. They agreed to expanded investigation responsibility for traffic officers but further delimited the arena of authority, excluding public street demonstrations and 48-hour detention. They also acceded to National Assembly criteria for excuse from jury service. However, on their initial reading of Chapter 4 on prison reforms, the Senators flatly rejected it.

The bill then shuttled back to the National Assembly, where the governing majority adopted all the senatorial amendments with the exception of Chapter 4, which was reinstated in its original form. In light of continuing disagreement over Chapter 4 of the legislation, the government called a conference committee. The conference committee report adopted senatorial preferences for the exclusion of Chapter 4 from the legislation. Returning the bill to the Senate for ratification, the government, according to its constitutional rights, reintroduced Chapter 4, thus earning a negative vote in the Senate. The government then sought a final National Assembly vote. But the National Assembly standing committee offered its own amendment to Chapter 4, requiring judicial review of prisoner movement rather than judicial control. This amendment was adopted by the National Assembly, and because of this modification to the legislation, the bill again shuttled to the Senate. The Senate remained adamant, rejecting the bill, which then shuttled back to the National Assembly for the final affirmative vote.[13]

In this case, some of the predictions of the three theories coincide; all three anticipate substantial senatorial influence over the legislative outcome.[14] However, the explanatory power of the theories can be evaluated on other grounds. Reference to senatorial expertise cannot explain why the navette proceeded four rounds before the National Assembly recognized its superior wisdom. Agreement should have proceeded quickly but did not. Furthermore, reference to the cordial relations between the Senate and the president fails to clarify why senatorial suggestions were not fully implemented. Although ideologically similar, the president and the Senate did not agree on all issues. When preferences varied, senatorial influence diminished.

[13]There is a discrepancy between the debate proceedings, which record a Senate rejection of the legislation on the fourth reading (June 30, 1978) and a request by the government for a National Assembly vote in last resort (July 1, 1978), and the publication of the law, which shows Senate adoption of the legislation, followed by National Assembly adoption.

[14]Grangé (1984: 967) considers the 1978 penal code reform a senatorial failure. However, as noted in the text, although the Senate was unable to gain its preferences, the legislation was modified to include judicial review of transfers, an important control over prison administration and a reinforcement of individual rights.

Empirical studies of bicameralism

Our approach explains senatorial influence in terms of the narrowness of the majority coalition. The National Assembly was impatient because it feared defections and made concessions to the Senate in order to conclude the navette quickly. Ultimately, it was unsuccessful in obtaining senatorial agreement and theoretically could have returned to its initial position in the final vote.[15] However, defections from its own majority ultimately prevented that. These defections are visible initially in the conference committee's recommendation to accept the Senate position. Given its power to ultimately prevail, had the National Assembly been patient – that is, if it had a broad majority – it could have returned to its initial position in the final vote. But by the time the government requested a final National Assembly vote, members of the National Assembly located a new majority-preferred position, which was presented in the form of a standing committee amendment. The government's acceptance of this amendment serves as an acknowledgment that there was no longer a parliamentary majority supporting the initial position.[16] Thus, in both "final" votes in the National Assembly, concessions were made to members of the majority coalition.

Case 2: Local government reform, 1971. The legislation on local government reform was introduced by the Pompidou government. He was supported in the National Assembly by a broad conservative majority, 354 seats of the 487-seat National Assembly, elected in the wake of the civil disturbances of May 1968. In addition, the Gaullist UDR (Union des Démocrates de la République) had won, for the first time ever, a solid majority in its own right, 293 seats.[17] With a broad and strong coalition, National Assembly patience was high.

On issues of local government, the Senate is both interested and expert (Delcamp 1991; Grangé 1984). The French Senate is an indirectly elected

[15]According to the constitution (Article 45), the government can submit either the conference committee's version or the version last voted in the National Assembly. And the government retains both the right of amendment and the right to accept or reject amendments from the legislative chambers.

[16]Constitutional commentary states: "Upon its return before the assemblies, the text of the conference committee cannot be the object of parliamentary amendments, unless they are accepted by the government. Thus the [National Assembly] deputies, by themselves, can only adopt or reject; they vote under closed rule and if the National Assembly rejects [the bill], there will be no new legislative text" (Luchaire and Conac 1987: 894). The threat to the government then, is rejection of the legislation by the National Assembly majority. The same commentary notes the ability of the "majority that sustains [the government] in the National Assembly . . . to obtain new concessions from the government by acceptance of its amendments" (Luchaire and Conac 1987: 894; both passages are translated by the authors).

[17]This is an earlier incarnation of the contemporary RPR, the Gaullist conservative party.

156

body whose electoral college is composed of local government officials. As a result, many senators are local officials as well. They therefore have intimate knowledge of the problems faced by the communes and departments and have political interests in protecting them. According to a recent analysis (Delcamp 1991: 57), "*The defense of the commune, in addition to* [representing] *a certain conception of society and of democracy, has appeared to many as a means to defend the Senate itself,* [which is] charged to represent it."

Pompidou's relations with the Senate were located somewhere between de Gaulle's ostracism of the Senate and Giscard's cordiality. Pompidou made an effort to rehabilitate the Senate into the legislative process after de Gaulle's efforts to exclude it. However, the Senate's centrist majority was ideologically at odds with Pompidou's Gaullist philosophy.

Local government reform has long been a political issue in France. In 1971, the basic unit of local government, the commune, had remained virtually unchanged since the 1789 Revolution. In the census of 1968, France still counted 37,708 communes, more than half of which had fewer than 500 inhabitants (*Journal Officiel* 1971, Assemblée Nationale No. 1730).[18] Despite efforts to encourage the fusion of these units in 1884, 1890, 1959, and 1966, little progress had been made.[19] The government argued that this structure was outmoded and inefficient and proposed a law that would allow the executive branch, through its representatives, to force the fusion of communes, with a goal of 2,000 units of local government. In opposition stood the Senate.

The debate centered on the degree of voluntarism associated with the reorganization of local governments. The government proposed and the National Assembly supported (351 to 99, first reading) a program that called on the departmental prefects (appointed by the central government) to publish a reorganization plan after consulting with locally elec-

[18]The layers of local government in France in 1971 were as follows, from the smallest to the largest unit: commune, canton, arrondissement, department, and region (Chapman 1953).

[19]The 1884 law encouraged the fusion of communes; the 1890 law created *syndicats*, or organizations grouping several communes for the purpose of providing a service to the member communes, such as water supply or trash disposal; the 1959 law created both *districts* (grouping urban communes) and *syndicats à vocation multiple* (organizations providing several services to member communes); the 1966 law created *communautés urbaines*, or organizations that grouped urban communes. With the exception of the 1966 law that dictated the creation of four *communautés urbaines*, these laws were voluntary. Therefore, by 1971, less than one-third of the nation's inhabitants lived under some form of intercommunal cooperation and the fusion of communes was almost nonexistent (*Journal Officiel* 1971, Assemblée Nationale No. 1730). Also see National Assembly and Senate debates listed in the official publication of Law No. 71-588 of July 16, 1971.

ted officials.[20] The plan was then presented to the affected municipal councils and ultimately to the departmental general council. However, in case of local disagreement, the prefect could promulgate the plan through a decree of the Conseil d'État. Alternatively, the prefect could poll the local population through a referendum; the electorate could defeat the reorganization plan only by qualified majority (two-thirds of the voters *and* one-half of the registered voters).

The Senate agreed to debate the legislation[21] but proposed three major amendments (as well as several minor ones). The first involved delegating control over the development of the reorganization plan to local elected officials; the second involved removing any administrative control over the implementation of the plan; the third sought to delay the implementation of the legislation until after appropriate legislation on local fiscal reform had been passed. These modifications were supported by the Senate overwhelmingly 169 to 34 (only the UDR parliamentary group voted against the proposals).

On the second reading, the National Assembly reinstated the government provisions, only to have them replaced by the Senate, in its second reading, with the original amendments. In the conference committee, the National Assembly did compromise, deleting measures that permitted the prefect to petition the Conseil d'État. However, the role of the prefect in formulating the plan remained substantial. In addition, the recourse to referendum, in which a qualified majority would be difficult to obtain, left too much power in the hands of the central government according to senatorial tastes. Finally, the National Assembly refused to subordinate the institutional reform to fiscal reform.

The Senate therefore voted twice against the conference committee's report despite the recommendation of the committee rapporteur, who warned that a Senate rejection would permit the National Assembly to vote on its original bill rather than the compromise version (*Journal Officiel* 1971, Sénat, Débats, June 30). Finally, the government asked the National Assembly to vote in last resort, which it did by voice vote. The loss was bitter. According to Senator Lefort (Communist parliamentary group), "This text is very far from that which had been adopted by the Senate" (*Journal Officiel* 1971, Sénat, Débats, June 30).

The senatorial expertise argument clearly fails to predict the stunning

---

[20]Communes elect a *conseil municipal* from which is selected a mayor. Departments elect a *conseil général,* headed by a president. The prefect is the Ministry of Interior's representative in the department and had, in 1971, extensive control over the formulation and implementation of policy (Chapman 1953).

[21]Article 91, paragraph 4, of the Senate's regulations defines the procedure of the *question préalable,* which determines whether deliberation of the legislation will proceed. In this case, the *question préalable* was defeated.

defeat of the Senate in this case. Given the senators' clear expertise in local government, as well as their interests in maintaining local bases of political support, the Senate's inability to defend its position belies an argument based on the Senate's "perfect understanding of the subject."

Both the presidential theory and our model predict that Senate preferences would essentially be disregarded. The former approach refers to the ideological differences between the Gaullist president and the centrist Senate; this is substantiated by the fact that only the Gaullist parliamentary group in the Senate supported the government proposals against an opposition uniting the remainder of the political spectrum. The latter refers to the breadth of the majority coalition in the National Assembly; because defections did not threaten the ultimate passage of the legislation, the National Assembly could afford to retain its initial preferences. However, the presidential approach cannot explain the National Assembly's willingness to offer some concessions to the Senate: the deletion of the prefect's power to implement reorganization over local opposition via the Conseil d'État. Given the ideological differences between the president and the Senate, from the presidential attributes perspective, there is no logical reason why the government did not revert back to its initial position each time the bill shuttled back to the National Assembly.

In contrast, our approach anticipated concessions, in this case minor concessions, in order to speed passage of the legislation. However, our approach must explain why, if the concessions granted were insufficient to win the desired senatorial support, the government failed to revert to its original position in the end game. It does so by pointing to the costs of negotiating a new agreement with its governing majority, when the compromise position has already been adopted.[22]

Case 3: Tax on wealth, 1981. This legislation was introduced under the Mitterrand presidency. In accordance with constitutional provisions, after his 1981 election, Mitterrand dissolved the National Assembly and called for new elections, resulting in a majoritarian Socialist assembly. Although the parliamentary alliance initially included members of the French Communist Party, Mitterrand had a solid Socialist parliamentary majority to support his legislative program. In the June 1981 elections, the PS (Parti Socialiste) gained 285 assembly seats, an outright majority. They were joined by the 44 deputies representing the PCF (Parti Communiste Français) and 6 other members of the Left. The opposition, in contrast, garnered only 150 seats, divided between the RPR and UDF

---

[22]This situation differs from the penal code reform case where the amendment was initiated by the Assembly itself, an indication that the previous majority support had eroded.

(Maus 1987). Therefore, the National Assembly's patience was high. This was also an issue on which the Senate was considered expert, fiscal reform (Grangé 1984). Mitterrand's position toward the Senate was nuanced. He actively included the Senate in the legislative process, introducing bills there regularly and reforming the National Assembly's conference committee selection process to coincide with the Senate's. Nonetheless, to a Socialist president, the centrist Senate represented the political opposition.

A prominent piece of the Socialist legislative platform, on which Mitterrand was elected, was the imposition of a new tax on wealth (*l'impôt sur les grandes fortunes*), included in the 1982 budget law.[23] This proposed legislation imposed a progressive tax on personal wealth exceeding 3 million francs (about $600,000).[24] Although the tax was not expected to increase tax revenue dramatically, it was viewed by the Socialists as a measure to enhance revenues and reduce tax evasion by requiring the disclosure of assets. The conservatives, not surprisingly, opposed the particular form of legislation that singled out their political constituents for new taxation. Because the Senate preferred the status quo ante, it was infinitely patient; that is, it had a discount rate equal to one. Legislation under these circumstances can be achieved only through National Assembly definitive vote. Because the government understood this, and because these provisions were included in the 1982 budget law, the government declared urgency, limiting the navette to one reading prior to the anticipated conference committee.

When the bill shuttled to the Senate after passage in the National Assembly, senators were presented with two alternative strategies. The first was to reject the legislation, thereby demonstrating their opposition but negating their ability to modify the legislation. The second was to debate the legislation and both delay it and modify it by amendment. The Senate chose the second path and couched its amendments in terms of legislative efficiency. A leader of the conservative opposition, Jacques Chirac, argued in a National Assembly debate that "the principle of a tax on capital is not shocking, in and of itself. Many western countries have introduced this measure in their fiscal panoply" (quoted in Mopin 1988: 350). His objections involved the form of the new taxes, the lack of coordination with current inheritance and property taxes, and the effects of the tax on productive assets that would discourage investment, all

[23]Articles 2–10 of Law No. 81-1160, promulgated December 30, 1981. See Senate and National Assembly debates and reports listed in the official publication of the law.
[24]This amount was raised to 5 million francs, or $1,000,000, when wealth included productive assets.

indicators that the suggested changes would be beneficial to the nation rather than to a specific group of conservative political supporters.

The Senate version that was ultimately discussed in the conference committee sought to limit the tax to one year, 1982, and to reduce the taxable assets through exemptions. Among other things, the senators raised the productive asset exemptions from 2 million to 3 million francs, excluded long-term savings, allowed for property tax deductions, provided marital and child exemptions, and reduced nonpayment penalties.

Because urgency was declared, the conference committee was called to reconcile the Senate and National Assembly positions before a second reading. Some areas of agreement were reached. The National Assembly accepted a number of efficient amendments, such as the inclusion of common-law marriages as fiscal units, equality of treatment for corporate assets, and clarification of the status of rural property under long-term lease. They also acknowledged concern with the effects of taxation on investment and job creation both by narrowing the definition of assets to be taxed and by broadening the types of wealth categorized as productive assets (which received a 2 million franc exemption). However, the redistributive dimensions of the conservative Senate's amendments were clearly recognized and rejected. It came as no surprise that the conference committee failed to reach agreement. The Senate then rejected the National Assembly version of the legislation and the National Assembly voted the legislation alone. The main lines of the law remained intact.

Here again, the senatorial expertise argument cannot explain National Assembly rejection of several senatorial amendments, given their supposed expertise in fiscal affairs. Both the presidential attributes theory and our own model predict Senate failure, the former based on ideological differences, the latter due to the National Assembly's broad majority and high degree of patience. For our explanation, recognition that the Senate's discount rate was equal to one meant that concessions were useless. Hence, only efficient amendments were adopted, amendments that were retained when the National Assembly voted the definitive version of the bill.

In the next three cases, the composition of the National Assembly remains constant, illustrating the variation in impatience across individual pieces of legislation. The National Assembly that passed all three pieces of legislation was elected in March 1973; the conservative coalition consisted of 183 RPR deputies, 55 deputies from the Républicains Indépendants, and 30 deputies from the Centre Démocratique. The Left comprised 175 deputies from the French Socialist and Communist parties. The period was marked by President Pompidou's death in April 1974 and the subsequent election of Giscard d'Estaing to the presidency, between the bill on employee dismissals and the ORTF legislation and in the midst of the abortion debate (Maus 1987).

Case 4: Office of French radio and television (ORTF), 1974. This legislation was introduced under the Giscardian presidency. There are several indicators of the National Assembly impatience related to the passage of this specific piece of legislation. Fiscal crisis clearly compelled the National Assembly to pass the bill quickly. The ORTF experienced a budget deficit for the first time in its history, a situation that called for immediate action.[25] In introducing the legislation, Prime Minister Chirac explained that "the new regime must be implemented at the beginning of a [calendar] year. . . . This is indispensable for financial reasons" (*Journal Officiel* 1974, Assemblée Nationale, Débats, July 23). Prime Minister Chirac also stated, "The desire of the government to move quickly [is motivated] by the concern to ratify the text starting October so it can take effect this year on future programming schedules" (*Journal Officiel* 1974, Assemblée Nationale, Débats, July 23).

Consensus itself was highly valued on this highly politicized issue. The role of the government in the media was controversial (Centre d'Économie 1974). As a government monopoly, the parties in power controlled – to a greater or lesser extent – news coverage and media access (Bourdon 1994). There was growing popular discontent over the perceived manipulation of the news that the opposition sought to exploit. Senatorial agreement, in essence, would provide a stamp of approval to government policy, reassure the public, and reduce the political fallout from this controversy. Should conflict arise, as was the case in two earlier iterations of ORTF reform, the National Assembly would seek to minimize its visibility through quick passage of the legislation.

Additional indicators of the National Assembly's impatience include the use of three institutional mechanisms that speeded the passage of the legislation. The legislation was proposed during the third extraordinary session of Parliament called by the newly elected president. Declared urgent by the government, the debate was condensed into two readings, one prior to a meeting of the conference committee, one subsequent to its meeting. The final bill, comprising a preface and five chapters, was passed by both houses on July 28, 1974, only 10 days after being introduced in the National Assembly. Furthermore, the government used the *vote blo-*

[25]The opposition claimed that the budget deficit was merely a pretext for the reform, while the real reason was political (*Journal Officiel* 1974, Assemblée Nationale No. 1162). And Bourdon (1994: 10) reports that two-thirds of the personnel laid off as a result of the reform were trade unionists. However, this interpretation doesn't clarify why the government chose to lay off personnel in 1974 rather than during the 1972 reform.

qué to limit debate after the conference committee. These tactics were not overlooked by the Senate, which objected strenuously to the speed with which the government forced the passage of legislation.[26]

The Senate was considered an expert in the broad issues of civil liberties and had also developed a considerable degree of expertise in the specifics of broadcast communications, as demonstrated by senatorial initiatives during the passage of ORTF reforms in 1964 and 1972. As noted above, relations between the president, Giscard d'Estaing, and the Senate were cordial, based on a high degree of ideological congruence.

At issue was the reorganization of the ORTF. French broadcasting began as a government monopoly, regulated by decree. Structural reforms were initiated in 1959 by executive decree and in 1964 and 1972 through legislation. The earlier reforms were opposed by the Senate but it failed to achieve influence. In 1974, however, the ORTF experienced a budget deficit for the first time in its history and a remedy was required.

Although there was substantial agreement on organizational decentralization, the government failed to guarantee ORTF independence from political influence. The Senate, on the other hand, argued that the legislation should include "the principles of objectivity, pluralism and independence" (*Journal Officiel* 1973–74, Sénat No. 288). The Senate therefore sought to guarantee access to all political opinions.

The bill submitted by the government and approved by the National Assembly dissolved the centralized ORTF, created six public corporations, defined executive and parliamentary control, required public service broadcasts, and dealt with the personnel issues created by the reorganization. The most important senatorial amendments dealt with the preface and Chapter 4 of the bill. The Senate inserted a clause in the preface ensuring media access for all political groups in France. The clause reads "[the national public service of radio and television broadcasting] assures equal access to the expression of the principal tendencies of thought and of the main currents of public opinion. Broadcasting time is regularly granted for their disposition" (*Journal Officiel* 1974, Law No. 74-696 of August 7, 1974). The Senate also redesigned the parliamentary oversight committee to ensure that freedom of access, granted in principle, was implemented in reality. Membership in the parliamentary delegation for ORTF was expanded to five deputies and three senators, but more importantly, the representatives were to be "designated to assure a balanced representation of political groups" (*Journal Officiel* 1973–74, Sénat No. 288).

---

[26]Senator Fillioud protested against the "excessive haste of the procedure" and Senator Chambaz emphasized "the limits of parliamentary power when called upon to decide in haste" (*Journal Officiel* 1974, Assemblée Nationale No. 1162).

In Chapter 4 of the bill, Senate amendments required annual parliamentary review of both the *cahier de charges* and the allocation of funds between the six corporations. The Senate also offered an amendment requiring the radio and television stations to allocate to the political opposition "broadcasting time at least equal to half of that allocated to the government and the parliamentarians of the majority."

Because the bill was declared urgent, the Senate amendments were reconciled to the National Assembly version in the conference committee, which adopted the vast majority.[27] Both houses then approved the committee's compromise legislation. The legislation introduced many reforms suggested by the Senate in the 1964 and 1972 debates. The National Assembly also made additional concessions regarding media access to the political opposition and enlarged parliamentary control over programming and budget.

Despite the use of several institutional techniques that sought to reduce input from the upper house, both the Senate and the government acknowledged senatorial influence in the ORTF legislation. The Senate records indicate that "the text negotiated [in the conference committee] confirms the fundamental orientation to which the Senate gave clear consent and, in addition, takes up almost all our amendments, in any case, the essential [ones]" (*Journal Officiel* 1974, Sénat, Débats, July 28). On the other hand, Prime Minister Chirac complained that although "a certain number of modifications, in my eyes, improve the bill . . . certain amendments, and among the most important, were not desired by the government" (*Journal Officiel* 1974, Sénat, Débats, July 28).

This is a case where all three theories predict substantial senatorial influence. In the case of senatorial expertise, agreement was reached quickly, conforming to the expectations of the theory. However, this explanation fails to clarify why the National Assembly recognized senatorial expertise in 1974 but failed to do so in the earlier reforms of 1964 and 1972. The predictions of our model in this case are based not only on the breadth of the political majority but on bill-specific characteristics. National Assembly impatience to see legislation passed arose from the

[27]Additional senatorial influence includes: Senate amendments to Chapters 1 through 3 specified the administrative as well as financial autonomy of the corporations and expanded parliamentary representation to the boards of directors of the broadcasting firm, specifically to ensure parliamentary opposition was represented. In Chapter 4, the Senate was able to ensure programming coordination between the three television stations that appeared problematic in light of the reorganization and decentralization of decision making. In Chapter 5, the Senate sought successfully to extend early retirement provisions for ORTF employees ages 55 to 60, whereas the National Assembly offered those benefits only to employees ages 60 and above. See Senate and National Assembly debates and reports enumerated in the official publication of Law No. 74-696 of August 7, 1974.

politicization of the issue and, more importantly, from the fiscal crisis, which required immediate resolution. However, the case does not enable us to distinguish between the presidential and institutional approaches.

Case 5: Legalization of abortion, 1973–74. Another politically urgent issue confronting the same legislature was the legalization of abortion. Legislation on abortion was initially introduced under Pompidou and reintroduced under Giscard d'Estaing. Because it involved civil liberties, it came under the umbrella of senatorial expertise. The urgency for passage stems from the odd political coalition formed to pass the legislation, a hodgepodge of socially liberal members of the Gaullist UDR and centrist political parties, combined with members of the Socialist and Communist parties. This coalition was politically awkward both because it indicated the inability of the conservative parties to provide a viable alternative and because it legitimated potential Left governance in France. Once the government realized the inability to pass legislation based on its own majority and its reliance on a politically embarrassing coalition, it determined to pass legislation posthaste. As noted above, Pompidou's relations with the Senate were marred by ideological differences, while Giscard's relations with the Senate were good.

There is no doubt that the salience of the abortion issue was growing in France. The newly formed feminist movement in France had declared abortion a *cause célèbre*.[28] In 1971, the "manifesto of 343 women" was published, signed by well-known women who had undergone illegal abortions, demanding legalized abortion. They noted that 300,000 to 900,000 illegal abortions were performed every year in France, resulting in innumerable injuries and some 300 deaths annually. Shortly thereafter, a second manifesto was published, in which 331 doctors declared that they had performed or aided in the performance of abortions, openly flouting the law. And the public debate was fueled further in late 1972 by publicity over the prosecution of a 17-year-old girl who received an illegal abortion aided by her mother and two friends. By October 1972, the number of articles dealing with abortion in six major daily newspapers skyrocketed from an average of less than 25 per month to more than 150 per month, an average maintained for the next two and a half years (Isambert and Ladrière 1979). In this nominally Catholic nation, 75 percent of the public supported the liberalization of abortion in February 1973. Moreover, 62 percent of those surveyed deemed the government "hypocritical" for failing to deal with the problem (Peyret 1974).

[28]In 1970, several dozen women placed flowers at the grave of the unknown soldier in honor of someone "even more unknown than the soldier – his wife," thereby marking the first public display of the feminist movement in France (Isambert and Ladrière 1979).

165

The abortion issue was a subject of debate during the March 1973 legislative campaign, and the government submitted legislation in the first legislative session after the elections. Since 1810, abortion had been considered a criminal act in France, punishable by imprisonment.[29] In the early 1970s, the laws governing abortion dated from the 1920s; the law of July 31, 1920, outlawed advertisement and the sale of abortion remedies and the law of March 27, 1923, admitted abortion only when the mother's life was "seriously threatened."

The position of the ruling conservative majority in the National Assembly reflected a recognition that the current situation was untenable, but the solution favored a modest expansion of therapeutic abortion and additional financial and social support for pregnant women. The Senate, on the other hand, was more liberal than the National Assembly and preferred outright legalization of abortion in the early weeks of pregnancy.[30]

The first government project was presented to the National Assembly on June 7, 1973. This bill reflected the position of the Gaullist UDR. It expanded the circumstances under which abortion would be permitted by extending the notion of a woman's health to include psychological as well as physical dimensions. However, the decision depended on the opinion of two physicians rather than the individual woman, who could only request consideration. But no majority could be found to support this legislation and it was referred back to committee in December 1973.

President Pompidou died on April 2, 1974; in the ensuing presidential race, Valéry Giscard d'Estaing was elected.[31] The legislative experience in 1973 revealed that there were no legislative solutions supported by the governing coalition. Therefore, the new secretary for health, Simone Veil, proposed an alternative that relied on the opposition for support, a coalition that was politically embarrassing. The government ultimately chose to offer a temporary solution: a five-year trial period during which abor-

---

[29]Background on the abortion issue in France as well as a presentation of the political debates can be found in *L'avortement* (1975) and Peyret (1974). Also see National Assembly and Senate reports and debates as listed in Law No. 75-17 of January 17, 1975.

[30]The Senate did not debate this first piece of legislation because the government, lacking a majority in the National Assembly, sent the bill back to committee. Nonetheless, we know the party positions on abortion (Peyret 1974, Chapter 13) and the political composition of the Senate, which indicates a majority favoring legalization. Furthermore, the debates and votes of the Senate on the second bill support our contentions.

[31]As noted above, the parliamentary majority did not change. The newly elected president was not clearly on the side of legalized abortion. His campaign speeches on the subject tended to obscure rather than clarify his position. Policy statements included both "respect for life" and "freedom of conscience for every woman" (Peyret 1974: 165).

tion in the first 10 weeks of pregnancy was legalized, but only after the pregnant woman underwent a series of administrative hurdles. Abortion continued to be viewed as a "last resort," an act to be discouraged by a series of constraints. The woman was required to undergo counseling from a doctor and a social worker, to wait for seven days, then to request the abortion again, this time in writing. As an additional disincentive, abortions were excluded from the state-supported system of national health insurance. The Left unanimously supported the liberalization, whereas only 32 percent of the UDR members, 50 percent of the centrists, and in Giscard's own party, the Independent Republicans, only 26 percent voted for it (*L'avortement* 1975).

The legislation passed in the National Assembly on November 29, 1974, and shuttled to the Senate. The areas of agreement were large because this second bill closely resembled the Senate's initial preferences. Still, the Senate failed to ratify Article 7 dealing with health insurance funding. It sought to include abortion procedures under national health care coverage, while the government bill specifically excluded it from coverage.[32] In addition, it responded to the Debré amendment, which was introduced in the National Assembly on the first reading, and sought to prevent the creation of "abortion clinics" by requiring that abortions performed at any hospital not exceed 25 percent of the total surgeries performed. The Senate broadened that clause to include 25 percent of "surgeries and obstetrical operations."

Returning to the National Assembly on December 19, the two main points remaining in dispute were the definition of abortion clinics and health insurance funding. In its second reading, the National Assembly rejected the Senate's wording on abortion clinics and repassed Article 7, which prevented payment for abortions through national health insurance. When the bill shuttled back to the Senate, the senators agreed reluctantly to Article 7 but rejected the wording on abortion clinics. In the conference committee, the senatorial wording was retained and passed by both houses of Parliament. The total legislative passage from introduction to final passage took only 25 calendar days, conducted during a regular legislative session with a busy legislative agenda.

The abortion case outcome coincides with all three theories that predict important senatorial influence over the outcome. However, the case provides some clues that permit us to distinguish between the presidential explanation and the one presented in Chapter 4. Given the supposed ideological congruence between the president and the Senate, it is odd

[32]The bill did permit poor women to apply for welfare funding for abortions, a procedure that required a separate application through the local government's social services department.

that the government was forced to rely on the Left opposition for passage of the legislation in the Senate. Not only did the Gaullist RPR defect from the parliamentary majority, Giscard's own party, the UDF, defected as well. Only 26 percent of the UDF parliamentary group voted for the government bill. While the outcome coincides with the prediction, the underlying antecedent condition – ideological congruence – was lacking. Our model on the other hand, can straightforwardly predict from the high level of National Assembly impatience the high level of senatorial influence. To minimize the visibility of a politically embarrassing coalition, the National Assembly sought rapid passage of the legislation. This was achieved by granting concessions to the Senate that ultimately won Senate support.

Case 6: Employee dismissals, 1973. In contrast to the ORTF legislation, which was the result of a fiscal crisis, and the abortion bill, which erupted into political controversy, the legislation on employee rights in case of dismissal was a routine piece of legislation that was associated with neither fiscal crisis nor widespread public debate. The bill was introduced under the Pompidou presidency. The lack of impatience on this issue is visible in a variety of ways. In contrast to the ORTF legislation, there was no particular crisis that needed quick resolution. The legislation was introduced as part of a long-term project by the Ministry of Labor, Employment, and Population to update the French labor code, and many of its provisions merely acknowledged prior government decrees, common practice, and prior legislation. It was initiated by the previous minister of labor and proceeded through the usual channels. A draft bill was submitted to the Economic and Social Council in December 1972 for comment. When the opinion of the Council was received the following March, the legislation was duly revised. It was finally submitted to the National Assembly on April 25, 1973. A major justification for the labor code revision was to coordinate employee job security with employee profit-sharing plans (*Journal Officiel* 1973, Assemblée Nationale No. 197); profit-sharing plans, however, were originally introduced under de Gaulle 14 years earlier, in 1959 (Liaisons Sociales 1961). Speed of passage clearly was not a priority; in other words, National Assembly impatience was low. Because it involved an issue of civil liberties, the legislation was considered an area of senatorial expertise. As noted above, Pompidou had normalized relations with the Senate but remained ideologically distant.

At issue were the conditions under which an employer could fire an employee.[33] Shortly after the French Revolution, feudal rights and corpo-

[33]This legislation dealt with individual dismissals and specifically excluded layoffs for economic reasons. See also National Assembly and Senate reports and debates as enumerated in the Law No. 73-680 of July 13, 1973.

rate privileges were abolished and contractual freedom recognized. A century later, with the rise of trade unionism, the law of December 27, 1890, recognized that unilateral cancellation of contracts may give rise to damages, the first legal recognition of an employee's right to job security. However, despite additional legislation in 1928, the burden of proof regarding arbitrary dismissals fell on the employee and damages were rarely awarded. Certain categories of workers (such as union representatives and pregnant women) gained special protection from dismissal, but most workers were still vulnerable to the arbitrary actions of employers. The majority of the 61,000 cases heard each year by the French labor courts, the Prud'hommes, dealt with arbitrary dismissals (*Journal Officiel* 1973, Assemblée Nationale No. 197).

The government bill, which the National Assembly approved, attempted to strike a balance between employer and employee rights: "a delicate equilibrium between the legitimate preoccupation of the worker with greater dignity and security and the equally legitimate concern of employers to assure the competitiveness of firms" (*Journal Officiel* 1973, Assemblée Nationale No. 352). The Senate, on the other hand, favored a broader and more systematic protection for employees from arbitrary dismissals.

The legislation served mostly to update the labor code according to prevailing practices, government decrees, and other legislation. The innovative aspects of the legislation dealt with three issues. The first was the introduction of a conciliation period before an employee could be fired. The second divided the burden of proof, in case of suit, between the employee and the employer, rather than falling on the employee alone. Finally, it introduced the rehiring of the employee as a method of resolving arbitrary dismissals. The text was voted in the National Assembly and shuttled to the Senate for review.

In the first reading, the Senate offered amendments to six articles; three were of an editorial nature; three were substantive. The first substantive amendment completely reversed the burden of proof on the employee and shifted it to the employer; the second extended these guarantees to employees with one-year continuous service rather than the two-year minimum proposed by the government; the third dealt with French employees in foreign subsidiaries.

When the legislation returned to the National Assembly, the standing committee report recommended retaining all the senatorial amendments. But the National Assembly as a whole, by government request, accepted only the editorial changes and the amendment on foreign subsidiaries, while reinstating the original burden of proof clause and two-year-minimum employment requirements. The Senate, in its second reading, again amended the legislation to reflect its original preferences on the burden of proof and extension of coverage. The conference committee was unable to reach agreement, and after a third reading, the government asked the National Assembly to vote in last resort.

Again, the senatorial expertise theory fails to predict the lack of senatorial influence. The Senate presented a case for expanded employee protection but failed to convince the National Assembly that this solution improved the initial legislation. In this case, the redistributive dimensions of the legislation are relatively transparent: extending employee rights reduced employer discretion and flexibility. The Senate favored a solution that shifted the balance further from employers to employees than the National Assembly desired. It is not surprising, then, that the Senate recommendations were recognized as redistributive rather than efficient.

The two other explanations are congruent with the outcome. From the perspective of the presidential approach, Pompidou was ideologically distant from the Senate and rejected its recommendations. Our theory emphasizes the high degree of National Assembly patience, minimizing the level of concessions.

4. SUMMARY AND CONCLUSIONS

Before summarizing the evidence, there is one point worth mentioning. In all six cases, the Senate had a nonnegligible impact on the content of the bill. This is true not only when the National Assembly made concessions in order to ensure the agreement of the Senate, but even in those cases where the National Assembly made the final decision, and even in the case when a majority of the Left dominated the National Assembly. This finding does not contradict any of the theories presented in this chapter. However, it does demonstrate that the Senate influences the decision-making process, even though it is a "weak" Senate in Lijphart's terminology.[34] Despite the institutional constraints of the French Fifth Republic, the Senate is hardly "useless," as some observers have claimed.[35] And as the model developed in Chapter 4 predicts, the mechanism by which the French Senate exercises influence is impatience.

Table 7.1 summarizes the analysis of the six cases. The conclusions we can draw from these six cases are limited by a number of factors. The first and most obvious is the small number of cases from which to generalize. The second is the inability to control for the various institutional constraints governing the navette in each case, some of which favored the Senate, others, the National Assembly. And because our initial concern is

[34]See Lijphart's definitions in Chapters 1 and 2.
[35]Quoted in Grangé (1981: 39), from J. Debû-Bridel in *Notre République* of April 29, 1966.

Table 7.1. *Summary of case studies*

	Influence	Expertise	Presidency	Impatience[a]	Rounds
Penal Code reform (1977-78)	Large	High	Giscard	High	4
Local government reform (1971)	Small	High	Pompidou	Low	4½
Tax on wealth (1981)	Small	High	Mitterrand	Low	2
ORTF reform (1974)	Large	High	Giscard	High	2
Legalization of abortion (1973-74)	Large	High	Pompidou/ Giscard	High	3
Employee dismissals (1973)	Small	High	Pompidou	Low	3½

[a]See text for definitions and operationalization of impatience.

to illustrate variation in the level of impatience, our cases do not reflect variation on another dimension, senatorial expertise. Nonetheless, we believe it is appropriate to draw attention to the advantages and disadvantages of the various approaches and to employ the process of bicameral negotiations illustrated by the six cases to differentiate between the usefulness of the approaches.

On the basis of this table, the flaws of the first theory – senatorial wisdom – are readily visible. The most common method of operationalizing senatorial wisdom is by defining those areas of specific interest and/or expertise. There is substantial consensus regarding those areas (Grangé 1981: 62, 1984: 965; Lassaigne 1968; Marichy 1969; Tardan 1988: 101): family law, civil liberties/civil rights, agriculture, local government, and fiscal reform. In our six cases, each fell under an area of senatorial expertise, yet the Senate was able to influence significantly the outcome in only three cases, penal code reform, ORTF, and the legalization of abortion.

Furthermore, if expertise or wisdom is the sole explanatory variable, the National Assembly should readily agree to the improved legislation and the navette should end in one or two rounds. Yet we see only two bills that were passed in two rounds, and these because urgency was declared rather than through voluntary agreement. The four other bills required

171

up to four and a half rounds, and in four cases, the National Assembly voted in last resort. These events are inconsistent with an explanation that bases senatorial influence on the level of expertise.

A wider interpretation of senatorial expertise, according to which wisdom is only one of the possible factors contributing to senatorial influence,[36] is incomplete rather than incorrect. As we noted earlier, there are two types of senatorial influence, efficient and political (redistributive). Expertise is undoubtedly a factor in the acceptance of some senatorial amendments, and our cases illustrate some efficient amendments. Examples include the protection from arbitrary dismissal of French employees in foreign subsidiaries (case 6) and the inclusion of common-law marriages as fiscal units subject to the tax on wealth (case 3). What the expertise theory fails to acknowledge and, therefore, cannot explain is the political influence of the Senate, where senatorial preferences are incorporated in the legislation despite different National Assembly preferences.

The other two theories fare equally well in terms of predicting outcomes in our admittedly restricted data set. The presidential attributes theory does well in predicting senatorial input in legislative outcomes: Giscard was consistently more willing to compromise on penal code reform, ORTF, and abortion than were Pompidou, on local government reform and employee dismissals, and Mitterrand, on taxes.[37]

The theory developed in Chapter 4, based on the level of National Assembly impatience, is also consistent with all six outcomes. For the first three cases we see that systemic impatience, based on the breadth and strength of the National Assembly, explains when the National Assembly will make concessions to the Senate. Table 7.2 summarizes the indicators of systemic strength for the three cases in question and the degree of Senate influence. In the two cases where the dominant party of the governing coalition held a wide majority in the National Assembly, 60 percent in one case and 58 percent in the other, it granted few concessions to the Senate. Where allies and opposition in the National Assembly were strong, the governing coalition granted large concessions to senatorial preferences. The evidence in the last three case studies demonstrates that where impatience is asymmetric, the house with the least patience tends to provide more concessions to the opposing house.

---

[36]See Grangé (1981, 1984), Lassaigne (1968), Marichy (1969), Mastias (1980), Maus (1985), and Tardan (1988).

[37]There is some readily available evidence that may cast doubt on this conclusion. For example, it is argued that Pompidou, had he lived, would have offered substantial concessions on the abortion issues (*L'avortement* 1975). Both Grangé (1984) and Mastias (1988) point to several pieces of legislation where the Senate was powerless under Giscard d'Estaing precisely because relations were good (see below). Certainly, the expansion of the analysis to include a larger number of bills would indicate whether one can rely on the theory of presidential attributes.

Table 7.2. *Summary of systemic measure of impatience*

Bill	Dominant party of majority[a] (percent)	Subordinate party of majority[a] (percent)	Strength of Opposition[a] (percent)	Senate influence
Penal Code reform (1977-78)	154 (31)	123 (25)	199 (41)	Large
Local government Reform (1971)	293 (60)	94 (20)	91 (19)	Small
Tax on wealth (1981)	285 (58)	44 (9)	150 (30)	Small

Note: Figures represent seats in the National Assembly. Percentages do not add to 100 percent because some deputies are not affiliated with any party.
[a]High dominant party of majority scores represent patience; high subordinate party scores and high opposition scores represent impatience.
Source: Maus (1987).

Once we examine the process or mechanics of bicameral negotiations, the usefulness of the institutional approach presented in Chapter 4 becomes evident. The presidential approach emphasizes both the attitudes of the president toward the Senate as a legislative institution and the ideological congruence between the Senate and the president. Valéry Giscard d'Estaing was favorably disposed toward the Senate on both dimensions. Yet, in case 1, the government rejected the Senate's position on prison reform and the Senate refused to ratify the bill, requiring the executive to ask for a National Assembly vote of last resort. Resort to a National Assembly vote *against* the opinion of an ideologically allied Senate contradicts the hypothesized outcome. In case 5, although the outcome is congruent with the predictions, the abortion legislation illustrates a wide degree of ideological disagreement. These examples point to a problem of internal logic; ideological congruence indicates similar preferences and therefore little need for influence. It doesn't explain why influence should exist where preferences are dissimilar.

Our approach provides a series of predictions concerning not only the outcome of bicameral negotiations, but also the process of these negotiations. The process of bicameral negotiations is congruent with the predictions in all six cases. For example, we mentioned in the beginning of this section that, in all six cases, the National Assembly made concessions,

173

and concessions increased as the number of rounds increased despite the threat of a unilateral decision by the National Assembly.

Similarly, the case of Penal Code reform illustrates the potential for defection from the initial position as the bill shuttles between houses of the legislature. In this particular case, the coalition was narrow and weak. The ability of the Senate to postpone the conclusion of the navette allowed defections from the National Assembly majority that ultimately forced a change in the legislation to ensure passage in the lower house. The National Assembly voted three times for its initial position, yet defections were visible beginning with the conference committee and forced the National Assembly to modify its original position. Ultimately, the sentencing judge was provided a continuing role in reviewing administrative decisions over inmates. The potential for defection motivates the impatience of the legislators to pass the legislation as quickly as possible.

Concessions are offered by the National Assembly to achieve early agreement. Yet in several cases, concessions failed to achieve the desired goal, either because the Senate had incomplete information about the National Assembly's discount factor or because the Senate had a discount factor equal to one. Thus, the National Assembly made good on its threat to legislate alone. Why, in these cases, did the National Assembly fail to revert back to its initial position, given Senate obstinateness? The cases we study suggest several reasons. Where the Senate's discount factor was equal to one, only efficient amendments were adopted, providing no reason to revert back to the original legislation. In the cases of local government reform and employee dismissals, small concessions were granted during the navette and ratified by the National Assembly. Introducing new amendments opened the government up to the possibility of failure. And in the penal code reform case, that threat was realized: the National Assembly rejected the government version in favor of an amendment offered by its standing committee. Although the government offered large concessions to the Senate, it miscalculated the level of concessions required to achieve Senate agreement; the space provided by the elongated navette allowed the National Assembly majority to locate a new majority-preferred position, which was ratified instead of the government version.

The evidence presented in this chapter is congruent with our hypotheses that legislative houses are driven by impatience to pass legislation and that variation in levels of impatience, along with the institutional rules governing the navette process, affect the power of the Senate to influence outcomes. The limited number of case studies makes it impossible to evaluate the effects of institutional variations on legislative outcomes systematically. This would require a much larger data set of legislative out-

174

comes, in order to hold the effects of systemic and bill-specific impatience constant. However, in combination with the more systematic quantitative analysis presented in Chapter 6, the evidence suggests the plausibility of the theory developed in Chapter 4.

8

Conference committees

Conference committees are frequently employed to resolve disagreements between chambers that remain after one or more rounds of the navette. In Chapter 5, we pointed out that the importance of conference committees lies in their ability to make proposals to the parent chambers under *closed rule*, that is, without amendments. Consequently the details of a bicameral compromise are worked out in the conference committee, without possibility of new input from the parent chambers. Delegating the power of agenda setting to the conference committee presents the parent chambers with a serious danger, a "runaway conference" in U.S. terminology (Longley and Oleszek 1989: 4–5). The runaway conference is a conference committee that proposes compromise positions that either differ from the common positions of the chambers or exclude common positions of the chambers.

To avoid this danger, the parent chambers have two ways to rein in conference committees. The first is the explicit, restrictive, and credible specification of the set of acceptable solutions. Where the lower and upper house versions of the bill follow the same structure and disagreements are located at specific points, the conference committee may be restricted to discussing only those aspects remaining in disagreement and to locating a compromise somewhere between the positions of the two parent chambers. Conversely, where the two versions of the bill differ widely, sharing only the topic of legislation, the leeway of the conference committee expands to the maximum. In Chapter 5, we noted that since the compromise must be within the bicameral restrictions, reducing the space contained within bicameral restrictions will reduce the freedom of choice of the committee.[1]

---

[1] This is true only if these restrictions are credible, that is, if the conference committee knows that any compromise not included in *BR* will be rejected by one of the chambers.

176

Conference committees

The second way that chambers can ensure an acceptable committee decision is by the selection of the conference committee members. Again referring to Chapter 5, the selection of the members determines the yolk of the committee, which, in turn, determines the location of the uncovered set (and the "induced on bicameral restrictions uncovered set") of the committee.

Table 8.1 presents the rules governing conference committees in five countries (France, Germany, Japan, Switzerland, and the United States) and one federation (the European Union) where such committees are important.[2] The committees in these six cases present important and interesting variations in the features discussed in Chapter 5.

Bicameral constraints are defined by committee procedures. The scope of the discussion can range from only those areas of the bill remaining in disagreement to the entire contents of the legislation. The scope of the compromise can be limited to some linear combination of the two houses' positions or can include entirely redrafted legislation. And the conference committee may or may not be able to trade a compromise in one issue area with a compromise in another issue area. The German conference committee appears to operate under a minimum regime (few constraints), while French and Japanese committees operate under a maximum regime (many constraints). Switzerland is located somewhere in the middle with the European Union located toward the minimum regime. U.S. committees have the greatest variability in bicameral constraints because the chambers themselves determine restrictions on a case-by-case basis. At the extremes, the two houses in the U.S. either pass a simple shell as legislation and leave the entire bill to be elaborated in committee or dictate extremely detailed instructions concerning the compromise.

The composition of conference committee members exhibits less variation. Conference committees are usually composed of an equal number of delegates from each chamber. The exception to this rule is the U.S. Congress, where each chamber can send any number of delegates. However, in the U.S., decisions are made by the unit rule, that is, by concurrent majorities of the delegations, so the actual number of delegates per chamber is irrelevant.

There are strict rules governing conference committee membership. The common denominator of all national rules is that conferees from each chamber are selected by some authority within the chamber itself. To the extent that the major bargaining occurs across the dimension where the two chambers differ, this rule places the outcome somewhere

[2]As noted in Chapter 2, several other nations employ conference committees. The cases presented here represent those nations with variations on the dimensions crucial to the theoretical framework.

Table 8.1. *Conference committees in selected countries*

	France	Germany	Japan
Membership			
Lower house	7	16	10
Upper house	7	16	10
Selection in lower house	Before 1981 from majority; after 1981 proportionally represented	Parties proportionately represented	Selected by majority of chamber
Selection in upper house	Parties proportionately represented	One for each state; reflects party in state	Selected by majority of chamber
Committee restrictions			
Scope of discussion	Areas of disagreement only	Entire bill	Areas of disagreement only
Scope of compromise	No innovation	Unlimited	No innovation
Availability of tradeoffs across issues	No, although may be informally	Yes	Yes
Decision procedures			
Decision rule	Simple majority	Simple majority	2/3 majority with 2/3 quorum
Control over vote	Some party discipline	None	Weak party control
Ratification procedures			
Right to introduce amendments to committee report	Government only	None	None
Closed rule	Yes	Yes	Yes

178

Table 8.1. *(cont.)*

	Switzerland	United States	European Union
Membership			
Lower house	Depends on size of perm. committee; smaller committee enlarged to equal membership of larger committee	Variable, mainly corresponding to standing committee	15 [European Parliament (EP)]
Upper house		Variable, mainly corresponding to standing committee	15 (Council of Ministers)
Selection in lower house	Parties proportionally represented	By speaker, upon proposal by committee chair	Parties proportionally represented
Selection in upper house	Separate selection of additional delegation	By presiding officer	One representative per country (weighted vote)
Committee restrictions			
Scope of discussion	Areas of disagreement only	Variable (maximum when second chamber passes amendment in the form of substitute)	Entire bill
Scope of compromise	No innovation	Innovation possible	Innovation possible
Availability of tradeoffs across issues	Yes, informally	Yes	Yes
Decision procedures			
Decision rule	Simple majority with quorum	"Unit rule" concurrent majorities of two delegations	"Unit rule" qualified majority by Council and 8 out of 15 for EP
Control over vote	None	Weak party control	National government control in Council; party control in EP
Ratification procedures			
Right to introduce amendments to committee report	None	First chamber may "recommit" bill to committee	None[a]
Closed rule	Yes	Yes	Yes

[a] In case there is no committee report, the Council can reintroduce its own proposal to the EP, including those EP amendments with which it agrees; the EP can reject by absolute majority.
Sources: See text.

between the two chambers. All conference committees are composed exclusively or mainly of members of the standing committee who examined the bill, with the notable exception of those in Germany, where the conference committee itself is a standing committee, composed of party leaders from each party. In fact, the state (*Länder*) delegates to this committee are frequently the minister presidents of the state.

We distinguish four types of decision-making rules: decisions by unit rule (concurrent majorities); decision by majority rule of the committee members of the combined delegations; decisions by qualified majority; and a mixture of the above rules. Of the countries we study, the U.S. belongs to the first category; France, Germany, and Switzerland to the second; and Japan to the third (a two-thirds qualified majority is required for agreement). The European Union, which also holds the record for the most unusual decision-making rules, belongs to the fourth category of mixed rules. The conference committee instituted by the Maastricht Treaty decides by concurrent qualified majorities of the two delegations: the Council of Ministers, the European Union equivalent of the upper house, decides by qualified majority of approximately 5/7 (weighted votes), while the European Parliament's delegation decides by absolute majority (8/15) of its members.[3]

If the committee decides by unit rule, in general the locus of the outcome expands. As we demonstrated in Chapter 3, Section 1, the uncovered set of a bicameral legislature is generally larger than the uncovered set of a unicameral legislature or committee. Consequently, the committee has more leeway to select the compromise. Even if the committee members are perfect representatives of the parent chambers, under the unit rule the final outcome can be located in a wider area in space. If the decision is made by majority rule, the locus of the outcomes is significantly reduced. Finally, if the decision requires a qualified majority of committee members, the role of the committee diminishes, since fewer compromise solutions can be supported by such a majority.

In this chapter, we illustrate the impact of various conference committee rules on outcomes. These cases are not necessarily typical but illustrate the boundaries within which these committees operate. As suggested above, the U.S. and the E.U. committees should be the most powerful, because of the unit rule. However, there is a caveat concerning the E.U. conference committees; if they fail to reach a compromise, the bill can still be reintroduced by the upper chamber. Of the remaining countries in our sample, the German conference committee should have the broadest ability to fashion a compromise, whereas the French conference committee's discretion is nominal. In Japan, compromises are nego-

[3]We give below the exact numbers and the rationale behind these convoluted rules.

tiated outside the conference committee; when it is employed, it merely rubber-stamps deals concluded elsewhere. Switzerland represents an intermediate case where compromises devised in the conference committee are endorsed, provided they fall within the appropriate boundaries.

1. GERMANY

German bicameralism exhibits some exceptional features. The membership of the upper house (Bundesrat) is not elected like legislatures of other federal countries but is appointed by the governments of the respective states (*Länder*). The state delegations vary in size, as an increasing function of the states' populations, but they vote as a unit in the Bundesrat. The state delegation's vote is never divided since the members represent the position of the state.

The composition of the conference committee (Vermittlungsausschuß) is structured around the Bundesrat membership. Each state sends one delegate to the conference committee – 16 delegates in total (11 prior to unification). These are matched by 16 delegates from the Bundestag, or lower house, appointed to reflect the parties on a proportional basis.

To provide the maximum latitude for compromise, the binding commitment to carry out the state instructions in the Bundesrat stops at the gate of the conference committee. Inside the conference committee, each representative (quite frequently the state's minister president) is free to make the proposals he or she wishes and accept or reject other proposals on the basis of his or her judgment.[4] The meetings are secret, and the minutes of the conference are declassified only during the next legislative session, to prevent party or state punishment of delegate votes. Decisions by simple majority are presented to the parent houses under closed rule.

The secrecy of negotiation, the lifting of binding instructions, and the submission under closed rule work to expand the power of the conference committee in Germany. The conference committee is employed frequently for important legislation at least when the two chambers differ in political makeup and for about 10 percent of all legislation. Although the government and the Bundestag have the right to convene conference committees, most are called at the behest of the Bundesrat. The conference committee provides the Bundesrat with a channel for input into the legislation that would be lacking otherwise, given their constitutional role of voting either for or against legislation proposed by the Bundestag.

We present a well-known case that illustrates the power of the German conference committee. This case was controversial because it introduced

---

[4]Article 77, paragraph 2, of the Basic Law, cited in Mastias and Grangé (1987: 109). The same freedom from (party) instructions is true of Bundestag delegates.

new issues into the legislative compromise. The resulting parliamentary criticism forced a review by the high court, which ultimately upheld the conference committee decision.[5]

The conference committee met in December 1981 to discuss the Second Budget Restructuring Law, which had been approved by the Bundestag but rejected by the Bundesrat. The law was a so-called package law, and tied together seven laws with 45 changes to taxes and social spending. At the time the government was controlled by a Social Democratic/Free Democratic (SPD/FDP) coalition that held the majority in the lower house, while the Bundesrat was controlled by the Christian Democratic/Christian Social (CDU/CSU) opposition. The committee was composed of 22 members with the following political affiliations: the CDU/CSU controlled seven state coalitions, the SPD/FDP four; the SPD and CDU each sent to the conference committee five members from the Bundestag, the FDP one. In principle the CDU therefore had a 12–10 majority. However, the representative from the state of Saarland, Klumpp, was an FDP minister in a state CDU/FDP coalition. This meant that in fact there was often an 11–11 standoff in the conference committee, and nothing could pass without a compromise (Herles 1981).

The SPD wanted a compromise as soon as possible. The SPD/FDP coalition needed the bill to enact the 1982 budget by the latter half of January 1982. The CDU appeared to have greater flexibility. It knew that a cooperative position in the committee could stabilize the ruling coalition and that an uncooperative stance could make the coalition unworkable. Ultimately, the CDU used this leverage to extract maximum concessions from the SPD/FDP coalition.

The members of the committee spent the first day of the proceedings setting out their positions. The CDU/CSU made clear that they would not accept the tax increases in the bill. They opposed new taxes on trucking firms and the proposed decrease in corporate tax exemptions (exemptions from taxes on realized profits, taxed at a 20 percent rate). Instead, they sought cuts in social programs and in educational grants. The SPD finance minister indicated his willingness to make some cuts, but insisted that any changes should not worsen the national budget deficit. For the states' part, there were several items in the federal budget they did not want cut because the states would then have to finance those items. They included certain unemployment payments, funds for handicapped employment, and maintenance payments to hospitals.

On the following day the committee met again, and Baden-Württemberg's Christian Democratic minister president, Lothar Späth,

---

[5]The report is based on an article written by a member of the conference committee itself, Friedrich Vogel (1989).

proposed making changes in public housing policy. He wanted to increase interest rates on public loans for subsidized housing built before 1960 from 4 percent or less to 8 percent; the surplus would be employed to finance new apartment buildings.[6] Späth argued that the change would produce 9.3 billion marks and would mean 6,000 new apartments in Baden-Württemberg alone. In the first reading of the budget restructuring bill, the Bundesrat discussed the lawful limits of such an increase in interest rates, and much of the debate in the conference committee centered around what the Bundesrat really had discussed (Vogel 1989: 222). Späth's position was supported by the other CDU committee members. The SPD wanted to package some additional items in the Späth proposal, and the committee decided to deal with the entire subject. However, the Bundestag *had not* voted on the housing issues. The Späth proposal was outside the content of legislation to be considered by the committee. Interestingly, according to Vogel's account, no one objected to the extension of committee jurisdiction to public housing even though the Bundestag had not voted on the issue.

A compromise emerged from the committee on December 8. The CDU/CSU forced several notable changes to the government's bill. These included cuts of 500 million marks in social spending and 400 million marks in public service funds. The compromise reduced the burden on states and localities and increased the national budget deficit by 1 billion marks. Lothar Späth's building proposals were also approved. In the bill's final version, interest on buildings constructed before 1960 was raised to 8 percent. These measures also included the removal of outdated housing subsidies and permitted states the choice of introducing fines for the misuse of public housing instead of increasing the interest rate, in municipalities with more than 300,000 inhabitants. This provision was added to gain SPD support. The compromise also gave the SPD finance minister credits and the ability to draw on the Bundesbank's profits to make up the federal loss. But the SPD tried and failed to include legislation on reductions in child support payments to parents and an increase in the value-added tax rate.[7]

After the committee arrived at the compromise, controversy arose about whether or not it had overstepped its authority. The Buildings Committee in the Bundestag was particularly miffed and, in the debate before the Bundestag vote, members complained that the conference committee had taken authority from them. The chair of the Buildings Committee, Dr. Schneider, declared: "One cannot grasp in a few days the

[6]Interest rates on subsidized residential housing built prior to 1960 were a mere 0.5 percent while interest rates on rental housing were 4 percent.
[7]"Nach vier Tagen und einer Krise."

content from almost 50 laws, especially when only generalists sit on the Joint Committee. That is simply asking too much." The Joint Committee's co-chair, Hans Koschnick (Social Democrat, mayor of Bremen), also lamented the Parliament's decline. He noted that "the parliament has lost its role as law maker and is only the author of concept papers for the Joint Committee."[8]

Vogel, who was a member of the conference committee, responded that the committee had to deal with the entire budget structure law, which includes all proposals, suggestions, and laws made in the two houses. Although the Bundestag had not voted on public housing, the Bundesrat had discussed an increase in the interest rates on two separate occasions. Therefore the committee had the right to deal with the buildings issue. This argument did not quiet the critics. An influential Social Democrat, Herta Däumler-Gmelin, complained in an April 1982 *Die Zeit* article that

the necessary establishment of a bill's content according to orderly and public consideration did not occur. The Bundestag did not form the content of the bill, the conference committee did. The Bundestag and its representatives were therefore robbed of their right to form laws and were thrown back to the more or less theoretical possibility to say yes or no to the entire package. This action is unacceptable.[9]

She added, however, that this problem could be avoided in the future if the Bundestag did not pass such comprehensive bills. If the Bundestag passed more restrictive bills the conference committee would have less room for compromise.

The debate about the powers of the conference committee did not end with the passage of the compromise. It became the subject of many juridical articles and was finally resolved some four years later, on May 13, 1986, by the German high court (Bundesverfassungsgericht). The court declared that the inclusion of a bill, introduced but not approved in the Bundestag, in the conference committee's proposal was constitutional (Vogel 1989: 223).

This case is interesting because the parent chambers imposed so few constraints on the conference committee. Given that the principal players (party and state leadership) were members of the committee, they were able to define what was important, what compromises were to be struck, when they needed party approval to strengthen their position, and, in the

---

[8]The discussions took place during the Bundesrat debate on the Second Budget Restructuring Law on July 10 and on September 25, 1981 ("Was darf der Vermittlungsausschuß?").
[9]Herta Däumler-Gmelin (1982).

end, proposed a complicated package that could not be undone, despite the objections in the chambers.

The German conference committee is considered extremely strong. The name "third chamber" has been attributed to it precisely for this reason (Mastias and Grangé 1987). In comparative perspective, similar cases of conference committee power can be found only in the U.S. Congress.

2. JAPAN

The most exceptional feature of the conference committee in the Japanese legislature is the requirement of a two-thirds majority of its members to reach a decision.[10] For that reason, it is rarely used. In fact, it has only been employed in the years prior to the formation of the Liberal Democratic Party (LDP) in 1955 and after the LDP lost its majority in the lower house in 1993. For more than 30 years, when the LDP controlled both chambers, all compromises were worked out in the party itself without resort to the conference committee. Even after the 1989 legislative elections, when the LDP lost its majority in the upper house (House of Councilors), it preferred to co-opt some independents in order to ensure the majority in this house rather than to take the constitutional route of reconciling intercameral differences through a conference committee.

On other dimensions, the Japanese conference committee would appear to have considerable flexibility. Each house appoints ten members, representing its own majority. All aspects of the bill are open to discussion (Shugiyin 1990). However, the onerous super-majority requirement of the conference committee limits its effectiveness. Here we report two cases. The first is a labor law dispute that was resolved by the conference committee; the second, electoral reform, indicates a case where a compromise in committee was impossible and intervention by party leadership was required to resolve the differences. Both cases indicate the circumscribed role of the conference committee.

Labor law reform became an issue in the early 1950s. After Japan surrendered to the Allies in August 1945, the country's labor regulations were controlled by the Allied General Headquarters. As power was shifted to the Japanese civilian government in the early 1950s, there was a consensus that labor legislation should be modified and developed. Thus, efforts were made to amend the Labor Relations Adjustment Law and to establish the Law of Labor Relations in Local Public Enterprises.

[10]Article 92 of the Diet Law of Japan specifies that "in a meeting of the Conference Committee, a draft compromise becomes a final compromise when it has been decided upon by a majority of two-thirds or more of the members present."

Between May and July 1952, the issue was debated in the two houses. In the House of Representatives, the progressive parties (Japan Socialist Party (JSP), Japan Communist Party (JCP), and other small progressive parties) held 80 seats (18.2 percent). The conservative parties (Liberal and National Democratic) held the majority of 347 seats (78.9 percent). And other parties held only 13 seats (3 percent). In the House of Councilors, the progressive parties had larger representation of 69 seats (27.9 percent), while the conservative parties retained a majority of 162 seats (65.6 percent). Other parties accounted for 16 seats (6.4 percent).

In general, a Left–Right ideological spectrum can be used to distinguish the parties. While the progressive parties shared the common goal of enhancing working-class interests, the conservative parties were more protective of the status quo. However, the conservative side was not unified. The government was controlled by the Liberal Party (Jiyuto), under the leadership of Prime Minister Shigeru Yoshida. The Liberal Party controlled 283 seats (64.3 percent) in the House of Representatives but only 80 seats (32.4 percent) in the House of Councilors. The Liberal Party was also divided by factionalism, with Yoshida's mainstream faction constantly assaulted by the opposing factions. The other conservative politicians gathered under the banner of the Democratic Party (Minshuto, formerly Kaishinto) and other small parties. Despite the ideological similarity with the ruling party, they sabotaged legislation from time to time to increase their power.

There were four main points of disagreement between the houses. With respect to the Labor Relations Adjustment Law, the lower house bill included provisions that empowered the Minister of Labor to make emergency adjustments concerning labor disputes and disallowed disputes for 5 days after the adjustment was made. The bill as amended by the House of Councilors specified that the minister's emergency adjustment must be ratified by the Central Labor Committee and that no dispute be allowed for 10 days after the adjustment.

With respect to the Law of Labor Relations in Local Public Enterprises, the bill passed by the lower house allowed employees of local public enterprises to join unions and excluded disputes over the management of public enterprises. In contrast, the bill as amended by the upper house extended the application of the law to enterprises run by the local public body (*kokyo dantai*) and excluded "conspiracy" and "provocation" from the prohibited actions.

The joint committee elaborated the following compromise, which was subsequently adopted by both houses. With respect to the Labor Relations Adjustment Law, the minister must *consult* with the Central Labor Committee before making an emergency adjustment and no dispute is allowed for 10 days after the adjustment is made. With respect to the Law of Labor Relations in Local Public Enterprises, the final compromise extended the application of the law to enterprises run by the local public body and excluded disputes over the management of the public enterprise. It also prohibited "conspiracy" and "provocation" actions.

On this occasion, the conference committee was able to propose as a compromise a linear combination of the two positions that was closer to lower than to upper house preferences. However, the conference committee is not always as effective, as the next story reveals.

Electoral reform was a major political issue in Japan in the 1990s, because the previous electoral system was believed to promote factionalism, legislative gridlock, and particularistic interests through campaign contributions. Proposals for reform periodically surfaced since the 1950s, but it was not until the outbreak of the Recruit scandal in 1988 that the Japanese Diet members began to consider the proposals seriously (Sekai 1994). Some reform elements within the ruling LDP, championed by Prime Minister Kaifu, proposed changes to the electoral system but were unsuccessful. In 1993, when the LDP lost its parliamentary majority, the newly formed coalition government – composed of the Renewal Party, the Clean Government Party (CGP), the majority of the Japan Socialist Party (JSP) members, and some reform elements within the LDP – renewed the efforts for electoral reform (for the dates of the reform process, see Seikaiohrai 1994, 1995).

There were two major issues to be decided in the electoral reform bill: the electoral system (both formula and size of the constituency) and campaign financing. The positions of the major political forces were as follows:[11]

1. The conservative LDP. In general the LDP preferred a single-member district system with no restriction over donations to politicians. When the proposal to combine single-member districts (SMD) and proportional representation (PR) became popular, the LDP proposed two methods to reduce the weight of the PR formula. First, each voter would cast only one vote. Second, prefectures were designated as the PR districts, thereby curtailing the ability of small parties to draw on widely dispersed support. In terms of campaign financing, the LDP proposed to reduce the 1,500,000 yen ceiling but to retain business donations.

2. The reform LDP and the other government parties. These parties favored a combination of SMD and PR, with a greater weight to SMDs. They proposed that each voter cast two ballots, with the nation as a

[11]The position of major parties changed over time. The situation is complicated by the fact that the reform accompanied the dissolution and establishment of parties. What follows is a rough approximation based on accounts of Nihon Keizai Shinbunsha (various dates).

whole serving as the PR electoral district. The government coalition also sought more restrictions over campaign contributions. After 1992, some reform LDP members defected from the LDP and formed new parties. Their coalition was joined by the reform Japan Socialist Party (JSP) members.

3. JSP, Japanese Communist Party (JCP), and other small parties. These parties preferred either the previous electoral system (single nontransferable vote) or PR and wanted to prohibit donations to politicians.

The balance of forces in the two houses was as follows. The government controlled 54.6 percent of the seats in the House of Representatives, but only 47.8 percent in the House of Councilors. The mainstream LDP had 41 percent of the seats in the lower house and 37.8 percent in the upper house. The antigovernment Socialists (JSP) and the Communists had 4.4 percent and 14.5 percent in each house, respectively.

On the basis of these positions, the government proposal was adopted in the House of Representatives. It specified a combination of SMDs and PR (mixture of 274 SMD and 226 PR), with the whole country as one PR district. The bill also specified that political contributions could be made to political parties, but not to individuals. The bill was rejected by the House of Councilors. A joint committee was convened to resolve the difference at the end of January 1994.

According to the rules, each house elects its delegation. The House of Representatives sent three Socialists, two from the Renewal Party, two from the Clean Government Party (CGP), two from the Japan New Party (JNP), and one from Democratic Socialist Party (DSP). The House of Councilors sent eight LDP delegates, one JCP delegate, and one from the Second-House Club. The composition indicates that each house was interested in representing its own majority.

The bargaining process within (and outside) the committee lasted three days. On the first day (January 26, 1994), the coalition government opened the session with a compromise proposal: an electoral system composed of 280 seats elected by SMDs and 220 by PR from seven districts. To reform campaign finance, the proposal abolished business donations to individual candidates after five years.

The proposal was rejected by the LDP representatives the next day, and the committee chair declared the committee meeting adjourned. The speaker of the House of Representatives proposed a top-level meeting between the prime minister and the LDP president, a meeting that was convened two days later, on January 28. On January 29, a compromise was reached and the conference committee met again. They accepted the compromise and presented it to both chambers, who adopted it the same day.

Conference committees

The new electoral law specified that 300 representatives will be elected in SMDs and 200 elected by PR from eleven districts. With respect to campaign finances, individuals can accept donations up to 500,000 yen for the next five years.

The final outcome split the difference between the LDP and the reform coalition. The case is interesting because, although the conference committee officially had no restrictions on its decision making, it was not able to reach a compromise solution. The intervention of the two leaders was necessary for a compromise to be struck. While the institutional setting of intercameral bargaining is original, the phenomenon itself is quite frequent. It is well known that bargains struck within multiparty governments may be rejected in Parliament, while compromises negotiated among party leaders (like the government program of a coalition) are more stable. Tsebelis (1995c) has argued that members of government are more moderate and more accommodating toward each other than toward the corresponding party leadership. Consequently the compromises struck by the former may not satisfy the latter, while compromises struck by the latter will always satisfy the former.

3. SWITZERLAND

Swiss bicameralism dates from the adoption of a new constitution in 1848. The legislative institutions are copied in part from the U.S. model. The National Council is similar to the U.S. House of Representatives; the councilors are allocated according to population and elected by PR with each canton (or half canton) forming an electoral district. The Council of States is similar to the U.S. Senate; each canton is represented by two councilors (one for the half cantons).[12] Like the U.S. Congress, legislation requires the consent of both houses. Until the turn of the century, no procedures for reconciling differences between the two chambers existed. Legislation simply shuttled between houses until agreement was reached or interest in the legislation was lost. But in 1902, procedures regulating the relations between the two houses were enacted. For the first time, a conference committee (*conférence de conciliation*) was available to break deadlocks between the two houses.[13]

---

[12]Cantons decide how to select their councilors, although there is a trend toward homogeneity of the selection process, by direct proportional representation elections.
[13]The 1902 law was entitled "Loi sur les rapports entre les conseils"; this was rewritten in 1962 and entitled "Loi fédérale sur la procédure de l'Assemblée fédérale, ainsi que sur la forme, la publication et l'entrée en vigueur des actes législatifs." The law is still commonly known by the original name; we follow Hughes (1954) in translating this as the "Law on the Relations between the Councils." All references will be to the 1962 law as amended.

The conference committee procedures are straightforward. Both houses must declare their positions definitive;[14] at this point a conference committee becomes mandatory.[15] The conference committee is composed of members of the two houses' standing committees that originally examined the legislation. Where the number of committee members varies, the smaller committee is enlarged to equal the larger committee.[16] The conference committee is presided over by the president of the standing committee that first examined the legislation.

The debate in conference committee is limited to those articles of the bill where disagreement exists.[17] There are no procedural constraints on the types of solutions offered. Usually, an intermediate position between the two delegations is chosen. However, occasionally, a tradeoff between articles remaining in disagreement is the preferred solution, where one delegation prevails on one issue, the other delegation on another issue. The solution offered by the conference committee is returned to both houses for approval under closed rule. If either house rejects the compromise, the legislation is defeated.[18]

Because no limits on the navette existed until 1992, most differences between houses were resolved through the shuttle system.[19] Conference committees are rarely called. In the 70-year period between 1902 and 1972, only 13 conference committees were called for the 4,803 pieces of legislation debated, or 0.27 percent of the time (Trivelli 1975: 288). In 10 of the 13 cases, a compromise was reached and ratified by the two houses; in three cases, either the conference committee failed to find a compromise or the proposed compromise was not ratified.

The distinctive procedural rules governing conference committees in Switzerland affected the ultimate legislative outcomes. One of the most important rules involves the selection of conference committee members. Because the chambers are relatively small (200 members in the National Council and 46 members in the Council of States), the conference committee is composed of the membership of the Councils' standing commit-

[14]Originally, there was no time limit or debate limit. Normally, at least three rounds of debates were necessary before the houses declared their positions definitive. In 1992, the Law on the Relations between the Councils was amended to limit the navette to three readings in each chamber (Switzerland, *Recueil officiel*, 1992).
[15]Article 17, Law on the Relations between the Councils (Switzerland, *Recueil systématique*, 1948, 1973).
[16]This is almost invariably the Council of States, whose membership was initially 44 members (from the 22 cantons) and 46 members after Jura became the 23d canton. In contrast, the National Council has 200 members.
[17]Article 17, paragraph 1, Law on the Relations between the Councils (Switzerland, *Recueil systématique* 1948, 1973).
[18]Articles 18, 19, and 20, Law on the Relations between the Councils (Switzerland, *Recueil systématique* 1948, 1973).
[19]See Introduction, note 9.

tees that originally examined the legislation. Both houses seek to replicate the political composition of the houses in committees. However, the upper house committees are almost invariably smaller than the lower house committees and, according to law, are enlarged to equal the membership of the lower house committee. This rule is significant when the position of the standing committee is different than the upper house position.

This was the case for the 1948 law on air transport (Loi fédérale sur la navigation aérienne) (Trivelli 1975: 325–34). The issue over which the two houses disagreed was the funding of modifications to future construction projects mandated by air transportation safety. The positions of the lower house permanent committee, lower house membership, and upper house permanent committee converged on a position that placed the burden on corporations initiating the new construction; the airport affected by the construction was relieved of all liability, and government subsidies were confined to extraordinary cases of where costs were large and the "public interest" dictated intervention. The upper house originally sought to divide fiscal responsibility between the construction companies, the airport operators, and the government. When this position failed to garner the support of the lower house, the upper house sought to limit strictly government subsidies and to divide the financial liability evenly between airport operators and new construction.

When the conference committee was called, the upper house permanent committee was duly enlarged from 9 to 13 members; the enlargement brought about a change in position of the Council of States delegation to the conference committee. In the absence of a change in the delegation, we would anticipate a compromise reflecting the common position of the two permanent committees; as noted above, this involved no airport operator liability and very limited government subsidies. But because of the expansion of the upper house committee delegation to the conference committee, the upper house position on airport liability and government subsidies was taken into consideration. The compromise solution did limit airport liability but extended government subsidies in the case of "necessary construction."

This case is also important from the perspective of conference committee decision making. Equal representation from each house was clearly written into the legislation. However, absences from conference committee hearings can unravel the parity between the houses. When the conference committee voted on the compromise in this case, only 6 of the 13 members of the National Council delegation were present, whereas 11 of the 13 members of the Council of States delegation were present. In the absence of parity, the position of the median voter shifted closer to the preferences of the upper house delegation. Experiences like these prompted reform of the conference committee. The 1962 law mandated that votes could not be taken without a majority quorum from both houses.[20]

Conference committee procedures are also important. The conference committee is instructed to debate only those areas of disagreement.[21] However, nothing prevents a tradeoff between issues remaining in disagreement, and the houses have explicitly retained areas of disagreement with the purpose of providing a larger potential for compromise in the conference committee. This was the case in the 1964 Federal Labor Law (Loi fédérale sur le travail dans l'industrie, l'artisanat et le commerce) (Trivelli 1975: 449–60). The law was formulated to recognize and extend the benefits gained through collective bargaining to most sectors and firms in the Swiss economy. There were three issues on which the chambers disagreed. (The permanent committee and the house membership in both cases took the same position.) The first involved the reduction of the work week. The lower house, closer to electoral pressure from the working classes, chose a more liberal position of a 45-hour work week in industry and a 50-hour work week for crafts and wholesale and retail trade. The upper house adopted a more conservative position with a 46-hour work week in industry, 50 hours in crafts, and 52 hours in trade.[22] On the second issue, the lower house favored 8 national holidays, while the upper house chose to provide more flexibility for cantons to determine up to 14 cantonal holidays (Article 16). Finally, although both houses acknowledged special provisions for certain sectors of the economy, the National Council sought mandatory legislation for those sectors, while the Council of States sought to make these provisions voluntary (Article 25).

What is interesting about this particular legislation is that a compromise later adopted by the conference committee was proposed but rejected in the lower chamber during the navette on the grounds that it was "premature." The compromise delayed the reduction in working hours from 46 to 45 until 1967, and implementation depended on favorable economic conditions. This compromise was rejected by the lower house in the third round because "the supercompromise . . . was premature and should be preserved for the case where there is required recourse to a conference committee" (Trivelli 1975: 457). Furthermore, the Council of

[20]This clause is contained in Article 18 of the 1962 law. It also clarifies the majority voting rule: once the quorum is obtained (established by majorities of both delegations), decisions are by majority of voters present.

[21]Article 17, paragraph 1, Law on the Relations between the Councils (Switzerland, *Recueil systématique* 1948, 1973).

[22]A complementary clause dealt with maximum overtime hours, but since these were calculated directly from the legal maximum working hours, we do not discuss them separately.

States was willing to compromise on the sectoral provisions clause but "decided . . . to maintain globally and definitively its position, thus leaving the most material possible for the conference committee and thus perhaps facilitating the task" (Trivelli 1975: 457). In other words, the legislators sought to arrive at the conference committee with bargaining chips rather than compromise during the navette.

Thus, the final compromise retained the "supercompromise" reducing the work week to 45 hours if the economic situation "authorized" it; the position of the National Council was maintained on the legal holidays, while the position of the Council of States was maintained on the sectoral provisions clause.

The Swiss conference committee also provides examples of Council delegations that are extreme vis-à-vis the Council but moderate from the perspective of reaching a bicameral compromise. In 1970, a rent control law was passed (Modification des règles du code des obligations sur le contrat de bail) (Trivelli 1975: 470–83). In the context of an ongoing housing shortage in many of the cantons, the government proposed to provide permanent protection for renters and to modify the landlord's ability to abrogate leases. The Council of States took up the matter first. Its committee recommended that, in case of renter hardship, landlords be required to extend leases for six months in the case of housing and one year for commercial leases. They also included provisions for cantonal discretion to extend protection to one year for housing and two years for commercial leases. The Council of States took a similar but more conservative position: it agreed to rental protection but extended cantonal discretion for only three years, until 1974. The National Council was considerably more liberal on the issue and sought to abrogate the landlord's ability to terminate leases altogether. That is, in the case of housing shortages, the landlord would have no ability to terminate a lease. The National Council's standing committee, which was identical to its conference committee delegation, took a position that permitted renter protection for a maximum of one year for housing leases and two years for commercial leases, with no cantonal discretion.

The National Council's delegation to the conference committee was extreme (on the conservative side of the issue) when compared with the broader Council membership but moderate given the desire to produce a compromise between the two houses. The moderation of this committee helped to produce the conference committee compromise that provided for two successive extensions of the lease; the initial extension was for one year and two years depending on type; a second extension in cases of particular hardship, for two and three years, provided a total of three years' protection for housing leases and five years' protection for commercial leases.

193

Ultimately, each house must ratify the compromise created by the conference committee; the solution must fall within the bicameral winset of the status quo. Where it does not, we would expect the bill to be defeated. This is the case for the ratification of the International Labor Organization (ILO) treaty on salary equity between men and women (Trivelli 1975: 438–48). The government, in 1960, proposed the ratification of two ILO treaties, one on discrimination in the workplace, the other on salary equity between men and women. The first treaty engendered little debate; the second became the issue of contention. The National Council followed the recommendation of its standing committee to ratify both treaties, contending that they were interdependent and it would be illogical to ratify one without the other. The standing committee of the Council of States was similarly persuaded, but the parent body refused to adopt its committee's recommendations. A conference committee was called after both houses maintained their positions definitively after three readings each. The conference committee attempted to meet the Council of States halfway. It recommended separating the ratification of the two treaties; the first treaty on discrimination in the workplace was to be implemented immediately upon ratification, while the implementation of the treaty on salary equity would be delayed for four years. This compromise, however, was flatly rejected by the Council of States and the legislation failed.

The Swiss cases illustrate various dimensions of the model developed in Chapter 5. The first case indicates the significance of committee membership; in Switzerland, the National Council's conference committee membership is fixed by the standing committee membership, but the Council of State may be strategic when it augments its standing committee to equal that of the lower house in order to obtain an outcome closer to its own preferences. Moreover, given the majority decision-making rule, committee member absence from deliberations may shift the outcome toward one house or the other – hence the reform to ensure a quorum from each house before decisions are taken. In the third case, the extreme position of conference committee members vis-à-vis the parent body often helps to facilitate the compromise.

The second case illustrates the possibility of tradeoffs across issue areas and the strategic decision to postpone the compromise until a conference committee meeting. And the last case demonstrates that where the conference committee fails to select an outcome within the winset of the two chambers, the compromise is defeated.

4. FRANCE

The French have a conference committee system similar to the Swiss but it is significantly more restrained. Because the constraints are so onerous, the conference committee is generally viewed as a political tool of the government rather than as a means of reconciling differences between the two legislative houses (Hamon and Cotteret 1960a, 1960b, 1961; Hamon and Emeri 1963; Luchaire and Conac 1987; Trnka 1963, 1967).

The conference committee is an innovation of the Constitution of the French Fifth Republic. However, most control over the creation of a conference committee and the ratification of the conference committee compromise lies in the hands of the government rather than within the two chambers. After two debates in each house, or after one if the government declares the bill to be urgent, the government may call a conference committee (*commission mixte paritaire*).[23] Each house sends seven conferees and seven substitutes. The substitutes are designated with the purpose of maintaining voting parity despite the absence of delegation members, although they can also participate in the debates (Trnka 1963, 1967). This parity of both membership and voting contrasts with the Swiss case, where parity of membership is not necessarily maintained for voting. It is in this context that the selection of the conference committee delegates can be understood.

The selection of conference delegates has evolved over time. Delegations are nominated by the standing committee responsible for initially reviewing the legislation. Senate and National Assembly rules permit independent nominations to be presented to the president of each chamber, but the practice of independent nominations was quickly defeated by the desire of the standing committees to retain a monopoly on the nomination process, backed by the parliamentary majority. The standing committee normally nominates its president and recording secretary (rapporteur) to the conference committee delegation. However, other members may or may not be members of the standing committee. Originally, priority was given to the individual's level of expertise regardless of committee membership. Trnka (1963: 497) provides examples from both the Senate and the National Assembly delegations that included participants from up to five different standing committees, based on their given areas of expertise. Although multiple committee representation remains the rule, other selection criteria have changed. After the Gaullists gained a majority in the National Assembly in the 1962 legislative elections, National Assembly members of the conference committee were nominated based

[23]Article 45 of the Constitution of the French Fifth Republic.

on party membership and loyalty rather than expertise, whereas the Senate was represented according to the political composition of its members.[24] This difference remained until the 1981 shift in parliamentary majority to the French Socialist Party, when the National Assembly rules were modified to resemble the Senate's procedures. As a result, for the first twenty years of the French Fifth Republic, conference committees were dominated by the Gaullist Party. They primarily served the political ends of the Gaullist government rather than as a means of dialogue between the two legislative houses. Parity representation translated into lower house dominance of the conference committee, as only one member of the upper house delegation was needed to ratify any solution. After the change in committee selection after 1981, conference committees became less likely to find compromise, but if a compromise was negotiated, that compromise was more likely to be approved by the two houses.

Like the Swiss case, the conference committee can address only those articles remaining in disagreement. A ruling of the Constitutional Council specifically limited the ability of the conference committee to reopen discussion on already agreed-upon clauses, even though this might facilitate a conference committee compromise (Luchaire and Conac 1987: 893).[25] Furthermore, the discussions must take place based on the texts voted by the two legislative houses, rather than "inventing a third text" (Luchaire and Conac 1987: 891). An early effort to expand the parameters of the conference committee came in 1963 (Trnka 1967: 751–52). The chambers disagreed on the definition of "conscientious objector." The conference committee decided not to take the submitted texts into consideration; rather it substituted a new article that directed the definition to be undertaken within the context of a new general law on military recruitment. The government permitted a vote on this text despite the uproar in both houses over the right of the conference committee to innovate in this manner. The proposal was voted down by *both* houses, providing a lesson for future conference committees: compromises must be found within the boundaries set by the National Assembly and Senate texts.[26]

The ratification procedures further limit the import of the conference committee in France. The conference committee compromise is voted by the two houses under closed rule except for amendments proposed or

[24]Membership in the lower chamber delegation was based on the "organic" majority in the lower house, that is, on the parties that supported the government rather than the parties that supported the particular bill (Luchaire and Conac 1987).

[25]This is contained in a Constitutional Council decision of December 28, 1976.

[26]Members of the conference committee do have the right of amendment. However, according to Trnka (1963: 500), "This right is rarely exercised, the transactional texts being more often the result of a common drafting."

supported by the government. This permits the government to reverse completely the conference committee compromise, if it so chooses. In many cases, it reinstates its preferred position, in direct contradiction to the efforts of conciliation and compromise pursued by the conference committee. When this happens, the Senate often rejects the legislation on principle. The National Assembly may also object to the high-handed tactics of the government, but the government can use its threat of dissolution and/or turn the vote into a question of confidence to discipline the lower house. Ultimately, the government relies on its majority in the lower house to pass legislation by a definitive vote of the National Assembly.

A single piece of legislation illustrates well the severe constraints on conference committee solutions in France. In 1980, the government introduced a bill for agricultural reform in its territory of New Caledonia (Projet de loi relative à l'aménagement et à l'établissement rural dans le territoire de la Nouvelle-Calédonie et dépendances).[27] The bill undertook to transfer fallow or uncultivated land from private owners or the state to the indigenous community. When transmitted to the conference committee, eleven of the fourteen articles remained in dispute. In the compromise crafted by the conference committee, four articles retained the exact wording of the National Assembly, three articles retained National Assembly wording with minor modifications of form, one article retained the exact wording of the Senate, and three articles were redrafted texts. In the latter cases, however, there was no real innovation; the texts merely reflected parts of the Senate text and parts of the National Assembly text. To provide an example, Article 9 retained the Senate's position on one issue: that of appointing three delegates from the French state and three delegates from the territory to the commission charged with the task of evaluating land, rather than the National Assembly position of two delegates each. And it retained the National Assembly wording on a second issue: that of providing the commission president with power of decision in case of a tie vote. The only real innovation was a technical revision where the conference committee adopted a new clause excluding those with a conflict of interest from serving on the commission. Thus, the procedural rules within the conference committee severely restrict the types of compromises that can be created. And membership selection from the parliamentary majority in the lower house ensured National Assembly dominance over the outcomes.

This bill is interesting also because it illustrates the power of the government to overturn even such a benign compromise. When the conference committee bill was returned to the National Assembly, the govern-

---

[27]From the annexes to the Senate debates of December 20, 1980, Nos. 205, 206, 208, and 209.

ment amended it to limit expropriations to 50 percent of the property owned, an amendment the government majority in the National Assembly duly approved. When it was submitted to the Senate for approval in this new form, the Senate flatly rejected it, primarily because the government overturned the conference committee compromise.[28]

The French conference committee provides an example where the procedural constraints, committee membership, and committee decision rules severely restrict the space within which agreement can be negotiated.

5. THE UNITED STATES

Our discussion of the United States is based on congressional literature, in particular the books by Smith (1989), Longley and Oleszek (1989), and Krehbiel (1991). What we add here is the examination of the rules, composition, and outcomes of the committee based on the models developed in Part II. The lack of party discipline in the U.S. Congress makes coalition building more difficult, legislative strategies more complicated, formal rules (when they exist) more important, and outcomes more unpredictable (particularly when formal rules do not exist, as in the case of conference committees). For these reasons, a discussion of U.S. conference committees is necessary.

Conference committees are not the sole method of resolving intercameral differences in the U.S. The two chambers may use the navette system and shuttle legislation back and forth until they compromise, or one chamber may adopt the other's legislation, or they may combine these methods with a conference committee. In fact, the use of conference committees is *rare* if one considers all bills, but *frequent* if one considers only the important bills. For example, in five Congresses between 1955 and 1986, conference committees were employed in 11.4 to 22.8 percent of all bills (Smith 1989: 206); when considering only key legislation, the percentages increased to 46.4 to 84.6 percent.

When a conference committee is requested by one chamber and accepted by the other, there is no fixed number of participants per chamber as required in the countries previously discussed. In fact, there is no requirement of equality of membership for each delegation. Each chamber can decide the number of its representatives. This number can range from a single digit, a common practice in the past, to several hundred members. A large conference committee is divided into several subcom-

---

[28]Ultimately, the bill was saved by a solution suggested by the Senate and adopted by the National Assembly in yet another round of debates. It limited expropriation to 50 percent of *cultivated* property.

mittees that decide on different issues. Senate Majority Leader Howard H. Baker wrote about the 1981 budget reconciliation conference, "Over 250 Senators and Congressmen met in 58 separate conferences to consider nearly 300 individual issues" (*Congressional Record* July 29, 1981: S8711).

The composition of the House delegation is determined by the Speaker of the House upon recommendation of the chairperson of the standing committee with jurisdiction. In the Senate the delegation is determined by the chairperson and the ranking minority member of the reporting committee. Before the reforms in the mid-1970s, the House delegations were almost exclusively from the committee that reported a bill. From the late 1970s on, other members of the House were included as "additional conferees," meaning that they had the right to vote on specific subjects. In addition, the practice of "exclusive conferees" was instituted, according to which designated members had exclusive voting rights on particular subjects. Additional complex amendments were introduced in the 1980s so that the major players who shaped legislation on each chamber's floor participate in the conference committee. The formal and informal rules are both changing and complicated, but for our purposes, the bottom line is simple. "When the House and the Senate go to conference, the members of each chamber delegation are traditionally drawn almost entirely from a single substantive committee of that house" (Longley and Oleszek 1989: 109).[29]

The conference committee meetings were secret prior to the reforms of the mid-1970s. Subsequently the meetings were open, but the delegations have found ways of working around the openness requirements with few complaints. Senator Russell B. Long (D, La.) colorfully describes the methods devised to avoid public disclosure of negotiations (*Congressional Record* February 1986: S1463; quoted in Longley and Oleszek 1989: 46).

When we started the openness thing we found it more and more difficult to get something agreed to in the conferences; it seemed to take forever. So what did we do? . . . We would break up into smaller groups and then we would ask our chairman . . . to see if he could find his opposite number on the House side and discuss this matter and come back and tell us what the chances would be of working out various and sundry possibilities.

Senator Long describes only one method of limiting openness. The whole array of methods is a monument to creativity in practices as well as in names: *squeeze play* (use of small meeting rooms), *committee caucus* (meeting in a back room to work out a compromise), *shuttle diplomacy* (sending staff back and forth between chamber caucuses), *football huddle*

---

[29]For a more detailed analysis and disagreements among the experts, see Shepsle and Weingast (1987a, 1987b) and Krehbiel (1987, 1991).

(whispering to each other in corners of the room in order to achieve secretly a compromise subsequently discussed in public).

This secrecy rule must be combined with and understood in light of the composition of conference committees. Since the members of the committee come in overwhelming majority from the standing committees that elaborated the legislation, for each subject matter the same representatives meet over and over again to decide on particular pieces of legislation.

The conferees are usually old colleagues. The subcommittee chairmen have been bargaining and trying to persuade one another sometimes for a decade or more. While a conference is ad hoc, it is also in a very real sense a continuing institution. In the short run the issues may change; the participants seldom do. (Horn 1970: 155)

This ongoing interaction creates particular conditions of knowledge and understanding of conference committee members – the anticipation of each other's strategies and the creation of different lawmakers' reputations.

Not only are the meetings essentially secret and the interactions ongoing, but the rules of the conference committee deliberations are nonexistent: no quorum rules, no proxy rules, no amendment rules, no voting procedure rules. There is an informal rule that the chair of the whole committee will alternate from one chamber to the other, but that is practically all there is. Of course, who presides is very important because he or she can formulate proposals and try to forge one particular compromise instead of another. The significance of the chair can be illustrated by the following example (reported in Longley and Oleszek 1989: 201). In early 1984 an important conference on tax reform was approaching, and it was the turn of House Ways and Means Committee's Chair Dan Rostenkowski (D, Ill.) to chair the conference. In the meantime a minor bill raising the national debt ceiling passed the House. The Senate, under Finance Committee Chair Robert Dole (R, Kans.), passed a slightly different bill (different termination date) and requested a conference. Dole's maneuver aimed to make Rostenkowski chair of the minor conference, while guaranteeing Dole the chair of the important one. Rostenkowski was able to prevail by persuading the House to adopt the Senate modification of the debt ceiling legislation, which made a conference on this legislation unnecessary.

This description indicates that conference committees in the U.S. are secret or quasi-secret meetings of representatives in an ongoing interaction without formal rules. In such a setting, the assumptions of cooperative game theory (no formal rules, binding agreements) are a good approximation of the fluid U.S. case. Consequently, the cooperative game theory assumptions used in Part II are appropriate not only with respect to the countries with strong parties, such as the four previous cases, but for the U.S. case as well.

The conference discusses only issues of disagreement between the two chambers and cannot reopen matters on which agreement has been reached. Consequently, if one chamber introduces amendments to the bill of the other chamber, the scope of the conference committee is automatically restricted to the discussion of these amendments. If, however, the second chamber introduces an amendment in the form of a substitute, that is, it rewrites the bill from scratch, the conference committee has the maximum degree of freedom because all aspects of the legislation are open to discussion.

The conference proposal is voted under closed rule in both chambers. The report goes first to the chamber that *accepted* the formation of a conference committee. This chamber has three options: to accept the bill as is, to reject it, or to recommit it to conference. If the bill is accepted the conference committee is dissolved, and the bill is presented to the second chamber, which can only accept or reject it. The incidence of successful motions to recommit is extremely rare. Smith (1989: 230) reports that, in the period 1971–86, only 20 motions to recommit were successful (16 in the House and 4 in the Senate), compared with more than 60 unsuccessful challenges. The option to recommit and instructions to the conferees are the two tools that the parent chambers have at their disposal, after they have selected the delegations, to restrict the space of the final outcome from the winset of the status quo to the set of bicameral restrictions (see Chapter 5). Of the two tools, the motion to recommit restricts conference committees more severely, because instructions for the most part are not mandatory.

The case study below demonstrates an atypical case, where no chamber had deliberated on a bill, so that the conference committee got the complete power to "work things out": the Gramm–Rudman–Hollings bill. As we will see, the two delegations developed positions on behalf of their parent chambers; these positions were approved by the parent chambers before the beginning of the real negotiation phase; then the intercameral compromise was worked out (taking into account the preferences of the White House).

In 1985, when the Senate was debating the extension of the debt ceiling limit, Senators Phil Gramm (R, Tex.), Warren Rudman (R, N.H.), and Ernest Hollings (D, S.C.) introduced a complex forty-page amendment on the floor, which aimed at balancing the budget in six years. The debate was limited by very severe deadlines because the Reagan administration wanted the debt ceiling extension in a matter of days, so there was little time to evaluate the implications of the amendment. Although some

Democrats complained about the lack of debate and comprehension of the amendment, it was adopted by an overwhelming majority.[30] The amendment specified the size of annual budget cuts; should the House, the Senate, and the president fail to produce the appropriate budget cuts, they would be implemented by "sequestration," that is, automatic reductions across the board.

When the House received the legislation, it did not have an alternative proposal, so it requested a conference committee and gave to its own delegation very broad instructions in favor of deficit reduction. The conference committee was composed of some 50 people, including all the major players in both the House and the Senate, with the notable exception of all three authors of the amendment (Gramm, Rudman, and Hollings). Officially, the first two were excluded because they lacked membership in either Senate committee with jurisdiction, while the third lacked sufficient seniority. The negotiations continued until each of the delegations presented a set of points to the other. Their differences covered the target deficit for the first year, which agency would forecast the deficit figures, whether the entire bill or part of the bill would fail if some part of it were found unconstitutional, and whether low-income programs would be exempt from budget cuts. At that point, they realized that no further progress was possible and they adjourned.

Each chamber confirmed its delegation's proposal by a comfortable margin, and new (larger) delegations were selected. The most interesting difference was the participation of all the bill's sponsors on the Senate side.

The new conference convened, but since discussions and agreement among 60 delegates were impossible, the actual negotiations were delegated to smaller groups. The final compromise was forged by two Republicans (representing the Senate) and two Democrats (representing the House). This compromise was approved by both committee delegations and introduced in both chambers.

In the Senate, the members initially objected that the committee had exceeded its scope. A point of order was raised to that effect with the purpose to kill the bill. When this attempt was defeated, a second attempt to defeat the bill by recommitting it to conference was fended off. Only at that point was the report adopted by the Senate. Several procedural points had to be defeated in the House before the report was adopted. Finally, the White House seemed to have some objections before it agreed to sign the legislative compromise.

---

[30]Perhaps the most accurate description of the climate of Senate discussion is offered by the following quote of Senate Majority Leader Robert Dole to a proponent of the bill: "Don't get up and explain it again. Some of us are for it" (Longley and Oleszek 1989: 310).

Conference committees

This short report (for details see Longley and Oleszek 1989: 306–34) demonstrates concretely the points about conference composition, procedure, and outcomes that we made in the beginning of this section. The composition is determined to a large extent by the members of the corresponding standing committees. The conferees act mainly as representatives of their chambers. The essential decision making is secret despite the appearance of openness, and the range of the compromise can be wide, particularly in this case, where the parent chambers did not have clear positions.

6. THE EUROPEAN UNION CO-DECISION PROCEDURE

European Union legislation can be produced in different ways depending on the subject matter. All procedures specify some rules of interaction between the Commission, which introduces bills, the European Parliament, which proposes amendments to these bills, and the Council of Ministers, which makes the final decision most of the time. Tables 2.1, 2.2A, and 2.2B present a summary of these procedures as special cases of the navette system. Only one of these procedures, the so-called co-decision procedure introduced by the Treaty of Maastricht in 1992, requires the creation of a conciliation committee composed of representatives of the Council of Ministers and the European Parliament under certain conditions.

According to the co-decision procedure (officially named "the procedure referred to in Article 189b"), a bill is introduced by the Commission to the European Parliament for a first reading and then shuttles to the Council of Ministers. The Council considers the parliamentary amendments and gives its common position. A second parliamentary reading follows and the amendments proposed by the European Parliament at this stage, if accepted by the Commission, must be incorporated in the final text by the Council; otherwise the Council is required to call a conciliation committee. This committee is, for all practical purposes, a conference committee of a bicameral legislature; the only point of departure arises from the fact that even if there is no compromise, the bill does not die necessarily. In a third reading the Council can confirm its prior position with all, some, or none of the European Parliament's amendments. Finally, the Parliament can either accept or reject the Council's confirmed text.

Due to the recent adoption of this procedure and the secrecy of its deliberations (they are held *in camera*), there is little evidence of how it has worked in practice and even fewer descriptions of its results. Most of the following information is based on an account presented by Gary Miller (1995) of the Conciliations Secretariat of the European Parliament.

Additional information can be found in the authoritative *The European Parliament* by Jacobs, Corbett, and Shackleton (1995).

The conference committee is composed of 15 members from the Council of Ministers (one representative of each country voting by weighted vote) and an equal number of members from the European Parliament. At the time when the institutional details of the committee were elaborated, the European Parliament was influenced by two models of conference committees – those of the U.S. Congress, composed mainly of members of the standing committees with jurisdiction, and the German conference committees, with constant composition (Jacobs et al. 1995: 205). As a result, the parliamentary delegation is composed of three members from the vice-presidents of Parliament (who serve for a whole year and ensure institutional memory), the chair and the rapporteur[31] of the standing committee having jurisdiction over the bill, and 10 additional members originating from committees with relevant jurisdictions, selected by the political parties. The political composition of the committee is a faithful microcosm of the Parliament, with (currently) six Socialists, five Christian Democrats, one Liberal, and so on. The parliamentary delegation is led by the president of the Parliament (16th member), who can delegate this function to one of the vice-presidents.

According to Article 189b, the Council is represented by "the members of the Council or their representatives." In practice, ministers are replaced very frequently by high- (or lower-)level bureaucrats. The composition of the Council delegation affects the committee's capacity to compromise, because ministers can promise and deliver compromises, whereas unelected bureaucrats cannot. The bureaucrats must go back to their respective governments and ask for approval, so the meetings of the conference committee are frequently adjourned. In general, the composition of the Council delegation increases the intransigence of the Council's position. The Parliament has complained about this absence of maneuvering margins.[32] One or more members of the Commission participate in the meetings without the right to vote. Their mission is to "take all the necessary initiatives to reconciling the positions." The committee has six weeks to reach a compromise.

Although the number of official committee members is 30, the actual number of people attending the conference may be multiplied by a factor

[31]Rapporteur is an institution unknown to Anglo-Saxon parliaments, but frequent in continental European ones. A specific member of the committee (and not the chair) is assigned the responsibility for putting together the committee's position on a bill, to report on the floor, to express the committee's positions by accepting or rejecting amendments on the floor, and to follow the bill on behalf of the Parliament.

[32]See the report of Mme. Nicole Fontaine (1995: 16), first vice-president of the European Parliament (Christian Democrat), which states: "De ce fait, les représentants permanents (adjoints le plus souvent) ne jouissent d'aucune marge de manoeuvre."

of 10. Each Council representative may be accompanied by up to 5 assistants, and the president of the Council may have an additional 5 Council assistants. The parliamentary delegation may include another 10 officials from the secretariat. The Commission representatives may also bring assistants. Add to that the interpreters for the 11 official languages, and the image can become quite interesting indeed! Informal meetings of committee officials become necessary to ensure the progress of negotiations.

The committee is jointly chaired by the leaders of the two delegations. The discussions in the committee are not restricted to the differences between the Parliament and the Council. The committee may discuss compromises including parts of the bill that were not amended by the Parliament. The decisions are made by concurrent qualified majorities: absolute majority of the EP delegation and qualified (currently 62/87) majority of the Council delegation.[33]

The compromise solution is presented in all 11 official languages of the Community to both the Council and the Parliament for a closed-rule vote and is considered adopted when both institutions approve it, the Parliament by *simple majority* and the Council by qualified (62/87) majority. If the committee is unable to reach a compromise, the Council may confirm its previous position (including as many parliamentary amendments as it wishes) and send it to the Parliament, which has six weeks to reject it by *absolute majority*.[34] If the Parliament rejects the bill, the status quo prevails, while if it fails to reject, the bill is adopted.

Out of the 32 bills completed under the co-decision procedure by the middle of 1995, 30 were adopted and 2 were rejected. From the 30 adopted bills, only 12 required convening a conciliation committee (1 was adopted despite a previous declaration of intended rejection by the Parliament). Of the 2 rejected bills, 1 was after the failure of the committee to reach a compromise (the Council confirmed its prior position without including any parliamentary amendments and the Parliament rejected the position), and the other was after the compromise position was rejected by Parliament.

The bill protecting biotechnological inventions provides an example to illustrate the application of rules described above. In the second reading the Parliament accepted three amendments, although the committee had approved fifteen amendments (the Parliament was not able to vote on the other proposed amendments because of intervening elections and tight

[33]On issues of framework research programs and culture, the Council delegation must decide by unanimity.
[34]Given the low attendance rate at the European Parliament (sometimes below 50 percent), an absolute majority requirement can be the equivalent to a two-thirds qualified majority or even unanimity of the members present.

schedule). The Council accepted without difficulty two of the three amendments. However, the crucial problem for the parliamentary delegation was to introduce the amendments that had not been voted by Parliament. After a series of prolonged negotiations in conference committee, the parliamentary delegation was able to achieve satisfactory compromises on the three amendments adopted by the Parliament, as well as the inclusion of three more amendments (from the ones not voted by the Parliament). The committee bill was accompanied by a series of interpretative declarations, but by the time it reached the floor of the Parliament the political climate had changed and the Parliament rejected the bill with 240 against and 188 in favor. The failure of this directive has raised questions in the Council about the "contractual capacity" of the parliamentary delegation.

This account indicates the wide range of compromises available to a committee deciding under the unit rule. It also demonstrates in the European context what U.S. legislators know very well, that final approval by the parent chambers is not a mere formality. In the European Parliament, a discrepancy of opinion between committee and parent chamber is very rare, since the political composition of committees mirrors the Parliament, but possible.

One aspect of the E.U. procedure makes the conciliation committee significantly different from the other conference committees we discuss. A failure to reach compromise does not abort the bill, but gives one more opportunity to the Council to make a "take it or leave it" offer to the Parliament.[35] This procedure strengthens the hand of the Council in the negotiations.[36]

In his excellent report on conference committees, Miller (1995) observes intransigence of the Council delegation in the conciliation committee:

The attitude of the Council often seems to be that its common position represents the starting point of the whole procedure and the reference point for any compromise. Since its quality as a legal text is taken to be self-evident, given the time and

[35]This is what happened with legislation on the liberalization of voice telephony: the committee failed to reach a compromise, the Council reintroduced its previous position, and the Parliament rejected it. Subsequently the Commission had to reintroduce legislation, and the parliamentary amendments were incorporated in the new bill.

[36]The result reported in the preceding note notwithstanding. In game-theoretic terms, the previous result can be considered the outcome of an iterated game. However, an iterated game can have many more possible outcomes, including new legislation that conforms to Council specifications and capitulation by Parliament. On the other hand, the equilibrium of the single-shot game is in favor of the Council, which can incorporate in its common position as many parliamentary amendments as necessary to make rejection by an absolute majority impossible. For a discussion of the issue, see Garrett (1995) and Garrett and Tsebelis (1996).

energy the Council has invested in arriving at a compromise, Council members behave as if they are the ones who have to be convinced and as if they have no need to persuade the Parliament that its amendments are not acceptable. Thus, if the Council has accepted any of the amendments, this is presented as a great concession on its part. Parliament can in other words "take it or leave it," there is no point in discussing the other amendments and if Parliament is so foolhardy as to persevere with them, it will be up to Parliament to carry the responsibility for the failure of the procedure and ultimately to reject the act outright. The members of the Council thus permit themselves the luxury of leaving the search for a compromise to others (their Presidency and the Members of the European Parliament). The compromise must be sufficiently attractive to persuade them to change their minds.

According to our models, the Council's intransigence can be explained not by some "attitude" or by the fact that high- or low-level bureaucrats participate in the conciliation committee instead of ministers, but by the default solution: if the conciliation committee fails, it will be the Council's turn to make a "take it or leave it" offer to the Parliament, so there is no reason to be conciliatory in committee.

7. CONCLUSIONS

These short accounts and histories of conference committee decision making cannot be used as confirmation of the models presented in Chapter 5. In particular, no direct test of Proposition 5.1 or its corollaries can be performed on the basis of this evidence. However, all of the data presented are consistent with Chapter 5 and the models constructed there help us understand what happened in the cases presented in this chapter.

First, conference committees' deliberations are, for all practical purposes, a black box. Consequently, noncooperative game-theoretic models based on specific sequences of moves and countermoves are of little use. Second, either because of the existence of strong parties, or because of ongoing interactions, the assumption of enforceable agreements (necessary for the use of the cooperative game-theoretic models of Part II) is approximated.

The U.S. and E.U. committees have the ability to reach many different compromises because of the unit rule in their decision making. For example, referring back to the Gramm–Rudman–Hollings discussion, the conference committee could adopt on any issue of disagreement the position of either delegation or some intermediate position. Similarly the E.U. conciliation committee could adopt any possible compromise involving the amendments adopted by the Parliament, as well as those not adopted. In contrast, a conference committee deciding by majority rule of all its members must adopt a compromise position on every issue, so that the final outcome would be located close to the center of the yolk of the committee (the multidimensional median).

The reason that all conference committees are powerful stems from their capacity to make the final proposals under closed rule. The French committees are weak because they have this right stripped by the government. As our case illustrates, the government can destroy agreements reached in committee by the introduction of additional amendments at the last stage. Because conference committees normally have the possibility of selecting out of all the possible compromise solutions the one that will become the law, they are able to influence legislation in an important way. The French case also illustrates the point that legislatures that want to rein in their conference committees give very detailed sets of bicameral restrictions.

Similarly the E.U. conciliation committee finds its right to make proposals under closed rule seriously circumscribed by the fact that, if it fails, the initiative for the bill returns to the Council, which can make a "take-it-or-leave-it" proposal to the Parliament. We saw that this institutional provision may be the cause for the intransigence of the Council delegation in the committee meetings.

The significance of conference committees can be reduced by making decisions difficult. Japan is the primary example, where a two-thirds majority is required for decisions. Our case illustrates a situation in which the committee could not decide on its own and was reduced to ratifying the decision of the party leadership.

The Swiss case provides a particularly clear example of the parent chambers' efforts to control conference committees through the appointment of members. Where the upper house's floor position differs from that of the standing committee, members are added to reinforce the floor's position to the detriment of the standing committee.

Finally, the reason that German conference committees are so powerful is that they operate under few constraints, and their composition is based on members of party and state leadership, so any agreement struck within them is rarely challenged, and even if challenged, it is sustained.

9

Implications

Some of the arguments made in this book, such as the proposition that bicameralism makes a change to the status quo more difficult than unicameralism, may seem intuitive, even trivial, to the reader.[1] Other arguments, like the rarity of a bicameral core in more than two dimensions, or empirical evidence, such as the connection between chamber composition and length of intercameral negotiations, dispute the conventional wisdom in the literature or point legislative research in a new direction.

In this chapter we review the different theories and arguments presented in the literature with a critical eye, explaining which are sound and justified, which require restrictions or modifications, and which are false and unsupported by the evidence. Finally, we raise other methodological, theoretical, and empirical issues that merit a more sustained investigation.

The chapter is organized in three sections, ordered from the more specific and the less objectionable to the more general and controversial. The first section deals with topics and ideas that are considered intuitive or at least well known. We show how we generalize these ideas or how we restrict their domain of application. The second section demonstrates that on a series of issues, we disagree both in theory and in evidence with the existing literature. The third part discusses the research agenda generated by this book. Given that some items fall into multiple categories, there is an overlap of subject matter among the three parts. For example, if there is a controversy in the literature and we side with and qualify one argument, we report the issue in both the first and the second sections;

[1]However, the two excerpts in the beginning of the book should serve as a reminder that what is obvious to one person may seem wrong to another. And if there is an important conclusion generated out of the plethora of social choice paradoxes (McKelvey 1976, 1979; Schofield 1978; Schwartz 1987), it is that our intuition is not a reliable guide and must be supplemented by careful evaluation of arguments. Consequently, what has to be evaluated is not how intuitive our arguments are, but how well founded.

and if we disagree with most of the literature and we believe that the issue merits further investigation, we report it in the second and third sections.

1. EXPANSIONS AND RESTRICTIONS OF KNOWN ARGUMENTS

In this section we present the approaches or arguments with which we agree and the limits of our agreement by demonstrating either that the argument can be expanded or that its domain of application is not as wide as previously believed. We deal with the issues of efficiency and redistribution, the privileged dimension of conflict, the selection of the conference committee's ideal point, the influence of both chambers on the outcome, and the importance of institutions.

Efficiency and redistribution. Figure II.1 presented a simplified but accurate idea of how bicameralism operates. The two chambers try to move the status quo to an area that both prefer. Such areas are likely to be located between the yolks of the two chambers. This movement of the status quo represents both an improved situation for both chambers along one dimension and a struggle between them along the other. In Chapter 1, we saw that beginning with the writings from ancient Greece, by way of Rome, and the classics of French and American constitutionalism, these two dimensions of bicameralism – the efficient and the political – have been recognized. In that respect, we provide a simple and intuitive geometric understanding of these diverse arguments, and we also demonstrate that the arguments hold if, instead of the simplifying single-actor representation of each chamber, we employ more realistic chambers with multiple members, without imposing any constraints on the position of the members' ideal points.

Privileged dimension of conflict. Hammond and Miller (1987) calculate the core of bicameral institutions in two dimensions, and they demonstrate that it is a straight line. Although they do not deal with the question of where on this line the final outcome of intercameral discussion will be located, they correctly identify that the points along the core cannot be defeated by other points in the two-dimensional space or by each other. According to their approach, this particular dimension of the core represents the zero-sum aspect of bicameralism, the set of points along which no efficiency gains can be achieved; consequently, the whole game of bicameral institutions becomes zero-sum. Their argument can be traced to Montesquieu ("One checks the other, by the mutual privilege of refusing") or to Madison ("No law or resolution can now be passed without the concurrence first, of a majority of the people, and then of a majority of the states"). We build on this concept of one privileged dimension of conflict and demonstrate that the argument is valid when the issue space is multidimensional, as well (see next section for further discussion).

Selection of conference committee compromise. Figures 5.1A–C demonstrate the likely proposal of a conference committee. The reader can verify that if the conference committee is conceptualized as a single player located at the center of the yolk of the actual committee, the prediction of the committee proposal as the legislative outcome is quite accurate. In fact, Shepsle and Weingast (1987a, 1987b) use similar illustrations, where the committee is a single player, and calculate the committee proposal as the point in the winset of the parent chamber that is closest to the ideal point of the committee. We simply generalize their argument by demonstrating that it holds for the more realistic setting of multimember committees *provided* that the members of these committees can make binding agreements (cooperative decision making). We believe that although the outcome remains qualitatively the same (the result we predict is an area that includes the result they calculate), our assumption of cooperative decision making is more realistic than the assumption of single-member committees, which is required for their results.

Influence of both chambers on the final outcomes. We also make the point that second chambers always exercise an influence on the final outcome of legislation. This is a trivial point when upper chambers can veto legislation, as in the United States, Switzerland, and Germany. However, it is our contention that all second chambers exercise influence even if they are considered weak or insignificant (Lijphart 1984). We demonstrate that the French Senate influences legislation, and we provide examples of upper house influence from countries like the United Kingdom, where the upper house is considered very weak. We also presented cases from Italy, where disagreement over important bills emerges even when the two chambers have the same political makeup. Our argument goes even further. To the extent that impatience for a compromise drives intercameral bargaining, even in the absence of manifest conflict, upper houses exercise some influence on legislation. This is because the absence of manifest conflict may not indicate the identity of viewpoints, but rather the anticipated reactions of the upper chamber and incorporation of its viewpoint in the process. In other words, to paraphrase the excerpt of Sièyes in the beginning of the book, second chambers may be bad (depending on one's point of view), but they are certainly not useless.

Importance of institutions. In an era of "New Institutionalism" (March and Olsen 1984), it is hardly an innovation to claim that institutions matter. What is required is the next step, that is, to demonstrate both theoretically and empirically *how* institutions matter. We believe that we make significant progress in this respect in Part II of this book. We present arguments concerning bicameralism in general, as well as specific institutional features of the navette and conference committees. Chapters 6 to 8 provide empirical tests of the claims presented in Chapters 3 to 5. We discuss these claims and findings in the next section.

2. DIVERGENT POINTS

In this section we contrast our arguments and findings with other approaches in the literature. For some of these issues, the existing literature provides opposing points of view; for others, there is no treatment of which we are aware. For the second time we address the questions of efficiency and redistribution, of one privileged dimension of conflict, and of the importance of institutions. For the first time, we contrast our arguments and results with the theoretical debates presented in Chapter 1, such as tyranny of minorities (Buchanan and Tullock), delaying qualities of bicameralism (Riker), effects of bicameralism in one and more than one dimensions (Riker), the role of bicameralism in the emergence of a strong Condorcet winner (Levmore), and the equivalence of bicameralism with qualified majority institutions (Levmore and Riker).

Efficiency and redistribution. As we mentioned in Chapter 1, historical arguments concerning bicameralism recognized both dimensions of bicameralism. But after the emergence of republicanism and the marriage of federalism with bicameral institutions, the bicameralism debate bifurcated. Theorists describing bicameralism in unitary states exclusively employed arguments concerning the efficiency and quality control of legislation, while in federal systems the common denominator involved issues of conflict and power distribution between the two houses. Our approach reintroduces both themes because it is only in extreme cases that one of the two dimensions of bicameralism – the efficient or the political – is completely absorbed by the other. In general, the status quo and the ideal positions of the two chambers (considered as unified actors) form a triangle, and consequently both houses can be made better off by moving away from the status quo, while each of them has a different idea about the best policy position.

Privileged dimension of conflict. In Chapter 3 we demonstrated that although some of the intuitions presented in the literature were correct, the arguments proposed in their defense were wrong. For example, unlike previous arguments (Brennan and Hamlin 1992; Hammond and Miller 1987), our defense of the one major dimension of conflict is not based on the concept of the core, but on other cooperative game-theoretic concepts like the uncovered set and the tournament equilibrium. We demonstrated in Chapter 3 that the core of a bicameral legislature rarely exists in more than two dimensions, and consequently it cannot be used as the basis for the privileged dimension of conflict argument. In contrast, the series of solution concepts that we present always exists. Consequently we can employ them to establish that *under the restriction of cooperative decision making,* once the decision to replace the status quo is made, the serious contenders for such a replacement will be located in the neighborhood of a straight line (see Figure 3.6). We find this restriction reasonably approximated in countries where parties operate under strong party discipline, that is, in parliamentary systems.

Importance of institutions. To our knowledge this is the first scholarly work to make specific predictions about the institutions used all over the world to resolve bicameral differences. We focus on the navette system and provide a way of studying it that enables us to understand the political effects of a series of institutional devices that have not been previously examined or that were considered administrative provisions for increasing legislative efficiency. Chapter 4 makes a series of predictions concerning these devices, and Chapter 6 uses these predictions to provide an alternative account of French legislative history. According to our account, where a bill is introduced or the number of times it can shuttle from one house to the next has political significance, because it shifts the balance of power between the two houses. In addition, we focus on a series of institutions regulating the activities of conference committees, in order to assess their significance. In particular, we argue that conference committees are significant because they can make a proposal to their parent chambers under closed rule, and thus that their composition, the restrictions under which they operate, and their decision-making rules are very important. With respect to their composition and restrictions, we describe the efforts made by parent chambers across the world to rein in these *third houses.* With respect to decision-making rules, we see that conference committees operating under the unit rule (U.S., E.U.) have greater leeway than conference committees operating under simple majority rule (the majority of countries with conference committees) and that this decision rule provides committees with more decision-making power than possible with qualified majority decisions (Japan). These expectations are derived from the size of the set within which the committee may make its proposal, the "induced on bicameral restrictions" uncov-

ered set (see Chapter 5). The empirical examples of Chapter 8 corroborated these predictions, although by no means can the claim of selection
bias be eliminated.

Impatience and uncertainty. The driving force behind our institutional
models, besides the institutions described in the preceding paragraph, is
the impatience of the two chambers to reach a compromise and the
uncertainty about this impatience. In Chapter 4 we argued that impatience will drive each chamber to accept less in order to reach a compromise today; this mechanism accounts for the influence of upper chambers
even if they do not have the power to veto legislation. We demonstrated
that institutional rules have an impact because they regulate this power to
delay or to veto, and we showed empirically in Chapter 7 that the more
impatient a chamber, the less input it has in the final outcome.

On the other hand, the length of the navette process is attributed, not
to the importance of the differences between the two houses, but to the
uncertainty about each other's impatience. While the standard explanation for the length of the negotiating process is the distance of the ideal
points of the two chambers, we place the explanation on the uncertainty
surrounding time discount factors. Chapter 6 provides statistical evidence
that the navette process lasts longer when the French National Assembly
is in the middle of its term and its discount factor can be estimated less
well by the Senate. Similarly, the navette lasts longer when the power of
the Gaullist allies is at intermediate levels, making it difficult for the
Senate to guess whether the National Assembly will insist on its proposal
or not.

How does this picture of bicameralism differ from other accounts
presented in the literature? In Chapters 6 and 7, we presented a series of
explanations from the French literature concerning the interaction of the
two chambers. They were based either on the wisdom of the upper house,
on the political weight of the president, or on administrative factors, such
as legislative expediency. We demonstrated there that our theory does at
least as well as any of these in explaining the events of French legislative
history. Here we want to make a different claim, which is, in our view, the
most important one. All accounts we encountered when reviewing the
French literature were local and do not generalize beyond the time and
place for which they were generated. In other words, these accounts are
not theories, or if one insists on the use of the term, they are *degenerative*
theories, to borrow Lakatos and Musgrave's (1970) terminology.

A series of arguments was presented in Chapter 1. It is time now to
review them. Buchanan and Tullock present an interesting argument that
bicameralism protects a polity from the tyranny of the minority, since
with two chambers it is impossible for a quarter of the population to

impose its will on the majority (it cannot have the majority in both chambers). While this argument is interesting, we are struck by its restricted applicability and by its contrived nature even in the countries where it is applicable. Indeed, the basic assumption for the argument is a plurality electoral system and a bicameral legislature where both houses have veto power. The set of countries with a plurality electoral system are all Anglo-Saxon, and of those, only the U.S. has a bicameral legislature where both chambers have veto power (Canada, another bicameral Anglo-Saxon legislature, has a weak upper chamber). Consequently, in the best of cases, Buchanan and Tullock's argument is applicable in a single country. But even in the U.S., it requires implausible assumptions about the distribution of voters in order to hold.

One argument presented by Levmore is equally contrived. He argues that bicameralism promotes a *strong Condorcet winner* if such a winner exists. According to his definition a strong Condorcet winner is an alternative that defeats every other alternative in both chambers. As we discuss in Chapter 3, Plott identified the conditions for existence of a Condorcet winner in more than one dimension and they are extremely restrictive. For each of the two chambers to have a Condorcet winner is a zero probability event, and for both of them to have the same point as a Condorcet winner, the probability is even lower.[2]

Bicameralism is also touted in the literature for reducing the power of the agenda setter and with reducing cycles (as argued by Levmore, Riker, Miller, and Hammond). It is true that certain cycles possible in unicameral legislatures are impossible in bicameral ones. At this point some reference to Figure 3.B1 may be necessary. While the winset of the status quo of a unicameral legislature is included in a cardioid, the winset of the status quo of a bicameral legislature is included in the intersection of two cardioids, one per chamber. Consequently, when a second chamber exists, some outcomes that can defeat the status quo in one chamber are eliminated as possible results of a bicameral legislature. However, as the figure indicates, the intersection of the two cardioids expands on the other side of line $C_L C_U$ further than the status quo. The figure indicates that the second generation of cardioids (the union of the winsets of the points that defeat the points that defeat points on line $C_L C_U$) expands even further. In fact, this is the area within which the uncovered set is included. One can continue like this and generate a sequence of points that defeat the preceding ones. It is clear that the last point of such a sequence (provided that one repeats the operation at least twice) may be defeated by points on the $C_L C_U$ line. Consequently, cycles can be gener-

---

[2] When the set of possible events is infinite, as is the case here, there are *possible* events with zero probability of materializing.

ated in bicameralism. The difference between bicameralism and unicameralism in this respect is a difference of frequency rather than a difference in kind.

How significant is the lower frequency of cycles in bicameralism? If one takes seriously the proposition that agenda setters are strategic actors, the difference between unicameralism and bicameralism is minor in this respect. A strategic agenda setter, with an agent in the other chamber, can generate a sequence of options that will cycle, and consequently can obtain his or her ideal point after a sufficiently long sequence of alternatives. Therefore, bicameralism improves the cycling situation but does not eliminate it. On the contrary, a qualified majority unicameral institution may eliminate cycles altogether. Figure 3.4 presents the 5/7 majority core of a legislature with seven members in two dimensions. Any point in the shaded area cannot be defeated at all. Comparison of this figure with Figure 3.3 indicates that the shape of the core of a bicameral institution (if that core exists) is very different. Even if the core does not exist, however, the fundamental confrontation in bicameralism still consists of selecting a point along the *UL* line. Even if the point does not belong to the line, the location of its projection along this line is the most important conflict of a bicameral legislature.

Here we come back to a point we make several times in the book. Bicameralism increases stability through promotion of the status quo; in other words, it makes the status quo more difficult to defeat. However, once the status quo is to be replaced, the main conflict is transposed along the line connecting the centers of the yolks of the two chambers (labeled *UL* or $C_U C_L$ in different figures).

Now we can address some of Riker's points. Riker claims that bicameralism in one dimension selects the median voter outcome, while in multiple dimensions it delays the decision until such a median emerges. The argument is incorrect. In one dimension, bicameralism does not select any particular point between the medians of the two chambers (see Figure 3.2). As a result, if selection of outcomes is the goal, bicameralism makes things worse in one dimension, because instead of the median voter (for an odd number of legislators), it presents a whole array of outcomes. In two dimensions, if there is a core, again it does not select one point of the core. In two dimensions without a core, or in more than two dimensions, bicameralism focuses the debate along axis *UL,* but it does not select any particular point, unless one wants to introduce a series of additional assumptions (as we did in Chapters 4, 6, and 7). In this case, the selected point is a function of all these institutional as well as political assumptions.

In conclusion, greater stability (in the sense of preserving status quo) and focus of conflict along one dimension are the main features (both advantages and disadvantages) of bicameralism. If an institutional designer desires policy stability as defined above, bicameralism delivers. In addition, as we argued in the introduction to Part II, this policy stability increases as a function of the distance of points U and L from each other, in other words, as a function of the degree of incongruence. On the other hand, if rapid change is desired, a constitutional designer would be better off avoiding bicameral (as well as presidential) institutions. Similarly, if the distinction between the two chambers represents a serious cleavage in the electorate, bicameralism is well suited to focus the political debate on that cleavage and to forge a compromise acceptable by both parts. If, however, the line of division of the two chambers is orthogonal to the main cleavages of the electorate, the legislative debate will focus on issues irrelevant to the electorate.

An example drives this point home. A major cleavage facing advanced industrialized societies is generated by a division between young and old generations concerning the issue of social security. On the one hand, the arguments are for fiscal responsibility and reduction of entitlements; on the other, the point is made that agreements are sacred and that how a society treats the elderly is a matter of society's self-image as a whole. Suppose that a federal country faces this debate and that the majority of one chamber represents the young and the majority of the other represents the old. This bicameral institution will be able to debate the issue thoroughly and come to a decision respected by the entire population. Consider now the case where both chambers represent one side of the coin; it makes no difference whether it is the young or the old. The major debate will be set aside, and both chambers will be willing to agree with very little debate. However, whatever their agreement, it will not be representative of the country as a whole.[3]

From this discussion, it is clear that our conclusions differ significantly from most of the literature on bicameralism. Now we turn to some points that are extensions of our approach, that are generated by other debates, and that have not been investigated in the text of the book. That is, now we focus on how the arguments made in this book can illuminate other ongoing debates in politics or in methodology.

3. AGENDA FOR FUTURE RESEARCH

In this section we focus on two substantive and two "methodological" issues. The quotation marks are used because, as becomes clear in the course of the discussion, methodology and substance are very closely

---

[3]The crusade of Senator Simpson against the American Association of Retired Persons may be a precursor of such a debate.

related. The substantive issues are the capacity of bicameralism to preserve the status quo to a greater degree than unicameralism and the implications of our analysis for the study of legislative politics. The methodological issues are the significance of accepting a set concept (like the uncovered set or tournament equilibrium set) as an outcome and the selection of one main dimension of conflict.

3a. Substantive issues

Preservation of status quo. The normative dimension of the preservation of the status quo will not preoccupy us here. Ultimately, analysts who dislike the status quo will be in favor of institutions that promote change, and analysts who like it will prefer institutions that tend to preserve it. Strong bicameralism (where both chambers have veto power) is one such institution.

In addition to this political alignment, there is an interesting professional one. Political scientists are often interested in the decisiveness of a political system, in other words, its capacity to solve problems when they arise. For example, in a thoughtful analysis of the effects of political institutions, Weaver and Rockman (1993: 6) distinguish 10 different capabilities that all governments need:

to *set and maintain priorities* among the many conflicting demands made upon them so that they are not overwhelmed and bankrupted; to *target resources* where they are most effective; to *innovate* when old policies have failed; to *coordinate conflicting objectives* into a coherent whole; to be able to *impose* losses on powerful groups; to *represent diffuse, unorganized interests* in addition to concentrated, well-organized ones; to *ensure effective implementation* of government policies once they have been decided upon; to *ensure policy stability* so that policies have time to work; to *make and maintain international commitments* in the realms of trade and national defense to ensure their long-term well-being; and, above all, to *manage political cleavages* to ensure that society does not degenerate into civil war.

While Weaver and Rockman are interested in the capabilities of governments, a great volume of economic literature is concerned with the credible commitment of the government *not* to interfere with the economy (Kydland and Prescott 1977). Weingast (1993) pushes the argument one step further and attempts to design institutions that would produce such a credible commitment. He suggests that "market preserving federalism" combines checks and balances that prevent government interference in the economy with economic competition among units to ensure growth.

Both literatures emphasize the benefits of stability as a dimension of good government. Bicameral legislatures provide such stability. We ar-

218

gued in the introduction to Part II that the larger the distance between the ideal points of the two chambers, the greater the capacity of a bicameral legislature to preserve the status quo. The examples of divided political majorities represented in upper and lower chambers in France (presented in Chapter 7), as well as in Japan and Germany (Chapter 8), illustrate the difficulties of agreement, slowing the passage of legislation. In France, resolving the disagreements required incurring the political cost of over-ruling the hostile Senate.

In Germany, new legislation required the support of an almost univer-sal coalition. In Japan, control of the two houses by different majorities significantly slowed the passage of legislation, up to the point of inca-pacitating the legislature itself. However, difficulty of changing the status quo is only part of the story. If bicameralism provides this desirable quality, it also comes with less desirable features.

Tsebelis (1995a) provides an analysis of different institutional settings that promote preservation of the status quo (labeled *policy stability*). In addition to bicameralism, such systems include presidentialism with a strong (in the legislative arena) president and multipartyism. Policy stabil-ity is then connected with a series of other properties in political systems. Tsebelis argues that increased difficulty in changing policies will result, under certain circumstances, in the change of government or change of regime. Consequently, policy stability is connected with government in-stability in parliamentary systems and with regime instability in presiden-tial systems.[4] In addition, he argues that policy stability will be connected with independence and significance of the judiciary and the bureaucracy.[5]

While most of these results have already been corroborated empiri-cally, the question remains whether bicameralism has only a mediated effect (through policy stability) on government and regime instability, as well as on the independence of the judiciary and bureaucracies, or a direct effect as well.

Significance for the study of legislative politics. As we made clear in the introduction to this book, the study of bicameral legislatures as if they were unicameral may be misleading, because the legislative outcomes are different and, consequently, so are legislators' strategies. In fact, strategic calculations by the legislators start from the last stage of the legislative process, the bicameral compromise (whether it is obtained by a confer-ence committee, by the navette system, or by a unilateral decision of one chamber), and work their way backward. In turn, if outcomes and strate-

[4]Tsebelis (1995a) provides evidence for both of these claims based on the work of Warwick (1994) and Shugart and Carey (1992).

[5]Recent work by Alivizatos (1995) corroborates this prediction with respect to the judiciary.

gies in bicameral legislatures are different than in unicameral ones, it may be that the structural characteristics of these legislatures cannot be studied in one chamber alone. Let us see how this proposition affects existing approaches to the most studied legislature of the world, the U.S. Congress.

Although there are numerous studies of Congress, most of them focus on the House of Representatives (Krehbiel 1991; Shepsle 1978; Smith 1989). There are some studies of the Senate (Fenno 1982; Sinclair 1989) but very few examine the interaction of the two houses (Longley and Oleszek 1989; Smith 1988). What is interesting about this literature is that although the models deal with both policy outcomes and structural features of Congress, the empirical research is almost exclusively based on structural characteristics of Congress.

For example, what have been labeled "distributive" models of Congress[6] predict that committees in the House will be powerful because they frequently submit their proposals under closed rule, while committees in the Senate will be less important, because their proposals are considered under open rule on the floor of the Senate. Consequently, the argument continues, there will be self-selection operating for committee assignments: members of the House will be interested in committees that reinforce their chance for reelection. Therefore committees will be composed of preference outliers, high demanders in the area of their jurisdiction. Shepsle (1978), who has made this argument, explicitly studied the composition of committees in the House and has found evidence corroborating his argument. To our knowledge, no one has made a similar claim about the Senate because Senate committees are not considered to be important.

On the other hand, what has been labeled the "informational" approach to Congress (Gilligan and Krehbiel 1990; Krehbiel 1991) expects committees to be agents of the parent chamber (since this parent floor decides both their composition and the rules for final votes). Consequently, committees will be composed of experts and moderates in order to provide the maximum amount of information to their principals.

A third approach, which considers committees as agents of the party that controls the majority of seats in the House (Cox and McCubbins 1993), expects the composition of important committees, that is, the ones that make procedural decisions, to be representative of the floor.

The empirical evidence concerns the composition of committees, not the policy outcomes. Even then, it is surrounded by methodological con-

---

[6]This is the terminology used by Keith Krehbiel (1991) in reference to a series of models the most representative of which can be found in the work of Shepsle (1979) and Shepsle and Weingast (1981).

troversies and the evidence is mixed.[7] What we would like to underline here is that none of these theories expects Senate committees to be composed of outliers, because Senate committees are not supposed to be powerful. However, empirical research by Grofman and Hall (1992) indicates that the Senate Agriculture Committee is composed of outliers with respect to their own jurisdiction (i.e., important agricultural issues). Why would this happen? Such a finding is a puzzle for one-chamber institutional approaches to legislatures[8] but can be illuminated by our approach.

We argue that committees are powerful in both the House and the Senate not only because of what they do in their own chamber (after all, the parent chamber can always decide to vote under open rule), but because participation in the standing committee provides a ticket for participation in the conference committee that makes its proposal under *closed* rule. As we described in Chapter 8, a U.S. conference committee makes a final proposal that cannot be modified. At most, a proposal can be recommitted to the conference committee by the chamber that examined the bill first, while the chamber that examined the bill second votes it up or down. In addition, as we argued in Chapters 5 and 8, the leeway of conference committees in the U.S. Congress is very high in comparative perspective, because it decides by the unit rule. This increases its uncovered set; that is, it is able to come to many different compromises. Our approach attributes the power of committees in *both* chambers (not only of the House) to participation in the bicameral institution (the conference committee), not to the relationship between each floor and the corresponding committee. Because of participation in the conference committee, these members can *propose* the compromise to their chamber. A crucial experiment in favor of our claim can be provided by the story of the German conference committee in Chapter 8. When the members of the standing committees differed from the members of the conference committee, it was the latter who prevailed despite protests on the floor of the lower house.

Anecdotal evidence from the U.S. Congress also supports our contention. Gold et al. (1992: 343) report the remark of "a seasoned conferee" to his staff: "When you come here [to Congress], they tell you to work within your committee to get what you want. But if you just wait until you can get on a conference committee, that's the best place I know to

---

[7]For the methodological controversy, see Londregan and Snyder (1994); for a substantive discussion, see Bawn and Tsebelis (1996).

[8]Of course, the argument can be made that committees in the Senate are powerful too, because of deference. However, in an institutional approach "deference" is a dependent, not an independent, variable.

sneak something into law."[9] Similarly, Republican Representative John Erlenborn claimed:

All too often . . . the House speaks its will by amending legislation from [the Education and Labor Committee] or adopting substitute bills and sending the legislation to the other body. All too often the other body passes a bill very similar to that rejected by the House. And almost without exception the conference committee members appointed by the House accede more to the provisions of the other body than they try to protect the provisions which the House had adopted.[10]

And Senator J. William Fulbright (D, Ark.) complained that "it is quite clear that regardless of what the common members of this body may wish, the conferees make the decision."[11] One can multiply the supportive quotes, but the essence of our argument is institutional: conference committees may face constraints from the parent chambers, but within these constraints, they control the agenda and can select the compromise they prefer.

Shepsle and Weingast (1987a) present a similar argument about the origins of conference committee power. They argue that standing committees are powerful because their members participate in a conference committee, which has "ex post veto power" over legislation (can abort legislation they do not like):

In the absence of some form of ex post veto power, committee proposals are vulnerable to alteration and, because of this, committees have agenda control in a very truncated form. It is unlikely, in our view that such a shaky foundation would induce individuals to invest in institutional careers in the committees on which they serve. (Shepsle and Weingast 1987a: 101)

Our argument is more general. Not only do conference committees, and therefore standing committees, have ex post veto power (the power to *block* outcomes they dislike); more importantly they have the power to *propose* to both chambers under closed rule.[12]

Bawn and Tsebelis (1996) provide another example that corroborates the approach of this book. They studied the passage of the 1977 Clean Air Act by locating the ideal positions of floor and committee medians in different dimensions. They found that with respect to a series of dimensions indicating protection of the environment, the positions of these four actors were arrayed in the following order: House floor, House committee, Senate floor, Senate committee. That is, the House committee posi-

[9]We thank Barbara Sinclair for the quote.
[10]Reported in Smith (1989: 224).
[11]Quoted in Longley and Oleszek (1989: 6).
[12]Nagler (1989) has made a similar point while discussing the strategic implications of conferee selection by the Speaker of the House.

tion was located between the Senate and the House floor positions, while the Senate committee was extreme in comparison with the positions of the parent houses. The final outcome was located somewhere between the House committee and the Senate. This final outcome jibes with the expectation of the distributive theories of Congress; it indicates that the House committee was strong and the Senate committee was weak. However, a close examination of the successive modifications of the bill as it comes out of each committee and each floor indicates that the House committee lost on the floor vote and the Senate committee prevailed on the Senate floor, that is, exactly the opposite of what prevailing theories would expect. Bawn and Tsebelis underline the fact that in the case of the Clean Air Act, when unicameral arguments are applied to each chamber alone the empirical evidence is against them, and when they are applied to the bicameral legislature, they come out correct. However, the explanation lies in bicameralism, not on the arguments of the corresponding unicameral theories.

Consequently, a close examination of the relationship between five different actors – two house floors, two house committees, and a conference committee – is necessary to understand legislation, strategies, and structural characteristics of Congress, as well as of any bicameral legislature. How can such a study be undertaken? This question takes us to the second part of the section.

3b. "Methodological" issues

Significance of a set concept as outcome. Thus far, we have implicitly applied a backwards induction argument. We considered the final outcome to be known and used it to calculate the optimal strategy in the preceding stage, then took these strategies for granted and calculated structural characteristics like committee composition. This is the standard approach in game theory. Its application is straightforward if there is only one (subgame) equilibrium at the end of the game. If, however, multiple results are possible, we may run into problems.

We first use a very simple game-theoretic example to drive the point across, then discuss the implications for legislative research. Consider the example presented in Figure 9.1, which we borrow from Fudenberg and Tirole (1992: 99–100).

Figure 9.1 presents a three-person game, where player 1 moves first and can choose to end the game and distribute 6, 0, and 6 to each player, respectively, or to continue. Then player 2 decides whether to end the game and distribute 8, 6, and 8 to each player, respectively, or to continue. At that point, players 3 and 1 move simultaneously, and if they coordinate (both select left or both select right), they distribute 7, 10, and 7 to

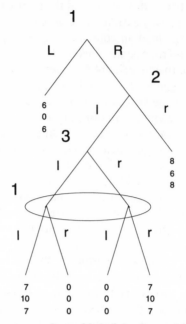

Figure 9.1. Game where uncoordinated beliefs lead to out-of-equilibrium results. Redrawn from Fudenberg and Tirole 1992: 99–100.

the players, respectively; if they make opposite choices (one left, the other right), all three players receive zero.

According to game theory, the correct way to play this game is by backwards induction. In the last stage of the game, when players 1 and 3 move simultaneously there are three equilibria: either they coordinate (both left or both right), receiving payoffs 7, 10, and 7 respectively, or they do not coordinate. We will take this lack of coordination to mean a mixed strategy where both players 1 and 3 use each strategy with probability 1/2, and consequently the players receive 7/2, 5, and 7/2, respectively.

Now let us move to the preceding stage. If players 1 and 3 are going to coordinate, player 2 is going to select to play the game, since she will receive 10 if the last stage is played out and only 6 if she selects to end the game when she has the choice. Similarly, player 1, knowing that player 2 will continue the game, will choose not to end the game, thus receiving 7 instead of 6. On the other hand, if players 1 and 3 are not able to coordinate (thus leading to the distribution of 7/2, 5, and 7/2), player 2 will end the game when her choice comes, in order to receive 6 instead of 5; consequently player 1 will select not to end the game in his first move, thus receiving 8 instead of 6. The conclusion is that whether players 1 and

3 can coordinate or not, *player 1 should not terminate the game in his first move.*

However, and here is the problem with the game-theoretic approach, the implicit assumption in all these calculations was that all three players were focusing on the *same* equilibrium in the last stage of the game. What if this assumption is incorrect? What if player 1 believes that he cannot achieve coordination with player 3, while player 2 believes that such coordination will occur? Under the assumption that players are unable to coordinate beliefs about the future of the game, player 2 will not terminate the game when it is her turn to play, and player 1, knowing that, will choose to terminate the game himself.

The notion that the beliefs of all players will converge to the selected equilibrium is built in in game theory.[13] In other words, in game theory players are *assumed* to have previously solved a coordination game concerning their beliefs. We want to argue that such an assumption is not always reasonable and to discuss the implications despite the fact that we have no good alternative proposal.[14]

We believe that frequently there is fundamental uncertainty surrounding outcomes of collective choice. It is possible that even the most well informed actors are faced with uncertainty over the predicted outcomes of a collective choice. It is possible that they cannot even assign probabilities to different possible outcomes. These are exactly the cases where multiple predictions or a set of predictions would be appropriate. For example, we think that the idea of participants in a conference committee who do not know the outcome in advance and are unwilling to make predictions is not just a creature of our imagination.

Under circumstances of radical uncertainty, it is possible that the expectations of different actors do not converge, and consequently their actions may not be in equilibrium. Although rational choice theory for the time being is not well equipped to handle such situations, we expect that such situations of uncoordinated expectations are common in case studies of legislatures, regardless of the number of chambers, and therefore, set predictions are appropriate.

Selection of one main dimension of conflict. This is a major theme of the book that we have touched on twice already in this chapter, once as a

---

[13]In fact, consistency of beliefs is a requirement of subgame perfect, or perfect (Selten 1975), or sequential (Kreps and Wilson 1982) equilibria.

[14]The standard game-theoretic approach would be to use incomplete information and model explicitly the different possible beliefs of each player as different types, then solve the incomplete information game. However, ultimately the different players would start from a distribution of different types that was "common knowledge" among them. For a different and promising approach to similar situations see Geanakoplos (1992).

point of marginal differences with some of the literature and once as a point of significant differences with other parts of the literature. We turn to it again under yet a different angle, its significance.

Why is dimensionality of the space so important in our eyes? For the simple reason that results generated for a specific number of dimensions often do not hold for a different number of dimensions. For example, the famous median voter theorem always holds for one dimension but rarely for more than one dimension (Plott 1967). Similarly, Hammond and Miller's (1987) outcomes about bicameralism do not generalize in more than two dimensions.

We would like to underline that, sometimes, results of theoretical research are conditioned by the dimensionality of the underlying space selected by the analyst. This should be a trivial statement since, in modeling, the conclusions of a formal theory carry the truth of its assumptions. As a result, if dimensionality of the space is one of the assumptions, the conclusions hold for this dimension and do not necessarily generalize.

Let us now apply this principle to two important theories of Congress, the distributive (Shepsle and Weingast) and the informational (Gilligan and Krehbiel). One essential assumption of distributive theories of Congress is that the policy space is multidimensional. This is how committee chairs and members extract gains from trade. They give up their positions in the less important dimension in order to gain in the more important one, their own jurisdiction. If the dimensionality of the underlying policy space is reduced to a single dimension, there are no possible gains from trade, and the approach collapses. Similarly, the essential assumption for the informational theory is a single dimension, along with incomplete information. Without the single dimension, there are no floor or committee medians, and the incomplete information games cannot be defined. Consequently, it is not surprising that the two approaches come to completely different results. Each carries with it the truth of the fundamental assumptions from which it was generated, in this case, the dimensionality of the underlying policy space.[15]

As we stated in the Introduction to the book, we believe that the underlying space for every legislature is multidimensional, because we share Riker's belief that strategic actors will try to alter the number of underlying dimensions in order to move from losing positions to winning ones. And here, in our opinion, lies the uniqueness of bicameralism. Through its institutional structure it selects one dimension of conflict out of a multidimensional space. Consequently, it can be approximated by one-dimensional models. Such models will include the five actors necessary to understand legislative interactions: the floor and committee medi-

---

[15]See the "Introduction" in Shepsle and Weingast (1995).

ans, as well as conference committees where appropriate. It may seem paradoxical, but one of the results of this study is that increasing the complexity of the legislative process (introducing two chambers as opposed to one) simplifies the models required for the study of the legislature (one-dimensional models as opposed to multidimensional ones).

As this agenda for future research suggests, the models of bicameralism presented in this book are partial because they do not include chamber committees. As a consequence, we expect our results to be partial as well. We believe we made permissible simplifications, since we began from the end of the game tree. However, more complete models as well as better-founded empirical research are necessary. We hope this book contributes to underscoring the necessity of studying bicameral institutions as such, not as unicameral ones, and in providing methods for these studies.

Conclusions

In this chapter we present a short recapitulation of our arguments and findings. We began with a review of the historical and geographic dimensions of bicameralism. We pointed out that bicameral institutions are protean and, like the ancient Greek god Proteus, change form. These different forms are accompanied by different analyses and justifications for such institutions. We know that our unscripted excursion in time and space impressed the reader with the variety of forms and functions.

In Part I we demonstrated that bicameral institutions can serve either functional (classes) or geographic diversity (federalism), but diversity does not require bicameral representation. Both stratified and federal societies may be represented by unicameral legislatures. From this account, we want to stress one historical point. Although currently federalism appears to be the only justification for an upper chamber's veto power, federalism was originally organized through unicameral legislatures with qualified majority or unanimity as the decision-making rule.

The institutions of bicameralism are diverse in their specifics, but they involve some form of the navette system, usually followed by some stopping rule: either conference committees, or joint sessions, or the possibility of one chamber to overrule the other. Financial legislation often elicited a different set of institutional rules. The wealth of institutional "details" in Part I may have seemed overwhelming in the beginning.

Part II aimed to organize this diversity and to demonstrate the bottom line consequences of bicameralism. We drew a series of conclusions, some of them singled out as "propositions" in Chapters 3 to 5, others simply discussed in the text. Here we recapitulate briefly. Our argument accords with those of most students of bicameral institutions: bicameralism promotes stability by making changes from the status quo more difficult. If changes occur, they happen through a process of both cooperation and conflict between the two chambers, what we have labeled the "efficient" and "redistributive" dimensions of bicameralism. Furthermore, redistribution occurs along one dimension of conflict; in this respect bicameralism differs from other systems that seek to preserve the status quo, such as qualified majorities.

The institutions that regulate bicameral interaction affect legislative outcomes. We argue that the process of intercameral bargaining is driven by the impatience of both chambers to achieve a compromise and by the uncertainty surrounding each chamber's level of impatience. And rules such as where a bill is introduced first, the number of rounds the process can continue before the application of a stopping rule, and the stopping rule itself all have predictable consequences on the outcome of bicameral negotiations. We claim that conference committees, a major means of resolving intercameral differences, are important because of their ability to make a proposal to both chambers under closed rule. Finally, we want to emphasize that without taking into account bicameral interactions, we are likely to be misled in our study of bicameral institutions.

Our empirical tests are more systematic with respect to the French Fifth Republic than with respect to other countries. We present evidence that impatience to conclude a deal does drive the interaction between the two chambers (case studies in Chapter 7). We also present statistical analyses (Chapter 6) indicating that the uncertainty (about one chamber's impatience or about one chamber's positions) affects the length of the negotiating process. Taken together these data provide the mechanisms of bicameral negotiations and consequently validate empirically (although indirectly) our argument that the rules of intercameral interaction (by specifying who reads a bill first, who last, how many rounds the navette process can last) do affect outcomes in significant ways. This is the foundation of the argument presented throughout this book: second chambers alter legislative outcomes even if they do not have the power to veto legislation ("asymmetric bicameralism" in Lijphart's terminology) and even if they have the same composition as the first chamber ("congruent chambers" in Lijphart's terms).

Turning to conference committees, we argued that their composition, their decision-making rules (mainly whether they decide as one chamber or replicate bicameral structures through the "unit rule"), and the constraints under which they operate systematically affect the outcomes of their deliberations. Examples from different countries (Chapter 8) were consistent with the argument, although, in order to test our argument in a systematic way, one would have to select samples of conference committee deliberations from different countries (an extremely difficult task given the languages involved and the secrecy of such deliberations).

Finally, we described the implications of our theory for the study of legislation and legislatures. In Chapter 9 we sorted out which of the arguments in the literature our analysis and findings support, which they modify, and which they refute. In every step of the way, we underlined the proposition that the study of bicameral legislatures as if they were uni-cameral ones biases the results, and we demonstrated alternative ways of undertaking such studies.

References

Adonis, A. 1988. "The House of Lords in the 1980s." *Parliamentary Affairs* 441 (3): 380–401.

Alivizatos, Nicos. 1995. "Judges as Veto Players." In Herbert Doering, ed., *Parliaments and Majority Rule in Western Europe*. New York: St. Martin's.

Allum, P.A. 1973. *Italy, Republic Without Government?* London: Weidenfeld and Nicolson.

Aristotle. 1959. *Politics and the Athenian Constitution*. Edited and translated by John Warrington. London: J.M. Dent.

Asahi Shinbunsha. Various dates. *Asahi shinbun.*

Asahi Shinbunsha. 1994. *Asahi nenkan deta bukku* (Databook of Asahi Yearbook). Tokyo: Asahi Shinbunsha.

Banks, J.S. 1985. "Sophisticated Voting Outcomes and the Covering Relation." *Social Choice and Welfare* 1: 295–306.

Barnett, James D. 1915. "The Bicameral System in State Legislation." *American Political Science Review* 9: 449–61.

Barnouw, A.J. 1944. *The Making of Modern Holland*. New York: Norton.

Baron, David P. 1993. "A Dynamic Theory of Collective Goods Programs." Working paper, Stanford University.

Baron, David P. 1995. "A Sequential Theory Perspective on Legislative Organization." In Kenneth Shepsle and Barry Weingast, eds., *Positive Theories of Congressional Institutions* (pp. 71–100). Ann Arbor: University of Michigan Press.

Baron, David P., and John A. Ferejohn. 1989. "Bargaining in Legislatures." *American Political Science Review* 89: 1181–1206.

Bawn, Kathleen. 1996. "Strategic Responses to Institutional Change: Parties, Committees, and Multiple Referral." *Public Choice* 88: 239–58.

Bawn, Kathleen, and George Tsebelis. 1996. "Congress Starts with a 'C', Not with an 'H': Committee Power or Bicameralism?" UCLA, manuscript.

Bourdon, Jean. 1978. *Les assemblées parlementaires sous la Ve République*. Paris: La Documentation Française, Notes et études documentaires No. 4463–64.

Bourdon, Jérôme. 1994. *Haute fidélité: Pouvoir et télévision, 1935–1994*. Paris: Seuil.

References

Brams, Steven J. 1989. "Are the Two Houses of Congress Really Coequal?" In Bernard Grofman and Donald Wittman, eds., *The Federalist Papers and the New Institutionalism* (pp. 125–41). New York: Agathon.

Brennan, Geoffrey, and Alan Hamlin. 1992. "Bicameralism and Majoritarian Equilibrium." *Public Choice* 74: 169–79.

Bromhead, P.A. 1958. *The House of Lords in Contemporary Politics: 1911–1957.* London: Routledge.

Bromhead, P., and D. Shell. 1967. "The Lords and Their House." *Parliamentary Affairs* 20: 337–49.

Brunschwig, M. Jacques. 1983. "Préface." In Aristote, *La Politique, Livre I,* translated by Pierre Pellegrin. Paris: Éditions Fernand Nathan.

Buchanan, James M., and Gordon Tullock. 1962. *The Calculus of Consent: Logical Foundations of Constitutional Democracy.* Ann Arbor: University of Michigan Press.

Burdette, Franklin L. 1940. *Filibustering in the Senate.* Princeton: Princeton University Press.

Burrows, H. 1964. "The House of Lords – Change or Decay." *Parliamentary Affairs* 17: 403–17.

Campion, Lord. 1953–54. "Second Chambers in Theory and Practice." *Parliamentary Affairs* 7: 17–32.

Canada. Department of Justice. 1989. *The Federal Legislative Process in Canada.* Ottawa: Canadian Government Publishing Center.

Casey, James. 1992. *Constitutional Law in Ireland.* London: Sweet and Maxwell.

Centre d'Économie de l'Information, Université de Paris I. 1974. *ORTF: L'agonie du monopole?* Paris: Librairie Plon.

Chapman, Brian. 1953. *Introduction to French Local Government.* London: Allen & Unwin.

Cicero, Marcus Tullius. 1929. *On the Commonwealth,* translated by George Holland Sabine and Stanley Barney Smith. Columbus: Ohio State University Press.

Colliard, Jean Claude. 1978. *Les régimes parlementaires contemporains.* Paris: Presses de la Fondation Nationale des Sciences Politiques.

Condorcet, Marie Jean Antoine Nicolas de Caritat, Marquis de. 1968. *Oeuvres.* Stuttgard-Bad Cannstatt: Friedrich Frommann Verlag.

Congressional Record. Various dates.

Cotturri, Giuseppe. 1982. "Abolire il bicameralismo?" *Rinascita,* no. 21, June 4, pp. 11–12

Cox, Gary W. 1987. "The Uncovered Set and the Core." *American Journal of Political Science* 31: 408–22.

Cox, Gary W., and Mathew McCubbins. 1993. *Legislative Leviathan.* Berkeley: University of California Press.

Cox, Gary W., and Richard McKelvey. 1984. "A Ham Sandwich Theorem for General Measures." *Social Choice and Welfare* 1: 75–83.

Däumler-Gmelin, Herta. 1982. "Ein beschämendes Ärgernis in Bonn." *Die Zeit* (April 23).

Delcamp, Alain. 1991. *Le Sénat et la décentralisation.* Paris: Economica.

Europa Yearbook: A World Survey. 1994. London: Europa Publications.

References

Fenno, Richard F., Jr. 1982. *The U.S. Senate: A Bicameral Perspective.* Washington, DC: American Enterprise Institute.

Ferejohn, John. 1975. "Who Wins in Conference Committee?" *Journal of Politics* 37: 1033–46.

Ferejohn, John A., Richard D. McKelvey, and Edward W. Packell. 1984. "Limiting Distributions for Continuous State Markov Voting Models." *Social Choice and Welfare* 1: 45–67.

Flanz, Gisbert H., ed. 1995. *Constitutions of the Countries of the World.* New York: Oceana Publications.

Fontaine, Nicole. 1995. *Les échos du Parlement Européen* 103 (March).

Freeman, Edward Augustus. 1863. *History of Federal Government, from the Foundation of the Achaian League to the Disruption of the United States; V. 1, General Introduction: History of the Greek Federations.* London: Macmillian.

Frickey, Philip P. 1992. "Constitutional Structure, Public Choice, and Public Law." *International Review of Law and Economics* 12: 163–65.

Fudenberg, Drew, and Jean Tirole. 1992. *Game Theory.* Cambridge, MA: MIT Press.

Galloway, George. 1955. "The Third House of Congress." *Congressional Record,* March 8.

Garrett, Geoffrey. 1995. "From the Luxembourg Compromise to Codecision: Decision Making in the European Union." *Electoral Studies* 14(3): 289–308.

Garrett, Geoffrey, and George Tsebelis. 1996. "An Institutional Critique of Intergovernmentalism." *International Organization* 50: 269–99.

Geanakoplos, John. 1992. "Common Knowledge." *Journal of Economic Perspectives* 6(4): 53–82.

Georgel, Jacques. 1968. *Le Sénat dans l'adversité (1962–1966).* Paris: Editions Cujas.

Gilligan, Thomas W., and Keith Krehbiel. 1990. "Organization of Informative Committees by a Rational Legislature." *American Journal of Political Science* 34: 531–64.

Ginsborg, Paul. 1990. *A History of Contemporary Italy: Society and Politics, 1943–1988.* London: Penguin.

Gladieux, L.E., and T.R. Wolanin. 1976. *Congress and the Colleges: The National Politics of Higher Education.* Lexington, MA: Lexington Books.

Gold, Martin, Michael Hugo, Hyde Murvy, Peter Robinson, and A.L. Pete Singleton. 1992. *The Book on Congress: Process, Procedure.* Washington, DC: Big Eagle.

Grangé, Jean. 1981. "Attitudes et vicissitudes du Sénat (1958–1980)." *Revue française de science politique* 31: 32–84.

Grangé, Jean. 1984. "L'efficacité normative du Sénat." *Revue française de science politique* 34: 955–87.

Greenberg, Joseph. 1979. "Consistent Majority Rule over Compact Sets of Alternatives." *Econometrica* 47: 627–36.

Grofman, Bernard, and Richard L. Hall. 1992. "The Committee Assignment Process and the Conditional Nature of Committee Bias." *American Political Science Review* 84: 1149–66.

References

Grossman, Sanford J., and Motty Perry. 1986a. "Perfect Sequential Equilibrium." *Journal of Economic Theory* 39: 97–119.

Grossman, Sanford J., and Motty Perry. 1986b. "Sequential Bargaining Under Asymmetric Information." *Journal of Economic Theory* 39: 120–54.

Hamilton, Alexander, John Jay, and James Madison. 1961. *The Federalist*. Cambridge, MA: Belknap Press of Harvard University Press.

Hammond, Thomas H., and Gary J. Miller. 1987. "The Core of the Constitution." *American Political Science Review* 81: 1155–74.

Hamon, Leo, and Jean Cotteret. 1960a. "Chronique constitutionnelle et parlementaire française." *Revue du droit public* 76: 648–58.

Hamon, Leo, and Jean Cotteret. 1960b. "Chronique constitutionnelle et parlementaire française." *Revue du droit public* 76: 986–1001.

Hamon, Leo, and Jean Cotteret. 1961. "Chronique constitutionnelle et parlementaire française." *Revue du droit public* 77: 99–131.

Hamon, Leo, and Claude Emeri. 1963. "Chronique constitutionnelle et parlementaire française." *Revue du droit public* 79: 243–65.

Håstad, Elis. 1957. *The Parliament of Sweden*. London: Hansard Society for Parliamentary Government.

Hempel, Carl G. 1964. *Aspects of Scientific Explanation*. New York: Free Press.

Herles, Helmut. 1981. "Manchmal die Bonner Hauptbeuhne (Sometimes the Principal Stage in Bonn)." *Frankfurter Allgemeine Zeitung*, December 3.

Hogg, Peter W. 1977. *Constitutional Law of Canada*. Toronto: Carswell Company Limited.

Horn, Stephen. 1970. *Unused Power: The Work of the Senate Committee on Appropriations*. Washington, DC: Brookings Institution.

Huber, John. 1992. "Restrictive Legislative Procedures in France and the United States." *American Political Science Review* 86: 675–87.

Huber, John. 1996. *Rationalizing Parliament: Legislative Institutions and Party Politics in France*. Cambridge: Cambridge University Press.

Huber-Hotz, Annemarie. 1991. Das Sweikammersystem – Anspruch und Wirklichkeit. In Parlamentsdienst, ed., *Das Parlament – "Oberste Gewalt des Bundes?"* Bern: Haupt.

Hughes, Christopher. 1954. *The Federal Constitution of Switzerland*. Oxford: Clarendon Press (reprinted in 1970, Westport, CT: Greenwood Press).

Inter-parliamentary Union. 1986. *Parliaments of the World*. Aldershot: Gower.

Ippolito, D.S. 1981. *Congressional Spending*. Ithaca, NY: Cornell University Press.

Isambert, François A., and Paul Ladrière. 1979. *Contraception et avortement. Dix ans de débat dans la presse (1965–1974)*. Paris: Éditions du Centre National de la Recherche Scientifique.

Jacobs, Francis, Richard Corbett, and Michael Shackleton. 1995. *The European Parliament* (3rd ed.). London: Cartermill International Ltd.

Jones, David R. 1993. "Policy Stability in the United States: Divided Government or Cohesion in Congress." Manuscript, University of California, Los Angeles.

Journal officiel de la République française. Multiple dates. Paris: Assemblée Nationale, Sénat.

References

Kanter, A. 1972. "Congress and the Defense Budget: 1960–1970." *American Political Science Review* 66: 1929–43.

Koch, H.W. 1984. *A Constitutional History of Germany.* London: Longman.

Koehler, D.H. 1990. "The Size of the Yolk: Computations for Odd and Even-Numbered Committees." *Social Choice and Welfare* 7: 231–45.

Krehbiel, Keith. 1987. "Why Are Congressional Committees Powerful?" *American Political Science Review* 81: 929–35.

Krehbiel, Keith. 1991. *Information and Legislative Organization.* Ann Arbor: University of Michigan Press.

Kreps, David, and Robert Wilson. 1982. "Sequential Equilibria." *Econometrica* 50: 863–94.

Kydland, Finn E., and Edward C. Prescott. 1977. "Rules Rather Than Discretion: The Inconsistency of Optimal Plans." *Journal of Political Economy* 85: 473–91.

Lakatos, Imre, and Alan Musgrave, eds. 1970. *Criticism and the Growth of Knowledge.* Cambridge: Cambridge University Press.

Lange, Peter, George Ross, and Maurizio Vannicelli. 1982. *Unions, Change and Crisis: French and Italian Union Strategy and the Political Economy, 1945–1980.* London: Allen & Unwin.

Lassaigne, Jean-Dominique. 1968. "Le Sénat dans la vie politique française." *Revue politique et parlementaire,* 37–46.

L'avortement. Histoire d'un débat. 1975. Paris: Flammarion.

Lees-Smith, H.B. 1923. *Second Chambers in Theory and Practice.* London: Allen and Unwin.

Levmore, Saul. 1992. "Bicameralism: When Are Two Decisions Better Than One?" *International Review of Law and Economics* 12: 145–62.

Liaisons Sociales. 1961. *Association ou intéressement des travailleurs.* Paris: Liaisons Sociales.

Lijphart, Arend. 1984. *Democracies: Patterns of Majoritarian and Consensus Government in Twenty-One Countries.* New Haven: Yale University Press.

Londregan, John, and James Snyder. 1994. "Comparing Committee and Floor Preferences." *Legislative Studies Quarterly* 19: 233–66.

Longley, L.D., and W.J. Oleszek. 1989. *Bicameral Politics: Conference Committees in Congress.* New Haven: Yale University Press.

Longley, L.D., and D.M. Olson. 1991. *Two into One: The Politics and Processes of National Legislative Cameral Change.* Boulder: Westview.

Luchaire, François, and Gerard Conac. 1987. *La Constitution de la République Française* (2nd ed.). Paris: Economica.

Lyon, Bryce. 1980. *A Constitutional and Legal History of Medieval England* (2nd ed.). New York: Norton.

Maddex, Robert L. 1995. *Constitutions of the World.* Washington, DC: Congressional Quarterly.

Manley, John. 1970. *The Politics of Finance: The House Committee on Ways and Means.* Boston: Little, Brown.

March, J.G., and J.P. Olsen. 1984. "The New Institutionalism: Organized Factors in Political Life." *American Political Science Review* 78: 734–49.

References

Marichy, Jean-Pierre. 1969. *La deuxième chambre dans la vie politique française depuis 1875*. Paris: R. Pichon et R. Durand-Auzias.

Mastias, Jean. 1980. *Le Sénat de la Vᵉ République: Réforme et renouveau*. Paris: Economica.

Mastias, Jean. 1988. "Histoire des tentations du Sénat de la Vᵉ République." *Pouvoirs* 44: 15–34.

Mastias, Jean, and Jean Grangé. 1987. *Les secondes chambres du Parlement en Europe Occidentale*. Paris: Economica.

Maus, Didier. 1985. *Le Parlement sous la Vᵉ République*. Paris: Presses Universitaires de France.

Maus, Didier, ed. 1987. *Les grands textes de la pratique institutionnelle de la Vᵉ République*. Paris: Documentation Française.

Maus, Didier. 1988. "Le Sénat, L'Assemblée Nationale et le gouvernement." *Pouvoirs* 44: 119–30.

McKelvey, Richard D. 1976. "Intransitivities in Multidimensional Voting Models and Some Implications for Agenda Control." *Journal of Economic Theory* 12: 472–82.

McKelvey, Richard D. 1979. "General Conditions for Global Intransitivities in Formal Voting Models." *Econometrica* 47: 1085–112.

McKelvey, Richard D. 1986. "Covering, Dominance and Institution Free Properties of Social Choice." *American Journal of Political Science* 30: 283–314.

Miller, Gary. 1995. "Post-Maastricht Legislative Procedures: Is the Council 'Institutionally Challenged'?" Paper presented in the 4th Biennial International Conference of ECSA, Charleston, South Carolina, May 11–14.

Miller, Gary J., and Thomas H. Hammond. 1989. "Stability and Efficiency in a Separation-of-Powers Constitutional System." In Bernard Grofman and Donald Wittman, eds., *The Federalist Papers and the New Institutionalism* (pp. 85–99). New York: Agathon.

Miller, Kenneth E. 1968. *The Government and Politics in Denmark*. London: Longman.

Miller, Nicholas R. 1980. "A New 'Solution Set' for Tournaments and Majority Voting." *American Journal of Political Science* 24: 68–96.

Money, Jeannette, and George Tsebelis. 1992. "Cicero's Puzzle: Upper House Power in Comparative Perspective." *International Political Science Review* 13: 25–43.

Money, Jeannette, and George Tsebelis. 1995. "The Political Power of the French Senate: Micromechanisms of Bicameral Negotiations." *Journal of Legislative Studies* 1: 192–217.

Montesquieu, Charles-Louis de Secondat, Baron de. 1977. *The Spirit of Laws*. Edited by David Wallace Carrithers. Berkeley: University of California Press.

Mopin, Michel. 1988. *Les grands débats parlementaires de 1875 à nos jours*. Paris: La Documentation Française.

Moran, Thomas Francis. 1895. *The Rise and Development of the Bicameral System in America* (repr. 1973). Baltimore: Johns Hopkins University Press.

Morey, William C. 1893. "The First State Constitutions." *Annals of the American Academy of Political and Social Science*, pp. 201–32.

References

Morgan, David Gwynn. 1990. *Constitutional Law of Ireland: The Law of the Executive, Legislature, and Judicature.* Blackrock, Ireland: Round Hall Press.

Moses, Bernard. 1889. *The Federal Government of Switzerland: An Essay on the Constitution.* Oakland, CA: Pacific Press.

"Nach vier Tagen und einer Krise in letzter Minute Einigung im Vermittlungsausschuss." 1981. *FAZ* (December 9).

Nagler, Jonathan. 1989. "Strategic Implications of Conference Selection in the House of Representatives." *American Politics Quarterly* 17: 54–79.

Nihon Keizai Shinbunsha. *Nihon keizai shinbun.* Various dates.

Norton, Philip, ed. 1990. *Legislatures.* Oxford: Oxford University Press.

Ordeshook, Peter C., and Thomas Schwartz. 1987. "Agendas and the Control of Political Outcomes." *American Political Science Review* 81: 179–200.

Passant, E.J. 1977. *A Short History of Germany.* Cambridge: Cambridge University Press.

Percival, R.W. 1953–54. "The Origin and Development of the House of Lords." *Parliamentary Affairs* 7: 33–48.

Peyret, Claude. 1974. *Avortement. Pour une loi humaine.* Paris: Calmann-Lévy.

Plato. 1966. *Plato's Republic.* Translated by I.A. Richards. Cambridge: Cambridge University Press.

Plott, Charles R. 1967. "A Notion of Equilibrium and Its Possibility Under Majority Rule." *American Economic Review* 57: 787–806.

Poole, Keith T., and Howard Rosenthal. 1985. "A Spatial Model for Legislative Roll Call Analysis." *American Journal of Political Science* 29: 357–84.

Poole, Keith T., and Howard Rosenthal. 1987. "Analysis of Congressional Coalition Patterns: A Unidimensional Spatial Model." *Legislative Studies Quarterly* 12: 55–76.

Popper, Karl R. 1962. *Conjectures and Refutations: The Growth of Scientific Knowledge.* New York: Basic.

Renier, G.J. 1944. *The Dutch Nation.* London: Allen & Unwin.

Riemens, Hendrik. 1944. *The Netherlands.* New York: Eagle Books.

Riker, William H. 1983. *Liberalism Against Populism.* San Francisco: Freeman.

Riker, William H. 1992a. "The Justification of Bicameralism." *International Political Science Review* 13: 101–16.

Riker, William H. 1992b. "The Merits of Bicameralism." *International Review of Law and Economics* 12: 166–68.

Rogers, Lindsay. 1926. *The American Senate.* New York: Knopf.

Rubinstein, Ariel. 1982. "Perfect Equilibrium in a Bargaining Model." *Econometrica* 50: 97–109.

Rubinstein, Ariel. 1985. "A Bargaining Model with Incomplete Information About Time Preferences." *Econometrica* 53: 1151–72.

Sassoon, Donald. 1986. *Contemporary Italy: Politics, Economy and Society Since 1945.* London: Longman.

Sauser-Hall, George. 1946. *The Political Institutions of Switzerland.* Zurich: Swiss National Tourist Office.

Schofield, Norman. 1978. "Instability of Simple Dynamic Games." *Review of Economic Studies* 45: 575–94.

References

Schwartz, Thomas. 1987. *The Logic of Collective Choice*. New York: Columbia University Press.

Schwartz, Thomas. 1990. "Cyclic Tournaments and Cooperative Majority Voting: A Solution." *Social Choice and Welfare* 7: 19–29.

Seikaiohrai. 1994, 1995. *Seikaiohrai*, 1994: vols. 1–5; 1995: vol. 1. Tokyo: Seikaiohraisha.

Sekai. 1994. *Special Issue* (vol. 594). Tokyo: Iwanami Shoten.

Selten, Reinhard. 1975. "Reexamination of the Perfectness Concept for Equilibrium Points in Extensive Games." *International Journal of Game Theory* 4: 25–55.

Shepsle, Kenneth A. 1978. *The Giant Jigsaw Puzzle: Democratic Committee Assignments in the Modern House*. Chicago: University of Chicago Press.

Shepsle, Kenneth A. 1979. "Institutional Arrangements and Equilibrium in Multidimensional Voting Models." *American Journal of Political Science* 23: 27–57.

Shepsle, Kenneth A., and Barry R. Weingast. 1981. "Structure Induced Equilibrium and Legislative Choice." *Public Choice* 37: 503–19.

Shepsle, Kenneth A., and Barry R. Weingast. 1984. "Uncovered Sets and Sophisticated Outcomes with Implications for Agenda Institutions." *American Journal of Political Science* 29: 49–74.

Shepsle, Kenneth A., and Barry R. Weingast. 1987a. "The Institutional Foundations of Committee Power." *American Political Science Review* 81: 85–104.

Shepsle, Kenneth A., and Barry R. Weingast. 1987b. "Why Are Congressional Committees Powerful?" *American Political Science Review* 81: 935–45.

Shepsle, Kenneth A., and Barry R. Weingast. 1995. "Introduction." In Kenneth Shepsle and Barry Weingast, eds., *Positive Theories of Congressional Institutions* (pp. 1–4). Ann Arbor: University of Michigan Press.

Shugart, Matthew S., and John M. Carey. 1992. *Presidents and Assemblies: Constitutional Design and Electoral Dynamics*. Cambridge: Cambridge University Press.

Shugiyin. 1990. *Gikai seido hyakunenshi – Gikai seido hen* (One hundred year history of the parliamentary system – Volume of parliamentary institutions). Tokyo: Shugiyin.

Sinclair, Barbara. 1989. *The Transformation of the U.S. Senate*. Baltimore: Johns Hopkins University Press.

Sloss, Judith. 1973. "Stable Outcomes in Majority Voting Games." *Public Choice* 15: 19–48.

Smith, Steven S. 1988. "An Essay on Sequence, Position, Goals, and Committee Power." *Legislative Studies Quarterly* 13: 151–76.

Smith, Steven S. 1989. *Call to Order: Floor Politics in the House and Senate*. Washington, DC: Brookings Institution.

Steiner, G.Y. 1951. *The Congressional Conference Committee: Seventieth to Eightieth Congresses*. Urbana: University of Illinois Press.

Stone, Alec. 1992. *The Birth of Judicial Politics in France: The Constitutional Council in Comparative Perspective*. Oxford: Oxford University Press.

Strom, Gerald S., and Barry S. Rundquist. 1976. "House–Senate Conferences

References

and the Legislative Process." Paper presented at the 1976 Annual Meeting of the Midwest Political Science Association, Chicago.

Strom, Gerald S., and Barry S. Rundquist. 1977. "A Revised Theory of Winning in House Senate Conferences." *American Political Science Review* 71: 448–53.

Switzerland. Multiple dates. *Recueil officiel des lois fédérales.* Berne: Chancellerie Fédérale.

Switzerland. 1948, 1973. *Recueil systématique du droit fédéral.* Berne: Chancellerie Fédérale.

Tardan, Arnaud. 1988. "Le rôle législatif du Sénat." *Pouvoirs* 44: 104–10.

Temperley, Harold W.V. 1910. *Senates and Upper Chambers: Their Use and Function in the Modern State.* London: Chapman and Hall.

Trivelli, Laurent. 1975. *Le bicamerisme – Institutions comparées – Etude historique, statistique et critique des rapports entre le Conseil National et le Conseil des Etats.* Lausanne: Payot.

Trnka, Henri. 1963. "La Commission Mixte Paritaire." *Revue du droit public* 79: 477–534.

Trnka, Henri. 1967. "Evolution de la procédure de la Commission Mixte Paritaire." *Revue du droit public* 83: 739–70.

Tsebelis, George. 1990. *Nested Games: Rational Choice in Comparative Politics.* Berkeley: University of California Press.

Tsebelis, George. 1993. "The Core, the Uncovered Set and Conference Committees in Bicameral Legislatures." Manuscript, University of California, Los Angeles.

Tsebelis, George. 1994. "The Power of the European Parliament as a Conditional Agenda-Setter." *American Political Science Review* 88: 128–42.

Tsebelis, George. 1995a. "Decision Making in Political Systems: Veto Players in Presidentialism, Parliamentarism, Multicameralism, and Mutipartyism." *British Journal of Political Science* 25: 289–326.

Tsebelis, George. 1995b. "Conditional Agenda-Setting and Decisionmaking Inside the European Parliament." *Journal of Legislative Studies* 1: 65–93.

Tsebelis, George. 1995c. "Veto Players and Law Production in Parliamentary Systems." In Herbert Doering, ed., *Parliaments and Majority Rule in Western Europe* (pp. 83–111). New York: St. Martin's.

Tsebelis, George, and Jeannette Money. 1995. "Bicameral Negotiations: The Navette System in France." *British Journal of Political Science* 25: 101–29.

Tsebelis, George, and Bjornerik Rasch. 1995. "Patterns of Bicameralism." In Herbert Doering, ed., *Parliaments and Majority Rule in Western Europe* (pp. 365–90). New York: St. Martin's.

U.S. Senate. 1987. *Creation of the Senate.* Washington, DC: U.S. Government Printing Office.

Vincent, J.R. 1966. "The House of Lords." *Parliamentary Affairs* 19: 475–85.

Vogel, Friedrich. 1989. "Der Vermittlungsausschuss." In *Vierzig Jahre Bundesrat.* Tagungsband zum wissenschaftlichen Symposion in der Evangelischen Akademie Tutzing vom 11, bis 14, April 1989. Baden-Baden: Nomos Verlagsgesellschaft, pp. 213–25.

References

Vogler, David J. 1970. "Patterns of One House Dominance in Congressional Conference Committees." *Midwest Journal of Political Science* 14(May): 303–20.

Vogler, David J. 1971. *The Third House: Conference Committees in the United States Congress.* Evanston: Northwestern University Press.

von Fritz, Kurt. 1954. *The Theory of the Mixed Constitution in Antiquity.* New York: Columbia University Press.

Walpole, Ronald E., and Raymond H. Myers. 1985. *Probability and Statistics for Engineers and Scientists.* New York: Macmillian.

Walsh, Correa Moylan. 1915. *The Political Science of John Adams: A Study in the Theory of Mixed Government and the Bicameral System.* New York: Putnam's.

Warwick, Paul. 1994. *Government Survival in Parliamentary Democracies.* New York: Cambridge University Press.

"Was darf der Vermittlungsausschuss?" 1981. *FAZ* (December 12).

Weare, V. 1965. "The House of Lords – Prophecy and Fulfillment." *Parliamentary Affairs* 18: 422–33.

Weaver, Kent, and Bert Rockman. 1993. *Do Institutions Matter?* Washington, DC: Brookings Institution.

Weingast, Barry. 1993. "Economic Role of Political Institutions." Manuscript, Hoover Institution.

Williams, Glyn, and John Ramsden. 1990. *Ruling Britannia: A Political History of Britain, 1688–1988.* London: Longman.

Wood, Gordon S. 1969. *The Creation of the American Republic, 1776–1787.* New York: Norton.

Wright, Vincent. 1989. *The Government and Politics of France.* New York: Holmes and Meier.

Index

Adams, John
  on legislative power, 25
  mixed government theory applied to
    legislature, 25–6
Adonis, A., 34
agenda setter
  in bicameral legislature, 36
  role in conference committee, 36n36
  in unicameral legislature, 36–7
agreements
  enforceable under cooperative game the-
    ory, 77
Allum, P.A., 53
Aristotle, 17–18, 40
  on aristocratic government, 20
  on Plato's ideal republic, 19
  simple government prescription, 19–
    20
  on tyranny, oligarchy, and democracy,
    19
auctoritas, 40

backwards induction. *See* noncooperative
    game theory
Baker, Howard, 199
Banks, J.S., 81
bargaining game
  French navette system, 130–1
  impatience as dynamic driving, 146
bargaining model
  See also noncooperative game theory
  Grossman and Perry, 102–4
  Rubenstein, 98–9
Barnett, James D., 27n23
Baron, David P., 77
Bawn, Kathleen, 2, 222
Bayesian perfect equilibrium, 102
beliefs (game theory), 224–5
bicameral legislatures
  in American colonies, 27

arguments for, 4–5
checks and balances system in, 35–7
conference committees, 110–11
congruent, 35
constituency base, 36
core of, 41, 80, 91–4
defined, 15
diversity of, 13
efficient dimension of, 15–16, 21, 28–9,
  32–3, 37–42, 210, 212
evolution of modern, 21–3
in federal systems, 33–4
German, 32, 181
interaction between chambers of, 3–4, 6
legislative outcomes, 40–1
Montesquieu's idea of, 24–5
from perspective of game theory, 76–7
political dimension of, 15–16, 21, 28–
  9, 210, 212
of post-medieval Europe, 29–31
privileged dimension of conflict and
  compromise, 91
procedures governing financial legislation, 63–9
procedures governing nonfinancial legislation, 55–63
representation in, 13
role in reduction of conflict, 76
stability with, 37–40
status quo ideal points, 73–6
status quo preservation in, 74–9, 89
strong, weak, and insignificant, 3, 16,
  33, 44–5
Switzerland, 31–2
uncovered set, 85–7, 94–6, 110–11
unitary form in the Netherlands, 32
in unitary systems, 34–5
U.S. constitution, 27–8
variations in conflict resolution in countries with, 54–69

Index

Index

existence and location of core in bicameral legislature, 41, 91–4
set of possible outcomes as core, 78n4
tournament equilibrium set as subset of uncovered set, 81, 209
tournament equilibrium set of bicameral legislature, 87–9
tournament equilibrium set of conference committee, 111–12
uncovered bound sphere of conference committee, 112
uncovered set as concept of stability, 8
uncovered set of conference committees, 110–11
uncovered set defined, 81
uncovered set induced on bicameral restrictions (IBR), 113–20
uncovered set of bicameral legislature, 85–7, 89, 94–6
uncovered set of unicameral legislature, 86
uncovered set subsets, 81
yolk if conference committee at center of, 211
Corbett, Richard, 204
core. *See* cooperative game theory
Cotteret, Jean, 195
Council of States, Switzerland, 189–94
councils, Greece and early Rome, 17–18
countries with bicameral legislatures, 3
covering, 85
Cox, Gary W., 80, 81, 90, 220
curia regis, 22
cycles
in bicameralism, 215–16
in unicameralism, 216
cycling hypothesis, 136–41

Däumler-Gmelin, Herta, 184
decision procedures
conference committees, 41–2, 110–13, 177
rules for conference committee, 180–1
defections
from coalition in French Assembly, 146–7
potential in French penal code legislative process, 153–6
de Gaulle, Charles, 142, 151–2
Delcamp, Alain, 156, 157
dimensions of bicameralism
efficient, 15–16, 28–9, 32, 37–42
political, 15–16, 27–9, 35–7, 42
discount factors
bargaining with complete information, 99–100
bargaining with incomplete information, 102–3

efficient dimension of bicameralism, 15–16, 32, 42
contemporary debate, 37–42
Madison's idea of, 28–9, 33
electoral system
direct election to select upper house members, 47–53
election of lower house, 46
elections in presidential systems, 1
electoral college in France, 47, 157
Emeri, Claude, 195
enforceable agreements, 77, 100–101
equilibrium outcome (under majority rule), 88
Erlenborn, John, 222
Estates General
medieval period in Europe, 30–1
Sweden, 29
Europe
federal pattern of institutions, 31–2
unitary pattern of institutions, 29–31
European Union (EU)
bicameralism, 7
conference committee, 203–7
decision-making rules, 180
rules of interaction, 203, 205
executive functions
John Adams's idea of, 25
Montesquieu's idea of, 24–5

faculté d'empêcher (Montesquieu), 25
faculté de statuer (Montesquieu), 25
federalism
bicameralism in systems of, 33–4
compromise of U.S. Constitutional Convention, 27
with republicanism in United States, 26
Fenno, Richard F. Jr., 220
Ferejohn, John, 34, 77, 86, 95
football huddle, 199
France
abortion legalization, 166–8
bicameralism, 7
conference committee, 195–8
government role in legislative process, 130–1
legislative process, 128
local government legislation, 156–9
model of one-sided incomplete information, 127
ORTF legislation, 162–5
penal code legislation, 153–6
power of Sénat, 34–5
presidential attributes approach, 149–51
representation in Senate, 133
tax on wealth, 159–61

Index

246

Index